BACKROOMS
AND BAYOUS

BACKROOMS
AND BAYOUS

My Life in Louisiana Politics

ROBERT MANN

PELICAN PUBLISHING
NEW ORLEANS 2021

The word "Pelican" and the depiction of a pelican are
trademarks of Arcadia Publishing Company Inc. and are
registered in the U.S. Patent and Trademark Office.

Library of Congress Cataloging-in-Publication Data

Names: Mann, Robert, 1958- author.
Title: Backrooms and bayous : my life in Louisiana politics / Robert Mann.
Description: New Orleans : Pelican Publishing, [2021] | Includes index. |
    Summary: "This autobiography by the communications director of Gov.
    Kathleen Blanco during Hurricane Katrina covers the political drama and
    intrigue he witnessed—and learned from—as a journalist, political columnist,
    and congressional aide since the late 1970s. He reported on and/or worked
    for Louisiana's top political leaders of the last forty years: Edwin Edwards,
    Russell Long, John Breaux, J. Bennett Johnston, and Mary Landrieu. He is a
    professor and Manship Chair in Journalism at Louisiana State University"—
    Provided by publisher.
Identifiers: LCCN 2020044436 | ISBN 9781455626052 (hardcover) | ISBN
    9781455626069 (ebook)
Subjects: LCSH: Mann, Robert, 1958- |
    Governors—Louisiana—Staff—Biography.
Classification: LCC JK4753.S8 M36 2021 | DDC 976.3/064092 [B]—dc23
LC record available at https://lccn.loc.gov/2020044436

Printed in the United States of America

Published by Pelican Publishing
New Orleans, LA
www.pelicanpub.com

For John Copes

To strive with difficulties, and to conquer them, is the highest human felicity; the next is, to strive, and deserve to conquer; but he whose life has passed without a contest, and who can boast neither success nor merit, can survey himself only as a useless filler of existence; and if he is content with his own character, must owe his satisfaction to insensibility.

—Samuel Johnson

Contents

Introduction

During a massive snowstorm one night in the winter of 1985, US Senator Russell Long and I sat on an airplane at Washington's National Airport for several hours. In the time it took the ground crew to de-ice the plane several times, and during a two-hour flight to New Orleans, Long regaled me with dozens of stories about his uncle Earl. Earl Long was the younger brother of Huey P. Long, Russell's father. A political legend in his own right, Earl had served three times as Louisiana's governor.

I've always treasured the memory of this evening and, through the years, I have chuckled at an innocent question he asked as our conversation ended. When he had finally run out of stories, Long turned to me, narrowed his eyes, and asked, "Did *you* ever know Uncle Earl?"

I never knew Earl Long. He died three days after my second birthday, about sixteen years before I worked in my first Louisiana political campaign. In recent years, I've thought often about that fascinating evening with Senator Long. And I realized that while I had not known Uncle Earl, I *had* known virtually every major Louisiana political figure since the mid-1940s. As a journalist, I had covered governors Edwin Edwards, Dave Treen, and Bobby Jindal. I interviewed former governors Jimmie Davis, Robert Kennon, and John McKeithen. I've known almost every statewide elected official since the early 1980s.

As a journalist and political historian, I interviewed many prominent national leaders, including President Gerald Ford; a host of US senators, including Mike Mansfield, George McGovern, J. William Fulbright, Herman Talmadge, Strom Thurmond, Mark Hatfield, Gaylord Nelson, Lloyd Bentsen, and John Danforth; and many former White House and Senate aides involved in passing the historic civil rights laws of the sixties and who grappled with the fallout from the Vietnam War.

As a journalist, US Senate staffer, governor's aide, and political operative, I wrote about or worked with many US House members from Louisiana, including Rodney Alexander, Lindy Boggs, Bill Cassidy, Don

9

Cazayoux, Garret Graves, Jimmy Hayes, Jerry Huckaby, Chris John, Bill Jefferson, Buddy Leach, Bob Livingston, Jim McCrery, Charlie Melancon, Henson Moore, James Morrison, Otto Passman, Buddy Roemer, Steve Scalise, Billy Tauzin, David Vitter, and Joe D. Waggonner.

For almost twenty years, I was a senior aide to two US senators from Louisiana: Russell Long and his successor, John Breaux. I was press secretary to the 1990 US Senate reelection campaign of J. Bennett Johnston, when he defeated former Klan leader David Duke. As communications director for the Louisiana Democratic Party in 1996, I helped elect Mary Landrieu to the US Senate. I was communications director to Governor Kathleen Blanco before and after Hurricane Katrina.

In my years in politics and journalism, I've been fortunate to witness and experience an amazing amount of political history—from the raucous governor's race of 1983 between Edwin Edwards and Dave Treen to my behind-the-scenes role as a senior aide to Blanco during and after Katrina in 2005. Over the decades, I've attended six national political conventions—two Republican and four Democratic. I have known every person who represented Louisiana in the US Senate since the early 1970s, and I have known every governor of the state since 1944. Except Uncle Earl.

I never knew Uncle Earl.

That's why I began writing this book. I realized my decades in politics and journalism had afforded me priceless, personal views of the major leaders of my state—people who governed Louisiana since the mid-1940s. I believed I could share some interesting, insightful stories about these men and women and play a small role in writing the history of Louisiana politics during this period. I hope I've done that.

What I didn't realize at first was that this book would prompt months of soul searching, as I contemplated my career in Louisiana politics and journalism. What I learned during those months is that I made many mistakes over the years.

At first, it was difficult to put on paper the many ways I had failed myself, my friends, my bosses, and the good people they represented. But as I meditated and continued writing, it became easier. It was cathartic and redemptive, in fact. As this book took form, I realized I was producing more than political history. I was penning a cautionary tale for young people interested in a career in government. It is very easy to lose your way in politics. It is too easy to compromise your principles and forget for whom you work (the people). I hope young people and others will read my story and learn from my mistakes. And I made a lot of them. But I also learned some valuable lessons from my screw-ups and ethical lapses. I hope that confessing them in this book might help those who will govern our state over the next seventy-five years to avoid some or all of the errors that I made.

No, I didn't know Uncle Earl, but his nephew taught me a lot about politics. Working for him and other Louisiana political luminaries over twenty years also taught me a lot about life.

BACKROOMS
AND BAYOUS

1

Where the Hell Have You Been?

My wife, Cindy, heard the banging first. It was seven o'clock on Saturday morning, September 3, 2005, less than a week after Hurricane Katrina and the levee breaches that unleashed devastating floodwaters into most of New Orleans. When I slumped back to our Baton Rouge home the night before, I had been exhausted. For the first time that week, I had slept for eight uninterrupted hours. Sometime after midnight, however, my boss, Governor Kathleen Babineaux Blanco, had started calling me to return to work to help with a crisis—a high-stakes dispute with the White House over control of the Louisiana National Guard. I was her communications director. And I had slept through the whole thing.

As Cindy rushed downstairs to answer the door, I stumbled to the second-story window at the front of our house. What I saw startled me. It was the black Suburban used by the governor's State Police detail. When I got to the door, I recognized two of the troopers who were always at the governor's side. My immediate thought was odd: "They have come to tell me the governor has died. Why else would two state troopers be banging on my door on a peaceful Saturday morning?" The troopers didn't smile. One of them said, "Bob, Coach wants you to call him right now." Raymond "Coach" Blanco was the governor's husband. The trooper dialed Coach's number and handed me the phone.

The fury on the other end was instant. "Where. The. Hell. Have. You. Been?!" I stammered a few words about having a dead phone. "Get your ass down here, right now!" he barked and then hung up.

Within thirty minutes, I arrived at the governor's temporary residence, a large ranch-style home in the city's Bocage neighborhood, not far from the state's Emergency Operations Center. The state had leased the brick-façade home while the Governor's Mansion underwent extensive repairs. Blanco and other staff members brought me up to speed. My head spun as they described what I had missed as I slept. They had been up all night struggling with President George W. Bush and his staff over Bush's desire to take over the Louisiana National Guard. To a national audience that witnessed the massive flooding and the breakdown of order in New Orleans in the chaotic days after Katrina, surrendering our troops to the president might have seemed like a sensible plan.

We all knew it was anything but a good idea, unless the plan was to rehabilitate Bush's image after the federal government had botched its response to Katrina the previous week. For four long days, Blanco implored Washington for more federal assets, including troops, trucks of ice and food, generators, and buses to evacuate thousands of souls stranded at the Louisiana Superdome and the New Orleans Convention Center. At almost every turn, Bush, Federal Emergency Management Agency (FEMA) officials, and other administration officials talked a good game, but the promised help never materialized. It wasn't until later in the week that US Army Lt. Gen. Russel Honoré appeared in Baton Rouge, after Bush named him commander of Joint Task Force Katrina. In the coming days and weeks, Honoré and his troops would help the Louisiana National Guard troops restore order to New Orleans. Until that point, however, the Guard was mostly by itself in the Dome and on the streets of New Orleans, performing heroic, lifesaving work. The storm had shattered the city's police force. Many officers abandoned their posts.

And while the National Guard (from Louisiana and other states), the state's Department of Wildlife and Fisheries, and hundreds of volunteers saved thousands of lives, the disaster was so immense that we were all left wondering for several days, "Where is our federal government? Why is no one helping us?" Other than the Coast Guard and a few FEMA employees, there had been little or no federal presence in New Orleans until Honoré arrived.

In the days after Katrina, Bush and his aides paid scant attention to the devastation in New Orleans and coastal Mississippi. On a tour of Western states earlier that week, an ambivalent Bush would not return to the White House until Thursday, four days after Katrina hit Louisiana. That day, he only made matters worse by refusing to land in Louisiana on his way back to Washington. Instead, Air Force One made a low pass over New Orleans. He compounded his ham-handed handling of the disaster the next day in Alabama when he told the incompetent FEMA director, Michael Brown, "Brownie, you're doing a heck of a job." (Brown was not doing a heck of a job and would resign in disgrace ten days later.) And it wasn't just Bush who was AWOL. Several top administration officials were in Greece that week for the wedding of Bush's communications director. Secretary of State Condoleezza Rice was in New York, attending a Broadway show and shopping for shoes.

Into this vacuum, and in damage-control mode, rushed Bush's top political advisor, Karl Rove. "In a reflection of what has long been a hallmark of Mr. Rove's tough political style," the *New York Times* reported on Monday, September 5, "the administration is also working to shift the blame away from the White House and toward officials of New Orleans and Louisiana who, as it happens, are Democrats." (The story failed to mention the National Response Plan, signed by many members of Bush's cabinet, which called for almost-automatic deployment of the US Army's 82nd Airborne Division in a national emergency, such as Katrina. This had not happened, but many news outlets declined to criticize Bush and his staff for that failure, at least in the early days of the crisis.)

For days, leaders of the US government abandoned and ignored Louisiana during its darkest time. I will never forget the overwhelming feeling of horror mixed with sadness as I saw a submerged New Orleans for the first time, on Thursday, September 1, the day before my forty-seventh birthday. I accompanied Blanco that afternoon on one of her daily trips down to New Orleans on a Louisiana National Guard Blackhawk helicopter. I thought I was prepared for what I would see. I'd watched hours of network television coverage of the flooded city over the past several days. When New Orleans came into sight, however, I couldn't believe my eyes. There was shimmering black water—up to the rooftops of whole neighborhoods—as far as I could see in almost every direction. "New Orleans, as I knew it," I thought, "doesn't exist anymore." Overwhelmed with sadness, I realized that most of those thousands of submerged homes represented the life savings of a now-homeless family. I was not just flying over the wreckage of a destroyed city; I was witness to the wreckage of hundreds of thousands of shattered lives.

These images were searing, whether one saw them in person or on television. Coupled with powerful footage of New Orleans residents stranded on rooftops or suffering in the Superdome or the Convention Center, it all spelled political disaster for the White House. Political commentators were opining about how Katrina would wreck Bush's legacy, already tarnished by the gratuitous war he started in Iraq two years earlier. (More than 3,200 Louisiana National Guard troops were in Iraq in September 2005 and unavailable to help serve in New Orleans.)

Struggling to recover from the public relations disaster that consumed the White House, the US Department of Homeland Security, and FEMA, Bush's worried staffers did the only thing they knew to do: they blamed Blanco. They first spun the narrative she was so derelict that she had neglected to declare a state of emergency in Louisiana. There was only one problem: Blanco issued the emergency executive order two and a half days before the storm hit the state. It was posted on the governor's website immediately after she signed it on the afternoon of Friday,

August 26. The lie about the state of emergency was just one part of the White House plan. The other one we had expected since Wednesday. That day, James Carville called me from Washington. "The White House is fixin' to start blaming Governor Blanco for everything," the former campaign manager for Bill Clinton told me. "Get ready." I passed the word along, but there was little we could do. Several of us on staff wanted to respond to the emerging White House narrative and make a case for how Washington's failures were hurting Louisiana. We barely got the words for the plan out of our mouths before Blanco shut us down. "We're not getting in any war with the White House," she instructed. We pushed back, but she was adamant. "We're going to need George Bush's help to get this state back on its feet. We won't get nearly as much if we're fighting with him." So it was settled. We would remain quiet as the White House and its allies trashed us to the national press.

I soon learned that the prohibition on fighting the White House did not include challenging Bush's efforts—launched on Friday—to seize our National Guard so he could make the state of Louisiana, and its governor, look weak and ineffectual. Blanco had felt the first heat from the coming political firestorm earlier that Friday, when Air Force One landed at the New Orleans airport. Blanco and New Orleans Mayor Ray Nagin met with Bush in the plane's conference room, where the president and his staff pressed her to relinquish the Louisiana National Guard to federal control. This demand wasn't a total surprise. Two days earlier, I was with her when the head of the National Guard Bureau, Lt. Gen. Steven Blum, arrived at her small office at the Emergency Operations Center to caution her about any federal effort to take away the Guard. "Don't let them do it," the diminutive, pugnacious Blum told Blanco. "If they nationalize the Guard, you'll lose its law-enforcement authority." We all learned about the federal Insurrection Act and the principle of *posse comitatus*. In short, federal troops cannot perform law-enforcement activities on US soil, except in the most extreme circumstances. (It's only happened twice since 1969.) The only way the Louisiana National Guard could fall under federal control in Louisiana was if Blanco turned it over to Bush or if Bush took the extraordinary step of invoking the act. Bush did not want to do that—he knew he would set a dangerous precedent and anger Mississippi's Republican governor, Haley Barbour—so he would need to push, prod, cajole, and intimidate Blanco to do it "voluntarily."

On Air Force One that Friday morning—with Blum's wise warning still ringing in her ears—Blanco asked Bush for twenty-four hours to consider the proposal. She didn't need that long to decide. She would reject the plan twelve hours later. But she wanted to consult her lawyers and assess the legal impact of Bush's extraordinary demand. Louisiana wanted more troops, pronto, and arguing over who controlled them, or withholding them until Blanco agreed to give Bush control, seemed to be an outrageous and indefensible White House request. Moreover, the White House pursued this course because the tide had turned in New Orleans. The Dome and the Convention Center were empty. Most survivors in New Orleans who wished to be rescued had left for Baton Rouge, Houston, Dallas, or another dozen cities that were welcoming residents. Order was returning to the city, and Bush and his advisors wanted to take credit for work none of them had done.

It was grotesque. The White House spent days trashing Blanco and other Louisiana officials for Bush's failures. And now they wanted to complete the plan by seizing control of the Louisiana National Guard. Blanco was eager to work with Bush to rebuild her state, but she would not let him bulldoze her in a public-relations scam that would make the city more dangerous.

BY THE TIME I arrived at the governor's house on Saturday morning, the drama was ending. Around midnight, the White House had faxed a memorandum to Blanco, demanding that she accept a federal takeover of the evacuation effort in New Orleans (the same evacuation that had been completed). She refused and held her ground all night. Bush, his chief of staff, Andrew Card, and everyone else at the White House misjudged her resolve. People often did. I was guilty of it myself sometimes.

Blanco was nothing like the outgoing, wisecracking politicos who dominated the State Capitol in Baton Rouge. She was not a member of their old-boys club. She was a mother of six and a grandmother who entered politics for the first time in her early forties. She could be shy. She sometimes struggled to find the right words. She was not the most inspiring speaker. But she was guided by a profound belief that God called her into public service. She was not self-righteous about that calling. She rarely talked about it, but I realized—as someone who knew her long before she ran for governor—that this was not a woman who would abandon a commitment or shrink from a challenge. Just as she would fight for Louisiana until the last day of her term, she fought for Louisiana on the night the White House tried to seize the National Guard troops who had saved thousands of lives and were maintaining order in New Orleans.

Throughout the night, as I slept, she and her staff fought with the White House. Bush's staffers even forced General Blum, who days earlier argued against this very move, to call Blanco to say she had no choice but to give in. Blum later confessed to one of our staff members that he made his appeal under extreme duress. His language describing the pressure he experienced was profane and graphic.

Late that morning, Bush and Card capitulated. My lone contribution to the drama was to proofread the letter that Blanco and others prepared for Bush a few minutes before she signed it and faxed it to the White House. In it, Blanco refused to give up the National Guard (a course that Governor Barbour also followed in Mississippi). The White House had no choice but to give Blanco what she had requested the previous Wednesday: 7,200 federal active-duty troops and another 10,000 National Guard personnel from other states to assist with recovery efforts and restore order in New Orleans. Could Blanco have requested these troops earlier in the week, as some Bush defenders have argued? Sure. Her appeals for federal assistance—"we need everything you've got"—might have sounded vague to anyone who wasn't working in the Emergency Operations Center in Baton Rouge in the hours during and after Katrina. But this criticism of Blanco's reluctance or refusal to demand a specific number of troops on Monday or Tuesday ignores an important fact: officials with FEMA and the US Department of Homeland Security were embedded with the state's team in the situation room from the beginning of the response. FEMA director Mike Brown met with Blanco at the EOC on the night of Sunday, August 28, the day before Katrina came ashore. Among those at the big conference table in the EOC at every meeting over the next week were FEMA officials whom we understood to be experts in advising governors and state officials about what federal assets were available. Why didn't Brown or Homeland Security Secretary Michael Chertoff or General Blum advise Blanco about what she should ask of the federal government? To my knowledge, none of them did. Several of them, however, were quick to attack her for not requesting what they should have offered her on Monday or Tuesday of that week.

SATURDAY, SEPTEMBER 3, was the chaotic end of an emotionally draining week for all of us. Looking back on those incredible days, I regret I could not see that we were grappling with a catastrophe the likes of which no other American city—not even New York on 9/11— ever experienced. Much of a major US city had been destroyed. Almost a million people were displaced for months or years. Communications among Baton Rouge, New Orleans, and much of the far-flung towns of the region had been shattered. I still marvel that the governor of Louisiana and the mayor of New Orleans could not communicate by phone for weeks.

In fact, the day before Katrina hit New Orleans, I was with Blanco in Mayor Nagin's office at City Hall. We had finished the second of two days of press conferences in and around the region to warn residents about the danger of the storm and the dire need for immediate evacuation. The governor, Coach, and I accompanied Nagin to his large office for a few minutes of downtime before we returned to the Superdome's helipad for the short flight back to Baton Rouge. Nagin pulled me aside before we left. He held a large device in his hand. "This is my satellite phone," he said, as I scribbled down the number he gave me. "Tell the governor to call me on this if she needs me. This will always work."

It never worked.

For the next few weeks, if Blanco wanted to speak to the mayor, she climbed in her National Guard helicopter, flew to New Orleans, and tracked him down (not always easy, as he fled New Orleans for Dallas for days on end). This radio silence from Baton Rouge only fed Nagin's paranoia and deepened his feeling of estrangement, as he no doubt imagined the state and federal governments had abandoned him and his city.

The communications breakdown between Blanco and Nagin was one of many consequences of the catastrophe that was Katrina. In all, at least 1,836 people died because of the storm's winds and the failure of the federal levees—1,577 in Louisiana. Tens of thousands of homes were destroyed and hundreds of thousands of families were displaced or separated. Cities and towns across the Mississippi-Louisiana Gulf Coast were wiped off the map.

My family was safe. Upriver from New Orleans by about eighty miles, Baton Rouge suffered significant wind damage, but we weren't surrounded by floodwaters. After about a week, the power at my house was restored, and our home life began returning to normal. That didn't mean that I didn't mourn what seemed like the death of a beautiful, major American city. While I never called New Orleans home, I had dozens of friends who did. Cindy lived in Metairie (a New Orleans suburb) when we began dating in 1990. Before the storm, I was in the city almost every week for business or pleasure. It was like a second home. Now it seemed gone and, with it, a large part of Louisiana.

My brother, Paul, who lived in Fredericksburg, Virginia, emailed me that week telling me we were welcome to stay with him and his family until we figured out our next move. While I appreciated the gesture, it was inconceivable that we would leave the state we loved and where our children were born. Still, I kept my emotions under control for the first week or so. We were all working long, hard hours at the EOC. There was just no time to stop and mourn. Then, early one morning, I drove to work through the dark, empty streets of Baton Rouge. A song familiar to most Louisianians began playing on the radio: Randy Newman's haunting ballad "Louisiana 1927." When Newman reached his emotional refrain—"Louisiana, Louisiana/They're tryin' to wash us away"—my pent-up grief burst forth. I cried. It was intense. I almost pulled over so

I wouldn't lose control of my car. But I kept moving through tears. The moment was cathartic. I arrived at work with a clearer sense of purpose.

What I didn't know was that Katrina not only shattered New Orleans and brought an entire state to its knees. The aftermath of this massive storm, and the other immense hurricane that would strike southwestern Louisiana a month later, would not only upend Louisiana politics; it was also the beginning of the end of my career in Louisiana politics.

2

BEAUMONT

The old man eased onto the subway car in the basement of the Russell Senate Office Building on a cold afternoon in February 1985. He slumped into the bench seat across from me for the two-minute ride to the US Capitol. I was on my way to see my new boss, US Senator Russell B. Long, in his "hideaway" office just steps off the second-floor Senate chamber. It took me a few seconds to recognize that my traveling companion was Barry Goldwater, a senator from Arizona and the 1964 presidential nominee of the Republican Party.

Part of me wanted to gush, "Senator Goldwater, I met you back in September 1971, when you came to Beaumont, Texas. Do you remember me?" But I said nothing. Goldwater glanced at me, grunted a brief hello, and then looked away, no doubt lost in thought about some important matter of state. When we pulled into the stop at the Capitol, he struggled to rise. His hips were worn out. I considered springing up to help him stand but thought better of it. I didn't know much about Goldwater, but I knew he was a proud, independent man. He would have refused my help. He limped off our car.

As he walked away, I thought about that afternoon fourteen years earlier when I had met him in Beaumont as he and his Texas Senate colleague, John Tower, flew into the Jefferson County Airport for a fundraiser for Tower. Goldwater headlined the event and was still very much the hero of the American conservative movement just seven years after Lyndon Johnson had crushed him in the presidential election. I was thirteen years old, fascinated by politics, and had persuaded my parents to take me to the airport so I could get Goldwater's and Tower's autographs. An experienced former Air Force pilot, Goldwater flew the small plane that brought the two men to our southeast Texas town. As they deplaned and ambled over to the small crowd gathered to greet them, I clawed my way forward and pushed index cards into their hands. Both scribbled their signatures on them. The cards, which I still have and treasure, were among the first items in an autograph collection I had started.

Most of the signatures I collected in those days were of politicians. In 1968, I wrote to Vice President Hubert Humphrey. He responded with a brief letter and signed photo and autographed the accompanying biographical booklet.[1] A few days after my 1971 airport encounter with Goldwater, the postman delivered a letter from Ronald Reagan, then governor of California, in response to my letter urging him to run for president. "I deeply appreciate learning that you hold me in such high regard," Reagan said, "and your support gives me added encouragement to deal with the rugged challenges we face here in Sacramento." Other politicians who responded to my letters from the late 1960s through the late 1970s included Alabama Governor George Wallace and former President Harry Truman. I wrote to Truman twice at his home in Independence, Missouri, over several years in the late 1960s. Both times, he sent back small photographs of himself, signed and dated. I wrote FBI Director J. Edgar Hoover, and I sent get-well wishes to former President Dwight D. Eisenhower and words of sympathy to his wife, Mamie, when Ike died in 1969. Each replied with a card. An older cousin in Houston who learned of my hobby gave me the congratulatory letter that then-US Representative George H. W. Bush sent her when she graduated high school in 1970. I kept the correspondence to my mother from our local Democratic congressman, Jack Brooks, after she wrote him of her worries about crime and creeping socialism. "Your father was a long time friend and supporter of mine as well as a staunch Democrat," Brooks wrote her in March 1972 of my late grandfather Charles Wellhausen. "[I] don't think he would share your views that 'the Democrats are going to more Socialist leanings.'"

Like many young people, I drank deeply from the well of my parents' political views. They were conservative Republicans who voted for Wallace in 1968 because they thought President Richard Nixon was too liberal. That lasted until House Democrats began impeachment proceedings in 1974, which brought them back into the GOP fold. In the early seventies, I was obsessed with Wallace, perhaps because of my parents' enthusiasm for him and the kind, personal-sounding replies he sent to each of my letters.[2] When Wallace came to Beaumont for a rally at the Southeast Texas State Fairgrounds in 1968, I begged my parents to take me. It was my first political rally. Four years later, as Wallace was revving up his campaign for the Democratic Party's presidential nomination in 1972, my mother took me to a meeting of local Wallace supporters at the Jefferson County Courthouse. A photo of that meeting, with me in it, would be the first time my picture appeared in a newspaper.

On the May 1972 afternoon when Arthur Bremer shot and paralyzed

Wallace after a rally in a suburban Maryland shopping center, my mother was waiting for me when school let out. That was unusual, because George C. Marshall Junior High was a one-mile bike ride from our house. "Bob, Governor Wallace has been shot," she told me when I climbed into the front seat. I cried on the short drive home and glued myself to the television set for the rest of the afternoon, hoping for any positive news on Wallace's condition. Early that evening, the phone rang. It was Ms. Marion Eady, one of my teachers, a young African American woman who knew of my admiration for—really, my obsession with—Wallace. "Bob, I heard about Governor Wallace," she said. "I'm so sorry." I don't remember much else about that call or even how I replied.

I did not comprehend the import—to Ms. Eady or me—of that gesture until many years later. I was well into in my forties when I began to consider the compassion and maturity it took for a Black woman in the South to express sympathy over the shooting of the country's foremost racist to one of that racist's young disciples. Many years later, I tried to locate Ms. Eady to tell her not only what her call had meant to me but also how my views on race and politics had evolved. I hoped she would rejoice that I had outgrown my worship of racist politicians. I wanted

Marion Eady, one of my teachers at George C. Marshall Junior High in Beaumont, Texas. She called to comfort me the night former Alabama Governor George C. Wallace was shot in Maryland. (George C. Marshall Junior High, *The Rebel*, 1972)

her to know I considered the most important work of my professional life was campaigning to defeat former KKK leader David Duke when he ran against Louisiana Senator J. Bennett Johnston in 1990. I never found her.

Before long, I learned at least two lessons from the letters and the budding autograph collection that consumed me in the late 1960s and early 1970s: I loved these brushes with fame and the pieces of history that arrived—addressed to me—in our mailbox. And I was in love with politics. "Unless I miss my guess," Mrs. Fitzhugh, my fourth-grade teacher at Sallie Curtis Elementary, wrote me in June 1969, "you will be an important political leader some day. You show such an interest in our government and our leaders. We need leaders of such fine character as you." I took her prediction to heart.

Since my earliest days, I was a dreamer. I'd lie in bed at night, mentally transporting myself to random places and situations. My favorite dream during my junior high days was that I was a US senator. Between classes, I roamed the halls, pretending I was 1,200 miles away in Washington, DC, where I was the nation's youngest senator. Never mind that I was about eighteen years too young to take office. I pretended that Congress had recognized my unique skills and had amended the Constitution to allow me to serve.

My parents—neither of whom worked in politics—were slightly alarmed by my obsession but tolerated and, occasionally, encouraged it. My mother, once a fan of the 1952 and 1956 Democratic presidential nominee, Adlai Stevenson, had become a passionate Republican. She supported Goldwater's 1964 presidential campaign, but I don't recall any political activism into the late 1960s or early 1970s. My father did not feel strongly about politics, other than to agree with my mother that the country's future was endangered by its leftward drift at the hands of liberals like Johnson and faux conservatives like Nixon. Neither parent evinced much confidence that a person could maintain his or her principles after entering the political arena. Theirs was the typical cynicism about politics that one might have found in most middle-income homes in America near the end of the violent 1960s, a period dominated by Democratic politicians whose policies brought about momentous social and political changes that, at times, reached even isolated corners of the country, like Beaumont.

My mom and dad were alarmed about the direction of the country and, because they were, so was I. The communists or socialists (nobody really knew the difference between the two) were about to take over the government. At least, leaders like Goldwater and Reagan told us they were. So, we believed it. For some reason, none of this spoiled or diminished my fascination with politics and political history. My upbringing was conservative—religiously and politically. I recall the first time I read Massachusetts Senator Edward "Ted" Kennedy describe himself as a "liberal." I was astonished. I had no idea anyone would admit to such a character defect. In my mind, he might as well have confessed to being a horse thief.

"People who go into politics usually get corrupted," my mother often warned me when she thought my fascination with a campaign or a candidate was going overboard. Maybe she believed, as Adlai Stevenson once said, "It is often easier to fight for principles than to live up to them." I didn't argue with her, but I also didn't believe her. Young people are impervious to the advice of their elders, deeming them alarmist, out of touch, or overly conservative. More than anything, I knew I would be the exception to the rule. My idealism and innate goodness would inoculate me from the malign influences and tawdry temptations of political life. I would never, I resolved, sacrifice my principles for political or personal gain.

FOR ALMOST TWENTY-FIVE years, my father had worked at Sun Oil Company, where he supervised the Gulf Coast Service Section. In that job, he helped develop enormous maps of oilfields, something that had not been tried until then. He worked on the fourth floor of the Petroleum Building downtown. I loved visiting his office, which reeked of photographic developing chemicals. I had never smelled anything like it. Sometimes, he would invite me into the developing room, lit dimly by a red bulb. I would watch, mesmerized, as he swished the photographic paper around in the chemicals and slowly brought forth an image before hanging the paper to dry. Each of the large rooms was packed with enormous photographic and reproduction equipment, some of which he had developed, modified, or perfected to meet the company's needs. Dad was an inventive man, with a high school education and a year of college in an era when that, plus an apprenticeship with an oil company, was more than enough to guarantee a good, well-paying job for life.

He was a friendly man who loved jokes, especially the practical kind. He would often recruit my mother and all three children to come along on his es-capades. We would creep up on an unsuspecting neighbor's house and plant a for-sale sign or a toilet in the front yard. He once told us to rake up the leaves in our yard and bag them. That night, we loaded down our car with the bags and dumped the leaves onto the yard of one of his good friends. Other times, at his direction, we would sneak into a parking lot where a col-league had left his car and fill the inside—to the roof—with crumpled news-papers. After he acquired a discarded police car siren, Dad loved slipping up to friends' houses late at night, setting off the siren, and then diving into the bushes to watch the perplexed inhabitants emerge from their front door.

Dad's coworkers and bosses in Beaumont and Dallas liked him and he could have risen through the company's ranks had he agreed to a transfer to the Dallas headquarters. But my parents regarded that metropolis as a Babylon where they would find it difficult to raise children. Beaumont was relatively small. It had a population of about 117,000 in 1970, virtually the same as today. Dallas was a city of 1.3 million. Sarah, Paul, and I could ride our bikes all over Beaumont unmolested. It wasn't tiny, but it was small enough and where almost all my family lived. When offered the promotion, Dad turned it down because it would mean uprooting our family from our wholesome, peaceful, and prosperous life. Tragic for him, however, was the 1968 merger of Sun Oil Company with Sunray DX Oil Company. Had he taken the position in Dallas, he might have been safe. After the merger, however, his position in the Beaumont office was superfluous. The company laid him off after almost twenty-four years of service. They gave him about a year of severance pay. He had earned no retirement.

Using the severance pay, he and my mother opened a used bookstore, the Brouz-A-Bit, which was an oasis for a kid like me, who loved to read. For several years, I hung out at the bookstore after school and helped staff the cash register on summer days. It was like having my personal library. I could "check out" any book that I wanted. For a while, Dad had secured a side job delivering newspapers for the *Beaumont Enterprise*. It had terrible hours. The *Enterprise* required him to rise around two or three each morning and collect the bound papers as they rolled off the presses. Then, he would fold them and stretch a rubber band around each paper or, if it was raining, insert each into a plastic bag. Many mornings in the summer, Dad roused me around three o'clock, put me to work folding the papers, and brought me along so I could help him fling them from the car as he drove his route. I can still see the car's backseat filled to overflowing with folded newspapers and smell the overwhelming odor of the still-damp ink that saturated the car and assaulted my nostrils. Even though I would one day work as a newspaper reporter, the distinctive aroma of newsprint and ink has never appealed to me. Still today, it reminds me of my family's painful, hard times.

FOR YEARS, MY father had also served as a part-time, lay minister in the Church of Christ. He preached on Sundays at a variety of small, rural churches across East Texas, in places like Woodville, Evadale, and Anahuac, and in Merryville, Louisiana. On the Wednesday night in April 1968 that Martin Luther King, Jr., was killed in Memphis, we were on our way to a Bible study at a small African American church he pastored in Beaumont.

It was in the Church of Christ—that conservative Protestant

nondenominational assemblage—that I learned my earliest lessons about racial tolerance. I will never forget the Sunday morning in the early 1970s when a Black woman arrived for worship at the Pinecrest Church of Christ, where my family attended when we were not accompanying my father to one of his congregations. The woman's car had broken down as she drove to her church that morning. When she noticed that our services were about to begin, she wandered inside and worshipped with us. Most members welcomed her courteously. And then our minister rose to deliver his sermon and began by noting the Black woman's presence. "She's only here this morning because her car broke down," he told the congregation. The implication was clear: don't worry; this Black interloper won't return. My mother fumed. She was incensed that he had made this woman feel conspicuous and uncomfortable in our presence. When church was over, my mother stormed up to the preacher—now greeting folks at the front door of the building as they left—and chewed him out for what seemed like five minutes.

Although I left the Church of Christ for the United Methodist Church in my adulthood, I would attend church with my parents when I visited them in San Antonio or Fredericksburg, Virginia. To this day, I am always amazed by the racial diversity in congregations of the Church of Christ. My parents were not civil rights leaders in our community. And I recall their distrust of Martin Luther King, Jr., and his movement in the 1960s. But I never heard them use a racial epithet. As children, my siblings and I were forbidden to use such words.

The Church of Christ might have helped me view those of another race with more enlightened eyes than some of my friends, but it also took us from our happy life in Beaumont. In 1971, my dad accepted a full-time job as the preacher for the Linwood Avenue Church of Christ in Shreveport, Louisiana. That move was traumatic enough, as we left behind my paternal grandfather and both my grandmothers. Our leaving Beaumont was the only time I saw my mother's mother weep. But at least we were only four hours away by car. We could, and did, make the drive in a morning's time. The next move, two years later, to Tucumcari, New Mexico, was far more difficult. Dad's preaching was uncompromising to the point of annoying and angering the less-devout members of his congregation. In Shreveport and Tucumcari, his strict, unbending sermons—informed by his arduous study of New Testament Greek— lasted about two years until members at both churches decided he needed to tone it down or move along. We moved along. In 1975, he found another job preaching at the White Park Church of Christ, about four miles west of Leesville, in rural Vernon Parish in west-central Louisiana. He lasted about two years in that job, too.

Our family's finances had suffered when Dad lost his job at Sun Oil. His preaching kept us alive, but there never seemed to be enough. We had no health insurance. He had no retirement and little savings. For years, money would always be short at month's end. In Shreveport, Mom and Dad found part-time work distributing "circulars," advertisements on newsprint that were sometimes inserted in the daily newspaper. In our case, however, the company wanted them attached to the doorknobs of homes on each route. For several days each week after school, the whole family would spend an hour or two folding circulars. Then, we would set off to walk whichever neighborhood was on that day's route. Whatever meager earnings this work generated helped keep us clothed and fed.

I will never forget my disappointment when I brought home my first paycheck in high school. (I worked at a gas station in Tucumcari.) My mother made me hand it over. Looking back, I understand. She simply needed it to pay the bills. In Tucumcari, Mom and Dad kept us fed by turning much of our backyard into a garden. They planted every vegetable imaginable. Many afternoons in the spring and summer found my sister, brother, and me pulling weeds in that garden. Dad read somewhere that mineral oil kept worms out of the corn, so he filled an oilcan and sent me forth to squirt a dollop of oil into the top of each ear on every stalk. It seemed to work.

Were we poor? Technically, we probably were. But I never remember going without a proper meal, decent clothes, or new shoes. Like many parents raising kids in tough times, mine did whatever they needed to keep their family together. They always loved us, taught us to be honest and caring people, instilled in us their strong faith in God, and provided for us as best they could. What more could a child want?

3

I'm in Trouble

Leesville, where we moved in the summer of 1975, was home to a 198,000-acre Army facility, Fort Polk, the headquarters of the 5th Infantry Division (Mechanized) and the site of the large-scale 1941 war game—the Louisiana Maneuvers—that drew to Vernon Parish a host of military giants, including Dwight D. Eisenhower, George Patton, Omar Bradley, and Mark Clark. We lived in the small parsonage behind the modest church building west of town. Our water came from the well with a motorized pump (the sulfurized water always reeked of rotten eggs), and when we wanted to make a phone call, we made sure the party line was clear. We shared the line with several families who lived in the small White Park settlement. The phone had a distinctive ring for each household. Life in the country was different, but I began to enjoy it. I could walk out our backdoor and into the woods that abutted the church property and roam the vast acreage north of Anacoco Lake. I hunted squirrels and rabbits. We fished for bream, perch, and catfish in the lake and I learned to water ski on Vernon Lake, two miles north of our house.

When I arrived at Leesville High School in the fall of 1975, it was my fourth school in five years. I was a bit lost. I had made good friends in Beaumont, Shreveport, and Tucumcari, only to leave them behind in each move. I didn't know it, but moving to Leesville would be a blessing. In two short years, I would find a mentor, a life's passion, and a vocation.

Our principal was Dr. Herschel Lynn Russell, a dapper, hard-charging disciplinarian who wore his hair in a pompadour. He was equal parts drill sergeant and motivational speaker. He reminded me of country singer Conway Twitty, if Conway had sported leisure suits. He took an immediate interest in me and my sister, Sarah, who was one year behind me in school. In time, she and I would often find ourselves at the spacious home the Russells built on Vernon Lake. Both welcomed us like the children they never had. This gave me self-confidence. Dr. Russell saw in me something I had not seen in myself—leadership. By the end of my first year at Leesville High, I had gained enough confidence to run for senior class president.

I'm not sure how I realized that my opponents, each of them White and longtime residents of Leesville, were ignoring the African American students who made up about a third of the 250-member class. So, I started campaigning among the Black students. "Look, none of these other guys are even talking to you," I'd tell them. "If one of them gets elected, you won't have much, if any, voice. I'll be your voice." I'm not sure they believed I could do anything for them, but I was the only candidate asking for their votes and that meant something. The last week of my junior year, my classmates elected me class president in a runoff by 140 votes to my opponent's 84. In the same voting, students from all the grades elected my friend, Dale Sibley, an African American senior, as student body president. For a high school in a rural part of the Deep South in 1976, this seemed like a major event. It didn't hurt that many of the students at Leesville High had parents who were Army personnel. They had lived in other regions of the country and the world. And they brought with them a more tolerant, worldly view about life and other people—especially minorities—that made Dale's election possible.[1]

Despite the relative racial tolerance of the high school's student body, Leesville was still a small town in the rural South. I recall the reflexive disgust my buddies and I felt when we learned that the Ku Klux Klan would hold a rally on the lawn of the Vernon Parish Courthouse. On the evening of the gathering, we loitered at the back of the crowd and chortled at the ridiculous and hate-filled show the hooded men staged from a flatbed trailer. The gathering was sparse. I don't recall recognizing anyone in the audience. I should have been outraged, but we all found it pathetic and amusing. I suppose it was a testament to our American belief in free speech that the local powers gave the Klan the run of the square. Or it could have been that some parish officials were members. I never knew whose faces the hoods concealed.

SINCE I WAS ten years old—maybe younger—commercial radio had fascinated me. Besides indulging my interest in politics, my parents also tolerated my obsession with becoming a radio disc jockey. In my bedroom, I created a make-believe sound board and microphone to complement my turntable. I would sit for hours spinning country records to an imaginary audience. "That was Hank Williams singing 'Your Cheatin' Heart.' Now it's time for a little Ernest Tubb. Here he is singing 'Walkin' the Floor Over You.'" I could play this game for hours. In Tucumcari, I had befriended a former disc jockey who explained that if I wanted to work in radio, I must take a test administered by the Federal Communications Commission to

Me, age seventeen, at Leesville High School.

get my third-class license with a broadcaster's endorsement. If I passed the test, it meant that I understood the basics of electricity, radio waves, and frequencies. I could perform elementary tasks such as turning a radio station's transmitter on or off. I could read and adjust the dials on the transmitter. And, most important, I could staff the station at night or early morning without the presence of a licensed broadcast engineer.

In the late spring of 1976, I drove to Beaumont to take the FCC test in a room at the federal courthouse. I passed and soon I had my third-class license and a summer job at a 1,000-watt radio station in Leesville, KLLA-AM. First, I had to learn how to operate the sound board and remember to switch off the microphone after announcing a song or going to commercial. There are few more embarrassing moments in a radio announcer's week than forgetting the mic is still hot and discovering that the audience heard everything you thought you said in private. The station owner, Nick Pollacia, patiently taught me the basics, standing behind me as I learned to work the board and switching off the mic when I forgot. Working the board, especially the mic switch, soon became second nature.

Before long, I was hosting a morning country music show. Later, after school started, I would play pop music. And at the top of every hour, I'd read state and national news, ripped off the Associated Press machine housed in a backroom of the station. The machine's keys never stopped clacking as it spit out all sorts of news. It was an art to determine how many stories would consume exactly the four or five minutes allotted for the newscast. I made most of my editorial decisions in the three minutes it might take Mel Tillis to sing "Good Woman Blues."

I worked at KLLA-AM until February 1977, when Colonel John Stannard, a retired Army chaplain, hired me to work for Leesville's rival station, KVVP, a larger 3,000-watt outfit that played "beautiful music"— easy listening or "elevator music"—and country and jazz. Stannard was a quiet, kind man. The closest I ever heard him come to swearing was, when frustrated, he'd sputter, "Sugar!" Much of the station's programming was automated, so my job involved announcing and changing tape reels that contained the "beautiful music" and Bible studies by J. Vernon McGee and Jimmy Swaggart. I also wrote copy for commercials and even produced a few of them.

After graduation from Leesville High, I left for college at Northeast Louisiana University (now the University of Louisiana at Monroe), where I found a job at KREB-FM (and, yes, the REB stood for Rebels). In time, I would host an afternoon and evening country music show six days a week. At first, it was a demanding job for a college freshman who was given the station's least-desirable job: signing on the station in the morning. For that duty, I arose at 4:30 and reached the station's front door by stepping over the drunks sleeping in the second-floor hallway of the hotel/flophouse where KREB rented space. I would warm up the transmitter, put the station on the air, and play country music until the morning drive-time host—a molasses-voiced Horace "Hoss" Logan, founder of the famed *Louisiana Hayride*—took over.[2]

Then, I rushed back to campus for my morning classes. More than once, sleep deprived, I dozed off during a lecture. That radio job lasted until February 1978, when I got fired for complaining about how my early-morning duties interfered with schoolwork. If I hadn't lost that job, I might never have been drawn into campaigns and elections. As it turned out, getting sacked sent me back to Leesville and headlong into my first experience with the cutthroat world of Louisiana politics.

EVER THE PASSIONATE Republican, I volunteered in the summer of 1978 for the congressional campaign of Jimmy Wilson, a former Democratic mayor and state representative from Vivian (in far northwestern Louisiana) who had registered as a Republican that year to run for Congress to replace the 4th District's longtime Democratic representative, Joe D. Waggonner. I volunteered to help organize Vernon Parish, in the southern part of the district, where almost no one knew Wilson. People in Vernon Parish knew well another leading candidate for Waggonner's seat, forty-six-year-old Democratic state Representative Claude "Buddy" Leach, who, besides serving in the Legislature, was the de facto boss of Vernon Parish. Leach was a hulk of man, a courthouse lawyer, wealthy from his wife's enormous oil and gas holdings, and renowned for presiding over the House Ways and Means Committee with an iron fist. More than forty years after that first campaign, I realize my stupidity in thinking I could garner support for Wilson in a parish where most people who weren't scared of crossing Leach were grateful for the pork-barrel projects he brought back from Baton Rouge. His law partner was the district attorney; his brother-in-law, Creighton Owen, was the superintendent of Vernon Parish Schools (I had briefly dated Creighton's daughter in high school). Leesville was a small town. Everyone knew Leach and his family.

Not content to do my campaign work for Wilson—I drove him and his wife around the parish on their one visit to Leesville that summer—I drafted a letter to the editor of the *Shreveport Times* defending my belief in Republican Party ideals. "What's so detestable about being a Republican?" I asked in the letter the *Times* ran on July 22. "I have felt like a leper ever since I registered as such about two years ago." Unsatisfied with this innocuous missive, I next wrote a letter attacking Leach's "liberal" voting record in the state Legislature and sent it to the *Leesville Leader.* "How many voters realize that in the current race for Congress, 'our' candidate is using conservative rhetoric, but his voting record shows a liberal legislator?" I asked, closing thus: "I think it is time to elect a man to Congress whose views correspond with our own. That man certainly *is not* Claude Leach." My attack appeared in the *Leader* in mid-August 1978. It did not go over well with at least one local Leach supporter. Someone called our house that morning and, when my mother answered the phone, he made a threat on my life.

Later that day, I was working a shift at KVVP when the station's secretary received a phone call from Leach's sister, Gloria Owen, the wife of the school superintendent and the owner of a local dress shop that advertised on KVVP. "Does Bob Mann work for your station?" she reportedly asked. Told that I did, she canceled all her shop's advertising. Advised of this, Chaplain Stannard called and tried to dissuade her. Afterwards, he told me "they" insisted I be fired or the store would no longer advertise on his station. He did not fire me. The next day, I called Representative Waggonner's office in Washington and the state Attorney General's office in Baton Rouge to tell them what happened. Wisely, both wanted no part of this insignificant, small-town political spat between a dress shop owner and a college sophomore. Whoever I spoke to in the Attorney General's office advised me to take up the matter with the Vernon Parish School Board. So, I phoned two board members and told them about the alleged threats on my job.

News of my complaint no doubt reached the superintendent within minutes of my phone calls. Later that night, while I pulled a shift at the radio station, the phone rang. It was Creighton Owen. He asked if I had phoned two of his board members to allege that he and his wife had tried to get me fired. I told him I had, to which he responded with a string of invective. I hung up on him, which was my second unwise decision that day. Within ten minutes, Owen's car roared into the gravel parking lot of the station and he began pounding on the front door. I was alone at the station and, foolishly, let him in. The flood of invective started again, this time accompanied by his finger in my face. He refused to leave, so I retreated into the studio, locked the door, and called the only person I thought might know how to help me: my former high school principal, H. Lynn Russell.

"I'm in trouble," I told him before briefing him on the details of the day. He was horrified by the whole drama but particularly the news that I had complained to the school board members. He knew how this would end for me, but he also knew he had to help me defuse the situation. On his advice, I called the Vernon Parish Sheriff's Department. In about fifteen minutes, two deputies arrived and, after another twenty minutes of negotiation, they persuaded my fuming superintendent to go home.

I doubt Creighton wanted me fired. His wife—like many family

Dr. H. Lynn Russell, principal of Leesville High School, was a friend and mentor. He guided me through my first political scrape in the summer of 1978. (Leesville High, *Wampus Cat,* 1976)

members of beleaguered politicians—only wanted to protect her brother, Buddy, whom she loved. She probably picked up the phone and called without thinking about the consequences. I recall Stannard telling me "the Owens" wanted me sacked, but the initial phone call was almost certainly not Creighton's idea.

To some of Wilson's local supporters, this episode was public relations gold. One of them urged me to tell the whole sordid story and bought half-page ads in the *Leader* in late October and early November to run my affidavit attesting to the events. "Strong Arm Tactics are being used in Vernon Parish," I wrote. "They will continue to be used as long as people like Claude Leach are in power. . . . We do not need this kind of man in Washington."

Maybe if I had done a better job of organizing Vernon Parish instead of inciting the local Leach supporters, Wilson might have won more votes in this hostile environment. In the first round of elections, the state's open primary, Leach finished ahead of Wilson, districtwide, by one-tenth of 1 percent—26.9 percent to Wilson's 26.8 percent. Bossier Parish business executive Charles "Buddy" Roemer came in a close third, followed by two other candidates. (In Vernon Parish, Leach won 7,331 votes, compared to 2,038 for Roemer and a paltry 856 for Wilson.)

Creighton Owen was superintendent of schools for Vernon Parish. We clashed in the summer of 1978 but later became friends. (Leesville High, *Wampus Cat*, 1976)

In November, Leach won the runoff by 266 votes, a result that Wilson contested. A subsequent investigation led to the convictions of thirty-five people for vote buying in Vernon Parish on Leach's behalf, including a member of the Vernon Parish School Board and the mayor of Leesville. Federal prosecutors put Leach, the district attorney, and one of Leach's law partners on trial for bribery in connection with the election, but a jury in Lake Charles acquitted them in November 1979. Despite no conclusive evidence of his knowledge or participation, Leach could not overcome the scandal. Wilson and Roemer ran against him again in 1980. That time, Roemer ran strongest, edged out Wilson for the runoff spot, and defeated Leach in the general election, 64 percent to 36 percent.

MY FIRST CAMPAIGN taught me valuable lessons about politics. Among them: it might not always be effective to inject yourself into small-town political affairs and think you'll be welcomed warmly if you're opposing the entrenched power structure. I was a newcomer to Vernon Parish. I had not paid my dues. My voice had little credibility there. Instead of writing the letter to the newspaper, it might have been smarter to persuade an established local to do it. I also learned that it's easy to get manipulated by people who don't care about you. Leach's opponents in Vernon Parish were happy to exploit my naïveté as a weapon against him, without regard for the potential costs to me. In the end, nothing bad occurred, but I'm confident the people who paid for the newspaper ads in which I told my story didn't care much about what might happen to me. I wasn't wrong to take a principled stand, but my response to the attacks on me came mostly from anger and indignation, not sober thought. I should have consulted someone I trusted, like Dr. Russell, who might have given me sound advice.

I also came to understand that the First Amendment protects your right to speech, but you can still get fired for speaking out. Moreover, I was trying to have it both ways. I was dipping my toe into journalism—I was delivering the local news on a radio station—while attacking the local state representative. That was not ethical. Gloria Owen had every right to call my station and complain, maybe even an obligation to do so. Why shouldn't my boss have fired me even before she phoned?

In the decades to come, Leach and I would bury our differences and always greet each other amicably. Later, when I worked for Senator John Breaux, I would call Buddy whenever our travels took us to Vernon Parish. He always welcomed us warmly. In my many interactions with him in the past forty-plus years, he never spoke to me about my spat with his sister and brother-in-law, nor my ill-advised letter to the *Leesville Leader*. Whenever we would visit Vernon Parish, I also called Creighton

Owen, who became a friend during his tenure as executive director of the Leesville-Fort Polk campus for Northwestern State University. Creighton always treated me with kindness when we visited his campus and, like Buddy, never said a word about our confrontation in 1978. He died in 2002, having helped educate several generations of Vernon Parish's young people.

At the time, however, I wasn't ready to learn any of those lessons. That would come later. All I knew then was that I loved politics, even if it meant getting into more scraps like the one I had with Creighton. What I learned that year was simple and something I'd have to unlearn in the years to come: there's nothing more exhilarating than a good fight.

4

Who's the Mayor?

Strolling from Walker Hall to the Student Union one afternoon in 1980, Professor Richard Baxter listened patiently as I fretted about my future. It was a warm spring day on Northeast Louisiana University's campus. I should have been on an innertube, floating between the moss-draped cypress trees of lazy Bayou DeSiard, or killing time at the Wesley Center. Instead, I wasted time worrying about what to do after graduation the following year. "I don't know what I could do with a journalism degree beyond writing for a newspaper or working for a radio station," I told Richard, who ran the school's journalism program. His response brought me up short. "You know, you could be a press secretary for a politician, like a member of Congress." Holding such a job, or even living in Washington, seemed like an impossible dream. I had been to DC once—a one-night, two-day school trip to the capital in eleventh grade. I had contracted an instant case of Potomac Fever, but the idea of working there seemed preposterous. Richard, however, planted the thought in my mind.

Maybe he saw the makings of a politician because of my evident fascination with politics. When I got to college, I had continued to volunteer in campaigns and got involved in campus politics. In 1979, when Republican US Representative Dave Treen of Mandeville made the runoff in the governor's election with Democratic Public Service Commissioner Louis Lambert of Gonzales, I encouraged Republican students to request absentee ballots for Treen. I probably didn't help more than two dozen students to vote, but I was thrilled when Treen won by about 9,000 votes out of 1.37 million cast and became the state's first Republican governor since Reconstruction. From my first days on campus, I had thrown myself into the maelstrom of the Student Government Association. Some students gravitated towards Greek life, but even if I could have afforded it, I had no interest in joining a fraternity. In my sophomore year, I ran for class president and won (a couple of years later, I would campaign for student body president and lose). I don't recall details of the many SGA battles we waged—they all seemed so important at the time—but I remember one heated debate in my junior year involving the contested election of the new student body president. When I argued passionately against certifying this student's victory, one of his fraternity buddies—a former classmate of mine from Leesville High—rose to inform the assemblage that I had been no less a troublemaker during my time in Leesville. He was right. Then, as now, I didn't back down from a political fight.

From almost the beginning, I clashed with another SGA member, Alfred Bakewell. Our dislike for each other was intense and visceral. We snarled and bickered for weeks at SGA meetings. Over what, I do not remember. And then one day, I found myself sitting next to Alfred outside an SGA meeting and, forced to make small talk, we began to converse, not bark. It took us only a few minutes to realize we had much more in common than we first imagined. Soon, he invited me to meetings of NLU's Methodist students at the Wesley Center, then served by the Reverend Jim Wilson. Although I was not yet a Methodist, at the Wesley Center I found acceptance and peace apart from the hubbub of campus life. Jim was cheerful, funny, and not at all pious, which confused me. He

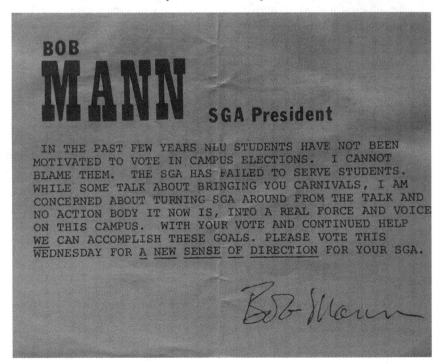

I ran for student body president at Northeast Louisiana University (NLU), now the University of Louisiana at Monroe, in 1980. Alas, I lost.

shocked me one day when I arrived at the center, telling me about a naked intruder he had discovered that morning in the sanctuary. "Really?" I said. "Yep," he replied, "we caught him by the organ." I laughed but wasn't sure if God wouldn't strike me dead. Jim taught me that religion and spirituality didn't mean you couldn't have a little fun.

After he graduated from NLU, Alfred went to seminary and became a Methodist pastor. Our friendship reminds me that enmity is often the product of misunderstanding and miscommunication. It's easier to dislike someone you're not talking with. It's easy to imagine what mischief or evil lurks in someone's heart but far harder to make the effort to talk to that person and discover his or her humanity, pain, struggles, and dreams. This would not be the last time I would learn this lesson.

I HAD NOT planned to study journalism in college. At Leesville High, I was active in the Future Business Leaders of America (FBLA) and let my enthusiasm for that group delude me into thinking I could thrive in accounting. By the end of my first semester, after struggling to earn a miserable D in my first accounting course, I knew I had overestimated my aptitude with numbers. I made a snap decision to change majors and settled on journalism. I had written for my high school's newspaper, the *Cat Talk*, and had been working in radio since my junior year in high school, so it seemed natural. Although I had lost my first college radio job because of my class schedule, I wasn't ready to give up on broadcasting. At the beginning of my sophomore year, I walked into the offices of KMLB-FM, a pop music station in a small building north of town, to ask for a job.

The owner was a slight, well-dressed, taciturn man, Bob Powell, who would soon be elected mayor of Monroe. Within a few minutes, I was sitting in his office. He hired me and assured me that the station would accommodate my classes. I often worked late afternoons, nights, and weekends. It was a fun job, but I was hungry for a station with a larger audience. After about a year, I moved to the mothership of northeast Louisiana radio stations, KNOE, which comprised AM and FM stations in a large complex in the center of town, also home to the local CBS television affiliate with the same call letters (the Noe family also owned WNOE-AM and FM in New Orleans).

It was a dream working at a station that wasn't run on a shoestring. Instead of cueing up records on turntables, I launched eight-track tapes with the push of a button. Once a song began, I could dash for the bathroom without worrying that the record would hit a deep scratch, get caught in a groove, and repeat the same line for two minutes (that happened to me more than once in previous jobs). It was a fun gig, made even more so when the station equipped my modest Ford Pinto with a cellular phone. Unlike the small, pocket-size devices of today, this contraption had a black handset that rested in a cradle mounted on the dash. It looked very much like a traditional landline phone of the day. The handset connected to a massive transmitter that the station installed in my trunk. In the late 1970s, Monroe had only four cell phone lines. If I needed to make or receive a call, at least one of those phone lines had to be open. Often, I'd try to make a call, but no line was available.

On the sides of my car, the station plastered two magnetic signs: *Mann on the Go.* For several hours each weekday, I would roam the town until I found something interesting to talk about. Then, I would phone the station and do a brief interview or report. Sometimes, I'd follow a car and announce its license number or its make and model. If the driver was listening to KNOE, he or she would know to pull over to receive an on-air reward—usually concert tickets for some country act. One afternoon, I went to a local motel and conducted a painfully long interview of an Elvis impersonator. Whoever was running the board cut me off in mid-interview and went back to playing country music for the two or three listeners who hadn't already switched channels.

My car phone was a source of pride and impressive to some young women I courted. But seriously, could any car phone make a powder-blue 1977 Ford Pinto appear sexy? One feature of the phone that offered amusement to some of my buddies in NLU's Sherrouse Hall, where I lived during my freshman and sophomore years, was the horn that would blare when someone called. Some nights, one mischievous friend derived great joy from waiting until everyone had fallen asleep before he dialed my number, which shattered the dorm's silence. The honking would stir half the residents, who'd pour out onto the balcony to see my Pinto as the cause of their sudden awakening. The only way I could stop the bloody tooting was to run out and answer the phone or disengage the horn. I could hear everyone's sleepy curses as I scurried downstairs and dashed into the parking lot.

I enjoyed playing country records, but I set my sights on doing full-time radio news on KNOE's big, 50,000-watt FM station, FM102. For years, Linnie Freeman had anchored the local news on the pop music channel, the highest-rated radio station in northeast Louisiana. When she switched to the TV station to work as a news anchor in late 1980, I applied for her job. Soon, I was arriving at the station each morning to read the news at 5:30. I would anchor the newscasts every half-hour until 8:00 or 9:00, then rush off to classes. Around 2:00 or 3:00, I would return to the station to gather news and conduct phone interviews—in the radio business they're called "actualities"—for the afternoon, drive-time broadcasts. The job was not only great fun; it also taught me how to write on a tight deadline and do so concisely. If you have only thirty seconds to tell listeners about last night's city council meeting, you cannot use extraneous words. The skill of writing tight would serve me well when I got my first newspaper job.

In my last semester at NLU, fate put me in a journalism class taught by one of the *Monroe News-Star*'s editors, Mike Albertson. He must have liked how I wrote, for he offered me a job working for his paper. After my graduation in August 1981, I moved to Ruston—home to Louisiana Tech University, thirty miles west of Monroe—where I became the paper's Ruston bureau chief. "Bureau chief" sounds lofty, but I supervised only a circulation employee who seemed to think she answered to me but who worked for someone back in Monroe. I covered news in a four-parish area from Union, Lincoln, Jackson, and Winn parishes, an eighty-by-forty-mile undulating, timber-heavy swath of Louisiana that stretched from Junction City at the Arkansas border to Winnfield, about fifty miles north of Alexandria.

One day, I'd be covering a town council meeting in Choudrant, just east of Ruston. "Well, it's time to decide which one of us will run for mayor this year," the incumbent mayor announced at such a meeting one night. (It was just me, the mayor, and the council in attendance.) The moaning began. "I can't do it," one member complained. "I just don't have the time." Finally, one of them agreed, under duress, to "take" the job.

Another day, I might cover a murder trial in Jonesboro. I'll never forget that afternoon in the Jackson Parish Courthouse when a flamboyant defense attorney from Monroe wheeled around and bellowed to a pitiful thirteen-year-old boy, tearfully testifying at his mother's murder trial, "*You* killed your mother, didn't you?!" The next day, it might be a disaster response drill in Farmerville. The day after that, a celebrity speaker at Louisiana Tech.

For nine months, I wrote about high school football games; police jury, school board, and town council meetings; fatal car wrecks; and local elections. I prowled curvy White Lightning Road—north of Ruston between Vienna (pronounced "*Vigh*-anna") and Homer—trying to discover the origins of the name. (Legend has it the road was built by chain-gang members who had been arrested for selling the illicit corn liquor.) In August 1981, when a truck loaded with 100 pounds of dynamite broke down at the intersection of Highways 167 and 146 in Vienna—closing the highways in all directions—I camped out for most of the day until the crisis passed.

I also wrote more than a half-dozen stories for a series the paper called "Your Town." For each, I wandered into some small town—many just wide spots in the road—and began interviewing people until I figured out how the town or village got its name and why anyone should care about its history. I quickly learned the best way to assemble an interesting history was to ask for the oldest resident. If that person was still lucid— and most were—I could collect some great fodder for my story.

I wrote about hilly Dubach, a town of 1,161 souls, thirteen miles north of Ruston. The place got its name from one of its early settlers, Fred B. Dubach, who moved there in 1899 and established the town's first sawmill. Intrigued by the name of a Jackson Parish village, Eros, just southwest of Monroe, I went there and discovered it was once the largest town in the parish (population 1,184 in 1920, down to 158 by 1980). The town got its name from the 433 Eros Asteroid, the second-largest near-Earth object, discovered in 1898 by a German astronomer. During its heyday, Eros had three hotels and the first high school in Jackson Parish. I also wrote about Downsville, a town that straddled the Union-Lincoln parish line (139 of the town's population lived in Union Parish, another 60 in Lincoln Parish). "My daddy said he remembered when they had twelve stores around here," eighty-nine-year-old Jim Hinton, a former state representative, told me, adding with a sly grin, "and all of 'em sold whiskey."

In Simsboro, a Lincoln Parish town of 300 residents, I met eighty-five-year-old Bruce Price, who had lived there since 1917. The five-foot-eight-inch Price informed me he had played baseball for the minor league Shreveport Gassers in 1921 and, as a pitcher, once faced Babe Ruth. As I later confirmed, when the New York Yankees played the Gassers in March 1921—the New York club held its spring training in Louisiana that year—Price took the mound one day in relief after his team's starting pitcher gave up six runs over three innings. Price tossed three scoreless innings and, in the high point of his brief career, forced Ruth to hit a weak infield grounder that Price easily fielded for an out.

I loved the "Your Town" series because it allowed me to meet so many fascinating people, including George Harmon Smith, then the mayor of the Union Parish town of Marion (population 1,096). Smith was also an award-winning novelist. Disney had made his 1964 book, *Bayou Boy*, into a television movie in 1972. For another story in July 1983, after I had moved back to the newsroom in Monroe, I wrote about John Julius Nelson, a 100-year-old resident of Lake Providence, a thriving town of 3,600 on the Mississippi River in East Carroll Parish. Still lucid and voluble, Nelson told me about traveling with his wife to nearby Vicksburg, Mississippi, in October 1907 to see President Theodore Roosevelt, who was nearing the end of his second term. "The children gave him a bouquet of flowers," Nelson told me about TR's rally at the Warren County Courthouse, "and he took [the children] up in his arms. He was a strong-looking man."

Besides writing for the "Your Town" series and working on human-interest stories, I had other interesting assignments, including interviewing former Governor (and Country Music Hall of Fame member) Jimmie Davis in September 1981 about his annual homecoming celebration at the Jimmie Davis Tabernacle in Beech Springs, just north of Jonesboro in Jackson Parish. On a warm Sunday in October, along with several hundred people who came for "dinner on the grounds," I listened as Davis crooned several of his hits, including "Suppertime" and his most famous composition, "You Are My Sunshine." In a nearby cemetery, not far from his boyhood home, was buried Davis's late wife, Alvern, who died in 1967. Eventually, Davis would rest there, too. "You have people telling [me] they want to be buried there," the former governor told me with a chuckle, "but they're not anxious to get there."

I covered an appearance at Tech by C. Brooks Peters, the *New York Times'* Berlin bureau chief in the late 1930s. Peters' description of his meeting with Hitler in September 1939 was mesmerizing. "He would start talking in a very low voice and gradually build it up until, at the end, he would be screaming," Peters said of the Nazi leader. "I was tremendously impressed every time I heard Hitler speak. There was something almost hypnotic about it." The following week, I covered a speech to students by Frank Abagnale, the professional con artist whom Leonardo DiCaprio played in the hit 2002 movie *Catch Me If You Can*. Looking back on my story about the event, I'm embarrassed by what I wrote about Abagnale's time posing as a pediatrician in Atlanta. "So convincing was his ploy," I wrote, "the hospital made him its chief resident pediatrician. What did he do if a friend came to him for medical advice? 'I just told them, I'd rather you see your own doctor,' he said. 'Whenever the girls came, I gave them a thorough examination and sent them on their way,' he said to the laughter of the crowd. 'I was young, but not stupid.'" Reading those words now, in which Abagnale bragged about sexual abuse, makes me sick.

OF ALL THE people I met in my travels throughout north-central Louisiana, none was more interesting and colorful than Winnfield Mayor Kenneth "Jack" Henderson. If small-town Southern politicians are made from the same mold, then Henderson must have been the prototype. He was rotund and balding and always seemed to wear a white, short-sleeve dress shirt with a clip-on tie. Enhancing his image of small-town political boss was his ever-present fat cigar. Henderson would serve three consecutive terms as mayor of Huey and Earl Long's hometown in Winn Parish, until his defeat in 1982. I met him early that year while working on one of my "Your Town" pieces. I drove into Winnfield that day intending to roam around, chat with a few locals, and get the feel of the place. After an unsuccessful attempt at conversation with the waitress at the café near the courthouse—who must have thought I was interested in more than casual conversation—I ducked into the mayor's office.

"Who's the mayor?" I asked his secretary (this was before Google would make that a stupid question). She told me his name. I asked to see him, telling her I hoped he could help me with a story. The waiting room was crowded, much more than one might expect for a small town—and even some larger ones. I soon discovered I was sitting among the mayor's closest friends. Upon learning I was a newspaper reporter, one man asked me to name my favorite liquor. That question took me by surprise, but I suppose reporters have always a reputation as hard drinkers. "Gin," I sputtered, without thinking. He nodded with slight disapproval. "I like bourbon," the man said, "but gin is all right." Somehow, I knew I was at home and welcome in this strange place.

Looking around the room, I noted that the brown-paneled walls were plastered with plaques and awards from civic groups, all honoring the mayor for his achievements and contributions to the community. Harshly lit with a humming fluorescent light, the room was a bit gaudy, but the plaques and pictures on the walls told a story about the mayor's civic involvement and leadership. It wasn't too long before Henderson burst into the reception area and invited me into his office for a talk. He was a little gruff, and seemed wary of me at first, but by the end of our thirty-minute conversation we were becoming friends. After that, I dropped in for a visit two or three times a month and, before long, Henderson included me in the day's activities whenever I stopped by.

One day, I lounged in his office listening as he and his friends bickered over whether the World War II Japanese general and prime minister, Hideki Tojo, was still alive. He was hanged for war crimes in 1948, but as Google had not been invented in 1982, I had no immediate way of helping settle the argument. Henderson, chomping on his ever-present cigar, leaned back as far as he could in his desk chair, wiped his glasses with his tie, and carried on three conversations at once.

"No. No. That Jap's still alive," he insisted to one friend, who swore back that he was certain Tojo was dead and had been that way for more than thirty years. Henderson turned to me. "What about it?" he asked. I suppose he thought college-educated reporters knew such things. I shrugged. About then, his secretary breezed in, bearing papers for him to sign. "You know if Tojo's still alive?" he asked her, as she held the stack of documents. "Nope," she said. To be honest, she confessed, she wasn't quite sure who he was. Then, while the group pondered this important question, the conversation turned to local politics—and then, just as fast, back to Tojo, and then to the weather—confusing me, but never our leader.

Another day, I appeared at the mayor's office for a chat and found Henderson readying to attend the funeral of an old friend. "Come along," he ordered. Reluctantly, I agreed. A few minutes later I settled into a pew in the Southern Funeral Home chapel, next to a politician incapable of whispering. The chapel was quiet as mourners took their seats. The open casket lay at the front of the pews, adorned with flowers. Several women wept. And Jack Henderson wanted to talk. He leaned his large frame my way. "We had a lot of good times together," he said, breaking the room's silence as he pointed to the casket. Several women turned around and glared at us. "We used to go hunting and fishing together. Drank a little whiskey with him, too." Several other mourners harrumphed and turned to give us annoyed glances. After a few agonizing minutes of this prattle, during which Henderson loudly recounted their wartime experiences and other escapades, the preacher mercifully appeared at the pulpit. I was relieved to be spared further embarrassment by the blessed beginning of the funeral service for a man I had never met. But my most awkward moment was still ahead. In a "whisper" that bounded off all four walls of the chapel, Henderson leaned over again and informed me, "Don't you worry 'bout a thing. This'll be over in about fifteen minutes. He's not too longwinded."

A younger politician, appealing to those who wanted a more progressive Winnfield, beat Henderson for reelection in the fall of 1982. Apparently, the townspeople were ready to shed their image of only producing wheeler-dealer politicians like the Longs and, yes, Jack Henderson. My heart was with him during the election. I followed him around town one day while he did some light campaigning. It was all low-key and ineffective. A friend told him of an older man who promised he could deliver five to ten votes but only if he were promised a job working for the town. Not caring that a reporter was listening, the mayor mumbled something about the man having been fired, but he promised to review his application. This was not the only questionable behavior I observed. One night, after covering a city council meeting, I followed Henderson into his office. He invited me over to a closet and opened the door to reveal boxes filled with various hard liquors. It looked like he was operating a small liquor store. "Take whatever you want," he told me. I demurred, explaining that journalism's ethical standards prohibited me from accepting such gifts from a politician. He squinted his eyes and said nothing in response, apparently not understanding the concept.

A week after his defeat, I threw my impartiality out the window and called him to offer condolences. As always, he was buoyant. "Aw, hell, I'm all right," he told me. I asked if he could find another job. He had more money than he needed, he assured me. He was, however, angry with some people who had supported his victorious opponent.

"Remember all those awards on the wall?" he asked.

"Uh huh," I said.

"Well, most of them were from those damned Jaycees," he replied, pointing out that the new mayor had been a Jaycee. "Next morning, I got a box, loaded 'em all up, and threw 'em in the dump."

Henderson's political career wasn't as dead as he thought. Eight years later, after the person who defeated him stepped down, he would run again and win a fourth and final term.

THE EXPERIENCE OF covering small-town Louisiana was invaluable for a budding newspaper journalist. I banged out my stories on an electric typewriter and edited them as best I could, before feeding them into the clunky fax machine to transmit my words to the newsroom in Monroe. This operation involved phoning the city desk to alert someone that my story would soon be on its way. Then, I'd attach the first page to a small cylinder that rotated as a small lens inched down the length of the thermal paper, burning an image of my type onto the page on the other end. It took an agonizing six minutes per sheet. To receive a fax from the newsroom required the same operation in reverse. The machine emitted a pungent odor as it burned the lettering into the fax paper.

I would sometimes cover a police jury meeting in Winnfield or Jonesboro that ran late. With no time to rush back to Ruston and type my story, I would find a phone booth. From there, I would call the newsroom, collect, and ask someone to type as I dictated my story, "writing" it in my mind as I consulted my notes. It was great practice for thinking and composing under pressure. Ever since, I can bang out a first draft of a column or story with little difficulty. I also learned to shut out most distractions when I write. In fact, I feel most comfortable writing in a noisy coffee shop or café.

Ruston is where I met Wiley Hilburn, the legendary *Shreveport Times* columnist and director of Louisiana Tech's journalism program. Although I was an NLU grad, Wiley and his buddy John Hays, the fearless, freewheeling editor and publisher of Ruston's weekly *Morning Paper*, took me under their wings. They schooled me in the ways of Ruston and Lincoln Parish. They gave me life advice. And they were friends and mentors. I drank my first bourbon, straight, in the backseat of John's car after a quick jaunt to a liquor store in nearby Grambling. Ruston was dry, except for the low-alcohol beer some local establishments sold. Wiley and I waited as John hopped out of the car and returned with a fifth of Jack Daniel's and three Styrofoam cups filled with crushed ice. We rode around country roads for an hour or two, sipping Jack as I listened to these two lifelong friends swap lies. Yes, I know we were breaking five or six laws and I'm not proud of it.

After nine months in Ruston, I was moved to Monroe. The *News-Star* in 1982 was a thriving, bustling enterprise owned by the Gannett Corporation. In those days, that meant we had ample resources to cover local news. The editor assigned me to cover West Monroe City Hall and the Ouachita Parish Police Jury. On both beats, I covered politicians who would become my lifelong friends. Frank Snellings, a young attorney who had been elected to represent the north side of Monroe on the parish governing body, became a valuable source and, eventually, a pal. A few years later, he met and married then-state Representative Mary Landrieu. And the new mayor of West Monroe, Dave Norris, had been my economics professor at NLU and was nearing the end of his first of ten terms.

Of all the people I met during my years in Monroe, none influenced me more than Dave. I'm sure when I showed up in his classroom in the spring of 1978, he took little notice of me. As I recall, I did well in his class but only after ferocious studying. I knew that Dave was running for mayor of Monroe's sister city across the Ouachita River, now known by many as the location for the hit cable TV series "Duck Dynasty." I remember hearing from someone that Dave would probably win his race. What I didn't know, however, was he would play a large role in my life, as a teacher, mentor, and friend.

Dave Norris was my economics professor at NLU. He ran for mayor of West Monroe that semester. He won and served ten terms. He became a mentor and dear friend. (Photo courtesy of Brad Arender)

I was intrigued by this dapper, dynamic leader who had transformed his once-sleepy hometown (population 13,000) by pushing and pulling it into the twentieth century. Dave was a brilliant man with an easy smile, a smooth singing voice (he has served as choir director of his Methodist church for decades), and a wicked sense of humor. He was a young mayor with a Ph.D. in business administration who applied sound business principles to running a city. The many reforms he enacted, and the new West Monroe that he helped build, were impressive.

I'm sure my reporting was not always to his liking. One of my stories in May 1982 was about an increase in residential garbage collection fees and water rates, approved during a council meeting. Afterwards, I noticed that the council had not posted the proposed rate increases on the meeting's public agenda, which, by state law, must be advertised at least a day in advance. My story forced the council to acknowledge that its actions had violated the state's Open Meetings Law. Dave had to bring the proposed increase before the council at its next meeting.

It was the first real government beat I had as a journalist, and I now recognize I did not always maintain my objectivity when covering Dave. I enjoyed his company, and he reciprocated, especially when he realized what a hopeless conservative he had on his hands. Many days, I would stop by his office, first visiting with his cheerful and loyal assistant, Jayne Norton, then engaging in a lively, fun, and always-educational talk with Dave. We would kick around official city business, but our conversations usually turned to my political education or, sometimes, my love life.

In the early summer of 1983, Dave would arrange for me to go on a date with the younger sister of one of his City Hall employees, a beautiful woman who was spending the summer in Monroe. She was a ballet dancer from Utah and a devout Mormon. After we had been dating a few weeks, I showed up one evening at her sister's house. A group of Mormon elders greeted me. Next thing I knew, I was enduring an hour-long tutorial on the benefits of Mormonism. I realized they were trying to convert me! I wasn't interested in Mormonism, but I was interested in the Mormon, so I went along. I don't recall another word being spoken about my potential conversion. Dave, however, roared when I told him the story. He also howled when I described taking the young woman to a local nightclub where we ventured onto the dancefloor. I could not—and still cannot—dance a lick. Imagine my embarrassment as the crowd parted when the Mormon professional dancer began twisting and twirling around me like a belly dancer possessed by the ghost of Joseph Smith. Meanwhile, I stood there in a state of semi-shock, bouncing up and down like Tucker Carlson on "Dancing with the Stars." To this day, Dave will not let me forget this embarrassing scene. The only thing I can add is my profound gratitude that the iPhone and its video camera would not be invented for another twenty-four years.

I've never understood how a liberal like Dave survived in conservative West Monroe for so long, except that his liberalism on most issues had little to do with the efficient operation of city government. To Dave's credit, he never criticized me for my ideology. Like the great teacher he was, he dropped facts and anecdotes into our conversations to help tug me in his direction. One day, he handed me an article about an academic study that began to alter my thinking about public assistance or "welfare." The researchers discovered that almost a quarter of all Americans depended on some form of public assistance at one time, but the majority who accepted welfare did so for just a short while—less than a year—before finding work or the help they needed to restart their lives.

Reading that article and talking about it with Dave made me realize I knew almost nothing about the lives of those on public assistance. To make up for that, I spent a few mornings in November 1982 at the local Louisiana welfare office, observing the people who were there to apply for benefits or resolve a problem. I overheard them as they cried about having lost a job and wondered aloud about how they would feed their children. I watched them fret over losing the Food Stamps they needed to tide them over to the end of the month, because the job they worked didn't pay enough to get them all the way through. I heard them agonize about losing their child support payments because the job they worked paid them just a little too much. Suddenly, these people were not abstractions to me but humans with real struggles, not entirely unlike those my family had sometimes faced.

In my story a few days later, I wrote: "It is shortly after 8 a.m. on a typical day at the Ouachita Parish Office of Family Services. Welfare clients drift in slowly—some by city bus, others by car. It's early, but not too early for anguish." After quoting a few clients about their struggles and humiliation, I observed: "Anguish is not all some of these people feel. Indignity, too, is a part of their lives. For some, it's not easy to ask for help."

All these years later, I consider that story one of my best, not because it was powerful writing—although I think there were flashes of that— but because it represented my political awakening to the complex world of poverty that had heretofore seemed so simple. I would never look at public assistance, and those who take advantage of it to care for and feed their children, the same. Later that year, a week before Christmas, I joined the West Monroe police chief as he drove around town, dropping off gifts that his officers had collected for the children of underprivileged families. As I entered these humble, ramshackle dwellings and observed the joy and gratitude on the faces of parents who had no idea how they would provide a Christmas for their kids, the ravages of poverty became even more concrete. Poverty was no longer an abstraction. I could not rest comfortable in the assurance that being poor was a symptom of laziness. These were hardworking people who, for whatever reason, did not earn enough to support their families. They yearned for a better job and for better lives for their children.

Seeing the financial struggles of hardworking people influenced my political views. I wasn't a Democrat yet but, after experiencing a wider, more complicated world, I was inching away from the conservative ideology I'd inherited from my parents. I had begun to consider, as Herman Melville wrote, "Of all the preposterous assumptions of humanity over humanity, nothing exceeds most of the criticisms made on the habits of the poor by the well-housed, well-warmed, and well-fed." Nothing shook me out of my comfortable, ignorant assumptions about poverty and the poor more than seeing firsthand what it looked like for a parent or a child.

AFTER SIX YEARS in the Monroe area—four in college and two more as a newspaper reporter—I was itching to make a move. I heard from friends that the *Daily Town Talk* in Alexandria was looking for a reporter. I applied and soon got an interview. I liked everyone I met that day, especially the publisher, Joe D. Smith, a kind, courtly man who insisted on interviewing me and spent more time talking with me than I deserved. It was a good paper in a sleepy town, much like Monroe, which is why I turned down the offer when it came a few weeks later. I wanted something bigger and was prepared to wait. And then I learned about the political writer opening at the *Shreveport Journal.* On Wiley Hilburn's recommendation, I got an interview and, a few weeks later, a job offer. The decision to go to Shreveport, not Alexandria, would change my life in profound ways.

5

A Three-Legged Monkey on a Democratic Pole

When I read the endorsement of Edwin Edwards in the *Shreveport Journal*, the paper where I began working in August 1983, I knew that covering that year's Louisiana governor's race would be fun. "Edwin Washington Edwards is a leader in the very best sense of the word," the September 23 editorial asserted. "He is one of those rare men whose style, energy and ideas can be transferred to the people, and thence to cooperative accomplishment. He exudes confidence, and it is infectious. We believe we can, therefore we can." I was the paper's new political reporter, assigned to cover Edwards' campaign for a third term. Although I had nothing to do with the endorsement, the enthusiasm of my editor and publisher for Edwards' campaign against incumbent Republican Governor Dave Treen could only help me. At the very least, I knew I would have easy access to Edwards and his staff.

While the paper confessed it had some concerns about Edwards' ethical standards, the former governor's interview with the editorial board had calmed those fears. "We were especially struck by the sincerity of his answers, and his obvious concern for his place in history," the board explained, adding that Edwards was "distressed" by polls showing many voters doubted his honesty. "We believe he will prove them, and his critics, wrong." Little did the *Journal* editors know that by March 1985, barely a year into his third term, a federal grand jury would indict Edwards and six associates on fifty counts of racketeering and fraud. He would beat those charges.

After more than five years in Monroe, I had been ready for a larger media market and one where I could write more about politics and campaigns. The *Journal's* politics beat opened up when my predecessor moved to Washington to work as press secretary to US Representative Charles "Buddy" Roemer.

At the *Journal*, I would work for someone who would be another great influence in my personal and professional lives. A native of rural Springhill,

Louisiana, Stanley Ray Tiner was a gregarious, tall, beefy ex-Marine who had served in Vietnam as a combat correspondent. Back stateside, Stan enrolled at Louisiana Tech in Ruston to pursue a degree in journalism under Wiley Hilburn, who was just four years his elder. Under Wiley's influence, he became editor of the school newspaper, the *Tech Talk*. After graduation, he wrote for the *Texarkana Daily News* and the *Minden Press-Herald* before landing the political writer's job at the *Shreveport Times* in 1970. During his years covering politics at the *Times*, Stan was among the most perceptive and prolific political journalists in the state. In 1974, the owner of the *Shreveport Journal*, the city's afternoon paper, hired him as the editor. It took me just a day or two working for Stan to understand why he had been such a successful reporter. His fertile mind rarely stopped churning. He could quickly conjure a workable theory about most any political question. His prose was folksy but elegant. It seemed he knew every political player in the state. And he could talk with anyone about almost anything—sports, politics, gardening, or the weather.

When Stan offered me a job in the summer of 1983, I was twenty-four and still green. I was not a bad writer and was a decent reporter with an innocent demeanor that prompted some people to share more with me than they wanted. But I thought I knew far more about politics than I did. After several months trekking around the state with Edwin Edwards, Dave Treen, and Jimmy Fitzmorris—a former lieutenant governor trying to win back his office—I would grow wiser about the rough-and-tumble nature of Louisiana politics and what a winning statewide campaign required. Watching and working with several talented press secretaries for these campaigns, I would also learn something about representing a campaign to the press—skills I would need in a few years.

Starting in August 1983, I began traveling with the fifty-six-year-old Edwards. I had never met the former governor before winning the assignment to cover his campaign and, under normal circumstances, he and his people should have been skeptical of a young reporter who wanted to tag along to every event for several weeks. Here is where the *Journal's* endorsement saved me. From almost the first day, Edwards and his aides, particularly Darrell Hunt and Wayne Ray, welcomed my presence. I would sit in the backseat of the campaign car, with Hunt or Ray at the wheel and Edwards riding shotgun. Edwards was solicitous, and sometimes even chatty, as we burned the backroads from meeting to meeting and rally to rally. The black sedan had a car phone, much like the one I once had in my car during college—only Edwards didn't need to wait for an open line before he made a call. During most rides, however, he resisted any temptation to use the phone and, when not talking, leaned back and took a nap. I've never known anyone who could fall asleep so quickly, snooze for five or ten minutes, and then awake as refreshed as if he had slept for an hour. Sometimes, as we zipped along, I'd ask a question or two. Mostly, I kept quiet and observed. Often, when Edwards and Hunt wanted to talk strategy, or just keep whatever they wished to say from me, they would converse in Cajun French. I did not understand a word of what they discussed.

Over several days in late August, I persuaded Edwards to spend several hours answering questions for the profile about him I was preparing for the *Journal.* I would interview his mother, childhood friends, and other family members over several months. One day, as we flew on a twin-engine King Air from Baton Rouge to somewhere in north Louisiana, I started peppering him. I discovered that, for all his flair on the stump, Edwards could be substantive and reflective.

"A few months ago, you told one of our reporters, I don't know who it was, that you were going to be so nice it's going to be disgusting," I said. "Do you feel like you've had to change your style of campaigning?"

"Only to the extent it was necessary to respond to [Dave Treen's] allegations," he said. "You got to spice it up a little bit."

"Basically, you think you've been the same Edwin Edwards you were back in '71?" I asked.

Edwards paused. "Ah, a little more subdued, a little more mature."

"How come? Why more subdued?"

"Well, I don't have to prove anything," he replied. "When I got elected in '72, almost half the people in the state thought I would not be a good governor. I don't have to prove that anymore. I think even my bitterest enemies recognize I'm capable of fulfilling what I set out to do. So, I don't have to be so caustic, so antagonist, so belligerent. And, as you grow older, you begin to have a deeper and better respect for other people's opinions and the fact that they may disagree with you. Besides, at the risk of sounding immodest—which I've never been—I really feel comfortable and secure in the knowledge that my predictions and projections for programs have all worked and came to be pretty much as I suggested."

I told him someone had recently stated to me that when he was elected to this third term, "unlike Treen says [more corruption], you'll do just the opposite, and be more concerned with the appearance of evil." I asked if Edwards really thought he would be watching his "Ps and Qs."

"I never was a person who placed form and appearance over substance," Edwards shot back. "I've been more concerned with the substance and still am. But I've learned to recognize that in politics appearances are sometimes just as important. But I would never substitute one for the other. I'll try to harness the two."

I have known few politicians as skillful and charismatic as Edwards.

He was movie-star handsome, with smooth, silver hair and a charming, roguish sense of humor. He seemed never to forget a name. I lost count of the times I saw him astound onlookers by pulling some seemingly unfamiliar person's name from the deep recesses of his mind. I have never known a politician better at summoning a clever, devastating rejoinder in a debate. And I have yet to meet his equal in conjuring electric energy on the stump. He exuded an astonishing, natural charisma when he mounted a stage. For attendees, an Edwards rally was a near-religious experience. Edwin Edwards had it all, except integrity. To his long-term detriment, his Cajun charm was exceeded only by his dishonesty.

For the first few weeks of my time covering the Edwards campaign, it had usually been just me, Edwards, and an aide plying the backroads. But on October 1, the campaign launched an ambitious, nine-day, 3,000-mile tour that would take the candidate to each of the state's sixty-four parishes. Suddenly, I was one of about two dozen reporters, some of them national and international writers, eager to observe the self-styled "Cajun Prince" at work. He launched the tour in his hometown of Marksville, in Avoyelles Parish in central Louisiana. In that speech on the courthouse square, Edwards recalled his mother, Agnes Brouillette Edwards, an untrained country nurse and midwife who often provided free healthcare to neighbors and friends. "I remember thinking how important it was to help people," Edwards told the crowd, "that my mother was always there to help, that people, no matter who they were, should be able to get help when they need it."

Edwin Edwards, campaigning for governor in 1983 somewhere in New Orleans. As a reporter for the Shreveport Journal, *I followed him around the state for months.*

With that, Edwards transitioned to attacking Treen for cutting the state's fifty-dollar-a-month allowance for those in the state's nursing homes. "I would rather my arm wither and fall off before I cut the little spending money that poor widows have who just want to live out their twilight years in peace and dignity." And then he sharpened his attacks, focusing on what he said was Treen's inability to help those looking for work. "They can't find a job and can't find anyone to talk to," Edwards said. "Have any of you ever called Dave Treen? Go ahead and try it and see if he calls you back. By the time you hear from him again, I'll be in the Mansion answering the phone." The audience roared.

At the next stop, in the parking lot of a Piggly Wiggly grocery story in nearby Bunkie, Edwards appealed to the gathering's farmers. "I'm aware of the fact there are more farms in Avoyelles Parish than in any other parish in the state," Edwards informed a crowd that included eager children perched on pickup trucks clutching balloons with *Edwards Now* printed on them. "I assure you as one who came off a cotton farm in Avoyelles Parish, I have not forgotten what it means to be a farmer." On the day's third stop, in a Winn Dixie parking lot in Ville Platte, Edwards claimed credit for the local vocational-technical school. "I like to remember that not everybody goes to school to be a lawyer," he said. "Some people want to work for a living." The audience cheered.

My most memorable stop on the tour came on day six, after we rolled into the town square in Lake Providence in northeast Louisiana, not far from the Mississippi River. It was noontime as Edwards climbed atop the stump of a 150-year-old oak tree and addressed his mostly Black audience, reminding them of his devotion to them during his eight years as governor in the 1970s.

"Are there any senior citizens?" he asked, pretending to search the crowd from his perch. Finally, he spotted someone, an elderly man. "Raise your hand, old man. I know you're a senior citizen. Look at him. He don't have a tooth in his mouth and he's trying to decide if he's a senior citizen. Boy, you'd make a good politician. You can lie with a straight face." The man beamed.

Then, Edwards wheeled around to another part of the crowd and took aim at his opponent, Dave Treen. "He cut taxes in 1980 to help the rich folk," Edwards said. "And now he's out of money. You know what he wants to tax now? Snuff. I know you're not going to admit it, but there are some snuff dippers in the crowd. And if you're a snuff dipper, you better go buy some snuff because he's going to put a tax on snuff." He was referring to Treen's proposal to increase state sales taxes on tobacco and alcoholic beverages. "When I could lower taxes, I lowered taxes for food and drugs, 'cause that's for you," Edwards continued. "When I could lower taxes, I took the property tax off so you wouldn't have to pay state taxes on your home."

Next, Edwards asked if there were any police jurors (in other states, county commissioners) in attendance. Several hands shot up. Edwards asked, "What's happened to your road fund, brother? Who took care of you when he was governor?"

"You did," the man replied.

"Tell them about it, Mike," Edwards said, impressing the crowd by recalling this local official's name. "You lost 25 percent of your rural road funds and that means that 25 percent of the people you would have taken out of the mud and the dust are going to be in the mud and the dust until next year when I get back in."

Everywhere Edwards went, it was clear he inspired many voters to long for a return to what they considered Louisiana's halcyon days before the austerity of the Treen years. One day in early October, after a rally at the Vernon Parish courthouse in Leesville, I asked an elderly White man if the candidate's speech had persuaded him. "Give me a three-legged monkey on a Democratic pole," the man told me, "and I'll vote for him."

As the tour went on, Edwards' attacks on Treen became harsher. And I had inadvertently given him one line for his stump speech. In the process, I learned that Edwards did not rely much on research or facts for his speeches. On a flight in his private plane on the way to Shreveport one night in September, Edwards began talking with me about Treen's lack of political acumen. In late September 1982, a train had derailed in Livingston, Louisiana, releasing a load of toxic chemicals and forcing the evacuation of thousands. On the campaign trail, Edwards told audiences that Treen had waited several days to return from a trip to Florida. In fact, Treen had rushed home when he got news of the crisis and toured the scene the following day. Nonetheless, Edwards hit Treen hard on this. "No matter where I was in the world," Edwards would tell audiences, "if I knew that coming back to Louisiana would save one life, I'd be on the next plane back, even if I was in Las Vegas on a hot roll." That always prompted the crowd to roar with laughter.

On the plane, as Edwards denigrated Treen's political instincts, I unwisely nodded in agreement. And then I compounded my error by telling Edwards that Treen, when I was a reporter in Monroe, waited five long days to show up in Ouachita Parish after the area experienced heavy flooding in late December 1982. During a press availability that day, I had questioned Treen about his delay, echoing complaints of some frustrated locals who wanted to know why it took Treen so long to appear. When I told Edwards this, his ears perked up. The story intrigued him. The next day, in Monroe, after he told the exaggerated Livingston derailment story, he mentioned that Treen waited five days after the 1982 flood to go to Monroe (at least *my* anecdote was accurate). The crowd applauded. In the car on the way to the airport, Edwards turned around and said to me, "They really liked that stuff about the flood, huh?" I mumbled an embarrassed assent.

At a rally one night where Lieutenant Governor Bobby Freeman, a close ally of Edwards, was a guest, Edwards shared the Livingston story again, this time telling the audience how Freeman tried to persuade Treen to return to the state. This was not true. After the rally, as we drove away, Wayne Ray spoke up. "You know," he told Edwards, "I talked to Bobby, and he says that story about the train derailment is just like you've been telling it." Edwards seemed surprised. "It's true?" he responded. "That's good." Despite what Freeman might have claimed, the story was still untrue, but Edwards did not seem to care.

Edwards' most memorable attack on Treen was one, thankfully, I had nothing to do with. At a rally in Metairie one evening, Edwards went after Treen's famous penchant for overthinking decisions. "He's been governor three and a half years and he hasn't made a decision yet. What can you do with a guy who takes an hour and a half to watch '60 Minutes'?"

Following Edwards, I not only witnessed his casual relationship with the truth; I also saw that his reputation as a Casanova was well earned. One day in late August, we flew from Baton Rouge on a rented King Air to Lake Bruin (outside St. Joseph in northeast Louisiana near the Mississippi River), to the home of state Senator Billy Brown, one of Edwards' biggest supporters, for a rally featuring the popular Cajun-Country singer Doug Kershaw. Afterwards, we headed for the plane for a short hop over to Shreveport, where Edwards would spend the night and I would jump off the campaign trail for a few days before rejoining him elsewhere. When we arrived at the airstrip, I noticed that a new passenger—an attractive young woman—was onboard, ostensibly as someone one of Edwards' aides had invited along. I suspected he had invited her along for Edwards, notorious for his sexual appetites. The woman appeared nervous. Maybe she had never flown before. More likely, she had never been picked up by a former governor thirty years her senior and flown off with him into the night.

When we landed at the Shreveport airport, I pulled the woman aside as the governor ducked into the bathroom before she, Edwards, and his entourage went off to a nearby Ramada Inn. I slipped her a piece of paper with my home number on it. "Call me if anything goes wrong and you need someone to come get you," I said as we parted. She gave me a slight smile. I didn't see her again until seven years later, in the summer of 1990, when I was traveling with Senator J. Bennett Johnston during his reelection campaign. She was with her now-husband, a local elected official, at a headquarters opening in northeast Louisiana. Although I could tell that she remembered me from that night, she said nothing about it.

I have wondered for years if I should have written about that incident. No one swore me to secrecy. Everything I saw and heard was on the record, unless I agreed otherwise. I didn't tell anyone about the encounter at the time—and maybe I should have mentioned this to Stan or another editor. But I decided that I had no story. I couldn't prove she wasn't accompanying one of Edwards' aides. I never saw her enter or leave Edwards' hotel room. Even if I had, I would have no way of knowing what happened inside. Besides, Edwards' serial infidelity was well known around Louisiana. He sometimes made it the subject of self-deprecating jokes. Any story I wrote about him and this young woman wouldn't have been news to anyone who paid attention to Louisiana politics. Still, it's always bothered me that Edwards regarded me so lightly as a journalist—maybe I deserved it—that they flaunted his infidelity in front me, knowing that I wouldn't write about it.

Edwards knew how to manage the press, if nothing else. He knew what I could not print and what I could. One day, as I settled in the backseat of his car after an event in Shreveport, I asked him some impertinent question. It annoyed him. Instead of giving me a long answer that amounted to nothing, he wheeled around, looked me in the eyes and said, "F--- you," and then laughed. He knew I couldn't quote him. He also reasoned, I'm sure, that I would be so rattled by his response that I would drop the questioning, which I think I did.

Sex wasn't the only part of Edwards' life that confounded me. Corruption accusations and federal investigations dogged him for years. As Edwards campaigned for his third term, a federal grand jury (the panel that would later indict him) was investigating him, and he was hounded by allegations he sold pardons during his first term. During his second term, he was accused of having received illegal contributions during his first gubernatorial campaign in 1971-72. In typical fashion, Edwards refused to deny the contributions, explaining that while it might have been illegal to make the donations, it was not against the law to accept them. "That's their problem," he said of the donors. In 1976, Edwards admitted that his wife, Elaine, accepted $10,000 in cash from South Korean businessman Tongsun Park during the 1971-72 campaign. Edwards claimed Elaine forgot to tell him about the gift until the Internal Revenue Service began investigating him. This and more were subjects of a 1977 book by a former Edwards aide, Clyde Vidrine, *Just Takin' Orders*. Vidrine's book included outrageous tales of Edwards' gambling trips to Las Vegas, his dogged pursuit of women, and alleged vote buying and kickbacks. I read it—wide-eyed—to prepare for covering Edwards. Imagine my reaction the first time I observed a supporter approach the former governor with a copy of Vidrine's book, a tome filled with lurid accounts of Edwards' alleged criminality. Any other politician would have declined a request to autograph the book. Not Edwards. Although he maintained the book was full of lies, I watched him sign every copy anyone pushed into his hands.

Despite his sizable lead in the polls, Edwards and his staff campaigned as if he was behind by ten points. Edwards and Treen spent an insane amount of money on that race. Edwards' campaign cost him $14 million (almost $36 million in 2020 dollars), while Treen spent a "mere" $7 million (almost $18 million in 2020 dollars). "In fact, in 1983," LSU political science professor Wayne Parent wrote in his 2004 book, *Inside the Carnival: Unmasking Louisiana Politics*, "when the state was still enjoying the fruits of the oil boom, more money was spent on [that] governor's race in Louisiana than in any nonpresidential election in American history up until that time."

Hijinks and dirty tricks were common. At almost every rally, a self-styled "Truth Squad" of Treen staffers—including Lanny Keller (now a columnist and editorial writer for the *Advocate* in Baton Rouge)—stood at the back of the crowd monitoring Edwards' statements. They would alert reporters to what they claimed were Edwards' untruths and misstatements, which annoyed the candidate's staffers. George Fischer, one of Edwards' close friends and a top campaign aide, was outraged to see these Treen staffers at rallies and initially tried to stop them from speaking to me and other reporters. One day in Breaux Bridge, I headed for my car to catch up with Edwards at his next rally when I noticed Lanny and his colleague staring at their vehicle. Someone, probably an industrious Edwards staffer, had let the air out of their tires. When we arrived in St. Martinville for the next stop, I asked Fischer if he knew anything about the sabotage of Lanny's car. "I assume they let their own air out," he told me with a straight face, "to make a good story."

The Edwards-Treen campaign gave me a crash course in hardball campaigning. When it was over, it felt as though I had learned a decade's worth of political lessons in six months. Watching Treen make an all-out push to woo the Black vote, I learned that—in Louisiana, at least—Black voters almost never vote for Republicans. Treen seemed to think he could close the gap with Edwards by campaigning hard in Black churches. In mid-October, I went with him to New Roads, where he addressed a mostly Black crowd and lamented that he won only 3 percent of the Black vote in 1979. In my story the next day, I wrote: "Treen and his advisors believe that if they can poll between 15 and 20 percent of the Black vote in the

coming election they stand an excellent chance of defeating Edwards."
That effort was not yielding the hoped-for results. That evening, at a
predominately Black, north Baton Rouge church, Treen's campaign
struggled to attract 200 people to the meeting. First Lady Dodie Treen
was angry at staffers over the pitiful turnout, which she blamed on poor
advance work. More likely, however, was the fact that her husband was a
Republican. On election day, Treen would win about 5 percent of Black
votes, slightly more than he earned four years earlier.

I also learned that public images rarely match private behavior. In
front of a crowd, Edwards was suave, charismatic, funny, and outgoing.
Treen was his exact opposite before an audience—dry, technocratic, and
often humorless. By the end of the race, having spent weeks watching
both candidates up close, I realized that their real personalities—who
they were when the crowds drifted away and the lights went off—were
far different from what most people saw. Edwards could still charm
in private, but his default demeanor was to withdraw into himself. He
did not crack jokes. He rarely smiled. Not that he wasn't friendly, but
I recognized he was an introvert who overcame those tendencies to
perform in public. I discovered that Treen was witty, warm, and down-to-
earth with me and others in ways that were difficult for Edwards. Treen's
charisma disappeared when he mounted the stage; Edwards' receded
when he stepped down from it.

Everywhere Edwards went, crowds greeted him like a messiah. One
evening we arrived for a big rally at the Fair Grounds racetrack in New
Orleans. This crowd was massive and particularly enthusiastic. Marsha
Shuler of the *Advocate*, John Maginnis of *Gris Gris*, and I were among
the reporters following the campaign that day, arriving in a staff car that
trailed behind his motorhome. When Edwards saw the crush of people,
he waded through the crowd to check on us. "You all right?" he asked.
We told him we were. He nodded. "Stay close to me." We stuck as close
to him as we could, plowing through the enormous crowd, protected by
a phalanx of police and security guards as we made our way to the stage.
We might not have arrived safely without Edwards' intervention.

FOR WEEKS, I had tried to persuade the most enigmatic person in
the Edwards campaign—his wife, former Louisiana First Lady Elaine
Edwards—to grant me an interview. She was reticent about talking to
the press and rebuffed me. Finally, I approached her husband.

"I've been trying to get Mrs. Edwards to talk with me," I told the
former governor. "Can you please help?"

"I'll see what I can do," he told me.

A few days later, word came that Elaine would see me. When I arrived at their spacious, well-appointed, ranch-style home on a large, wooded lot off Highland Road in Baton Rouge, Elaine escorted me to a patio. She was ill at ease. It was clear she was talking with me under duress. Her husband had begged—maybe ordered—her to speak with me. She answered tersely the first few questions I threw at her. I later discovered it was the first interview she had done in three years. "I sat here for two years, bored out of my mind," she eventually confessed, adding she tried her hand at interior design before starting a successful business creating custom dresses. "I don't need to make a living. I need something to enjoy."

To her credit, Elaine admitted she hated speaking to journalists, doubting she had anything interesting to say. "It's like my having to remember what the governor's mansion looked like the first time I saw it," she told me, adding that now "it's just another public building." In my story, I wrote of Mrs. Edwards: "To her, the political life is just like any other. Familiarity breeds contempt, or in this case, ambivalence." Mrs. Edwards confessed to me she still grieved over the shocking murder of Edwin's brother Nolan—a disgruntled client shot him that August in his Crowley law office—and the recent death of her and Edwin's good friend and constant companion, Gene Jones. She acknowledged the depth of her grief and how it crippled her. "I miss him a whole lot," she said of Jones. "I haven't really left this house but twice since Gene died." Edwin, she said in a revealing quote, handled his grief differently: "I think he is as human as everybody else is, but he has this thing about not wanting to lose or not wanting to be wrong. So, he builds this wall or barrier or resistance so that he won't ever be hurt."

Towards the end of the interview, I drew her into discussing her experiences as a United States senator in 1972, during Edwards' first term. Then-Senator Allen Ellender had died and Edwards appointed his wife to serve until a permanent replacement could be elected. At the time he appointed her, Edwards vowed Elaine would not seek the job in the fall 1972 special election. Once she got to Washington, she told me, she regretted the pledge. "If he had not made that promise," she said, "I would have run. I had no idea I could handle that situation. That was the highlight of my life."

AFTER I TRAVELED with Edwards for a month, Stan decided that Ronni Patriquin—the *Journal*'s Capitol reporter—and I were at risk of becoming inured to our respective candidates. This did not feel like a problem for me. Having spent weeks with Edwards, I still leaned towards voting for Treen. Despite his charisma and many kindnesses to me, Edwards represented so much of what I despised about Louisiana politics. And it wasn't just Edwards. I liked and respected many of his staffers, but some of them seemed to be in the game only for what financial benefits or raw power they could accrue. Several—including Wayne Ray, Andrew Martin, and Edwards' son Stephen—would later go to prison for various federal crimes. My disdain for the Edwards crowd only increased when I later heard that Ray, disgruntled over some story I wrote about his boss, began telling people, falsely, that he had sent a prostitute to my hotel room one night and I welcomed her.

One day, while in Shreveport with Edwards, I asked one of the candidate's staffers to give me a lift to the Caddo Parish courthouse so I could vote absentee. He did, probably assuming he was putting at least one vote in the bank for his boss. Instead, I voted for Treen. While I didn't want Edwards to serve another term as governor, covering his campaign was more interesting than writing about Treen, if only because it was clear he would win a third term. The Edwards camp was where the action was. Unfortunately, I would not get to cover Edwards all the way until election day. Stan made me switch candidates with Ronni Patriquin for the last ten days of the campaign.

By then, Treen's campaign had run out of steam. He and his staff tried to keep up the pretense that he could pull out a win, but it was painfully obvious to anyone who followed the campaign that Edwards would breeze to victory. Everywhere Treen went, small, lackluster groups greeted him. In some cases, when an audience failed to show, Treen resorted to prowling grocery store aisles and asking shoppers for their votes. It was an embarrassing, humiliating end to a respectable but politically inept term as governor. No matter how hard he tried, Treen could not persuade voters that his time as governor had made the state richer or stronger. By the night before the election, as a group of reporters gathered for drinks and dinner at Poet's, a popular Baton Rouge hangout, the outcome was nearly certain. Treen would lose. "This campaign ended," I told the group, "not with a bang but a whimper."

6

THE *SHREVEPORT JOURNAL*

The day after the election, which Treen lost 62 percent to 32 percent, I wrote about the false image voters had of the two candidates, based on my up-close view. "While Treen was beating the pavement, pouncing on housewives in the vegetable sections of Piggly Wigglys, Edwards was busy being worshipped by throngs of supporters on courthouse squares and shopping center parking lots, soaking up their adoration and love," I wrote. "There they were, Dull Dave and Fast Eddie: The former, the biggest bore and lackluster politician since Calvin Coolidge. The latter, the most exciting figure since Robert Redford. Right? Wrong." I observed that Edwards, "not at his best in a one-to-one situation, is nonetheless able to discard a reserved private manner in public and project the image of an evangelical preacher whose congregation believes he will lead them to salvation." Treen, for all his charm, could never translate his private charisma for the crowds or television cameras. "While Treen supporters might take consolation in that their candidate played great with the ladies in the grocery stores," I concluded, "they know all too well that Treen, at least in public, offered people a bland diet, when all along they craved ice cream and cake."

The governor's race was over, although I would cross paths with Edwards many times over the next thirty-five years. And I was happy to move on to covering other political campaigns, including the runoff in the fall of 1983 for lieutenant governor between two Democrats: incumbent Bobby Freeman and Jimmy Fitzmorris, who had held the office from 1972 to 1980 as the first full-time lieutenant governor after the state's new constitution took effect in 1974. Fitzmorris narrowly missed the runoff for governor in 1979 and was one of several Democrats who endorsed Dave Treen and were awarded jobs in the Republican governor's administration. Fitzmorris (his friends called him "Fitz" or "Jimmy Fitz") became Treen's special assistant for industrial development, a continuation of the economic development role the state's lieutenant governor had in those days.

By the time I showed up, Fitzmorris and Freeman had advanced to the late-November runoff. For all his personality and energy, the voluble Fitzmorris was running an uphill race. Edwards endorsed Freeman, whose backroom political style better matched his. Fitzmorris was as old-school New Orleans as they came. The phrase "hail-fellow-well-met" was not coined to describe Jimmy Fitz, but it could have been. The man never met a stranger and never saw a crowd for which he did not have an inspirational, patriotic speech. I followed him around for a day or two that November. Jimmy Fitz welcomed me onboard with a wide smile, a hearty handshake, and a slap on the back. It was as if he had been reunited with a long-lost friend.

The first day, we climbed onto a helicopter in New Orleans and took off for a whirlwind day hopscotching around south Louisiana. That afternoon, as we approached Houma, the pilot got lost trying to find the offices of a local dentist Fitzmorris promised to visit (probably to pick up a campaign check). As we buzzed around in circles, Fitzmorris spied a small, white, wood-frame farmhouse next to a cow pasture. "Set it down there," he directed the pilot, pointing at the pasture. The pilot put the chopper down. As soon as we landed, Fitzmorris bounded out, hustled across the pasture, up to the house, and rapped on the back door. A stunned elderly couple answered and let him inside. He was soon back with directions to the dentist's office. We were airborne again within minutes. Imagine the fantastic story the couple must have told their friends and family later that day. I have often wondered if anyone believed their amazing tale about the former lieutenant governor of Louisiana pounding on their door after landing his helicopter in their pasture. Despite running a spirited campaign, Fitzmorris would lose to Freeman by twenty points.

Covering campaigns was thrilling work, even if it involved spending weeks on the road, choking down bad food, and staying up late in a cheap motel to file a story. I loved politics, and following Edwards or Treen gave me the chance to be as close as any average voter would ever get. When I wasn't covering a race, I looked for an excuse to contact former Louisiana governors for profile stories. I soon learned there's almost no one hungrier for attention than a retired politician. When a reporter, like me, calls and asks for a few hours of their time, it's an opportunity to influence how history will remember him or her. I think former governors, especially, understand that history is kinder to them than daily journalism.

So, when I called up former governors Robert Kennon, Jimmie Davis, and John McKeithen to ask for their reflections on their many years in Louisiana politics, none of them hesitated. Each was available to talk as

Me in the Louisiana House chamber, covering a press briefing by Governor Edwin Edwards immediately after his third-term inauguration in March 1984.

soon as possible. Davis, a film and recording star, was retired from politics, but music was still very much his vocation. Even during his two terms as governor, he always found time for recording and performing. "I'm still going," he told me. "As long as they'll buy, I'll try it." I had interviewed the courtly, eighty-one-year-old Davis when I worked at the *News-Star*, but this time I wanted to take a broader view of his career, including his embarrassing civil rights record. I didn't do it justice, and didn't question him enough about it, but I noted in my story published in February 1984: "The compelling issue [in the 1960 governor's race] was segregation. Davis [and one opponent, state Senator Willie Rainach] were for it."

A lesser-known former governor, eighty-one-year-old Robert Kennon, who served from 1952 to 1956, was also eager to speak with me. A quiet, serious man who governed as a reformer—which usually means only one term in Louisiana politics—Kennon welcomed me to his spacious home in the Bocage subdivision in Baton Rouge one April morning in 1984. He was as slender as when he was governor. He sported a trim, white mustache. His trademark large ears remained his most prominent feature. I was still a few years away from working for Russell Long, who defeated Kennon in 1950 when they both ran for the US Senate. Kennon lost his bid for governor earlier in 1950, finishing a close third behind "Uncle Earl" Long—the winner—and reformer Sam Jones of Lake Charles. That fall, in the US Senate race, Kennon lost again to a Long, this time to Russell Long, by only 10,000 votes. When I spoke to him thirty-four years later, he was adamant that the Long machine stole the election, but any bitterness about the outcome had faded. "I've never let it bother me," he insisted. "I never did fuss with young Russell Long. I kind of got to know him and he got conservative and did a very helpful job. In lots of ways, he's been a very useful senator to the state of Louisiana."

None of the former governors I interviewed that year fascinated me more than "Big John" McKeithen, the first governor to serve consecutive terms, from 1964 to 1972, after voters amended the state constitution to allow him to run again. One morning in early February 1984, I drove two hours from Shreveport to Columbia, where McKeithen lived out in the country in a spacious, well-appointed, ranch-style house, a stone's throw from the scenic Ouachita River. As I sat in the living room waiting for him to emerge, one of his sons, an awkward man with a strange name— "Fox"—greeted me.[1]

Finally, Big John appeared. He was tall and erect. His hair was gray but still ample. His large frame still dominated any room he entered. His wide smile, easy manner, and supreme confidence gave me an immediate insight into his enormous success in Louisiana politics.

In my story, published in early March, I wrote: "John Julius McKeithen is still an imposing man, a tall, larger-than-life figure who would look more at home fighting bad guys in a John Wayne movie. His 65 years have not made him elderly. Rather, he has grown into an older version of his rough-hewn, plain-spoken youth when he ruled the state's political scene. . . . His face is rugged terrain, as if carved from stone—a cross between Bear Bryant and Leonid Brezhnev. His hands are large, built for manual labor, for a farmer and rancher, not an attorney and former governor."

Reading the story for the first time in over thirty years, I was surprised to see I omitted a charming anecdote McKeithen shared with me about his on-and-off relationship with his political mentor, Governor Earl Long. At one point, he told me, the two men fell out. I don't remember the year or the circumstances McKeithen described, but the former governor told me when he went to see Long, perhaps at his Pea Patch farm in Winn Parish, he arrived with a sack of squirrels as a peace offering. I cannot imagine why I left out such an interesting anecdote.

For years, I would run into McKeithen at political and other functions around the state. Although he had not sought political office since he got into the 1971 US Senate race against Bennett Johnston at the last minute, McKeithen always struck me as the person Central Casting might send if you asked for someone who looked like a governor. I was beguiled by him, as my story reflected. I continued describing him for four full paragraphs before I got around to his political career. I ended my description thus: "Longish gray hair, a bit askew, covers his head. Below blue eyes, crowned by bushy, black eyebrows, reveals a fierce blend of fire and compassion."

WORKING AT THE *Journal* and covering state and local politics was almost as interesting as working for Stan Tiner. A former political writer— he would quit the *Journal* to run for Congress a few years later—Stan brimmed with ambitious ideas about what I should cover. His instincts were usually sound. Often, when I broke a political story, it wasn't my sleuthing but because Stan scooped up a rumor about something and suggested I track it down. He always seemed to be two steps ahead of me.

For example, in the summer of 1984, I heard rumors that Don Owen, the popular, longtime news anchor on the local CBS affiliate, KSLA, might run for a seat on the state's Public Service Commission. I asked Owen's son, Daryl (then Bennett Johnston's chief of staff), about it. "Yes," I was told, "he's thinking about running, but this is off the record. You can't use it." I took that to mean I could write nothing about it. It never occurred to me to ask Owen about it on the record until Stan called me into his office one day. "I'm hearing that Don Owen might run for the PSC," he said. "Yeah," I replied, "I've heard that, too." Stan was incredulous that I had this tidbit but had failed to write a story on it. Embarrassed, I confirmed it for the record and broke the story the next day.

Stan also had superb instincts about the kinds of questions that would make good news. It was Stan who went to see Governor-elect Edwards at his Baton Rouge transition office in late 1983 for an interview. During a break, he asked to use Edwards' private restroom. There, he noticed that the governor-elect kept a Bible beside the toilet. When he emerged, he questioned Edwards about his religious beliefs, including the resurrection of Jesus. When Edwards said he did not believe in the resurrection—"that's too much against natural law"—Stan knew he had a blockbuster. Stan's story quoting Edwards sparked a firestorm that forced Edwards to backtrack after an uncomfortable meeting with a group of alarmed Catholic clergy. "Natural law is an obstacle," a chastened Edward announced, "that is overcome by my faith in God and my personal belief in the Scripture which teaches that Jesus is the God-man who was sent to this world to redeem mankind."

Not every idea of Stan's was a winner. One day, he summoned me to announce he wanted me to go to Ethiopia—then experiencing a severe famine—for a series about Christmas in that impoverished country. One of the editors suggested there were plenty of poverty-stricken people in

Shreveport within walking distance of the *Journal* offices. Stan couldn't argue with that and dropped the matter.

Another day, in March 1984, Stan sauntered up to my desk.

"How soon can you get to Florida?" he asked.

I was stumped. "Huh?"

"I want you to go and do a series on all the Louisiana college students who go to Florida for spring break," he explained.

Someone booked me a flight to Miami, and by the next afternoon I was wandering around a beach in Fort Lauderdale looking for Louisiana college students. I never found any. I had not been fortunate enough in college to make a spring-break trip because I was too poor and always working. Little did I know that Louisiana college students who went to the beach usually spent their spring break not in south Florida but in the Florida Panhandle, near Destin or Pensacola. Whatever the case, I came back and published a comprehensive, three-part series about the beachside exploits of college kids from New York and Ohio. That misadventure, however, was on me as much as Stan. I should have inquired about which beaches Louisiana college students preferred.

Stan also enjoyed having a little fun at the expense of self-important politicians. One morning in early 1984, I sat in his office, chewing over the latest news and what I planned to cover that day. I mentioned that a certain statewide elected official was holding a press conference at the Holiday Inn across the street from the *Journal*'s offices in downtown Shreveport.

"What's *he* doing in town?" Stan asked, with disdain.

I told him the official would talk about a subject unrelated to his prescribed duties.

"That guy sticks his nose into everything," Stan grumbled. "I'll bet if you asked him if he's being considered for baseball commissioner, he wouldn't deny it."

Stan paused for a moment. "In fact," he finally said, "here's what I want you to do. After the event is over, pull him aside and tell him we've heard a rumor he's being considered for the job. See what he says."

I swallowed hard and agreed to do it. So, I walked across the street and waited until the event was done before I approached the politician. When we stepped aside, I said, "We're hearing rumors you are in the running to be baseball commissioner."

The guy did not miss a beat. "I've heard those rumors," he said, launching into a two-minute disquisition about why he might be perfect for the job.

I wrote down what he was saying—even though we would publish no story about it—as I suppressed a laugh and then hustled back to the newsroom to tell Stan that his instincts were correct. Soon thereafter, Peter Ueberroth replaced Bowie Kuhn as the sixth commissioner of Major League Baseball.

Writing for the *Journal* was more good training in the art of reporting and writing on a tight deadline. I wasn't standing in a phone booth dictating to a clerk, as I had done while working out of the *News-Star*'s Ruston bureau. I was rising at five o'clock each morning to be in the newsroom by six, because the *Journal* was of that dying breed—now mostly dead—of afternoon papers. That meant whatever was going into that day's paper had to be written, filed, and edited by noon, sometimes sooner. Working at the *Journal* was a little like my first radio news job in Monroe. I had to wake up, sweep the cobwebs from my head, and get my brain and fingers into gear. One of the early-morning assignments we all hated became known as the "super obit," a mini-profile of an average person in the area who died. Famous people got news-story obituaries, the thinking went, so why not feature an average person each day and give him or her the same attention? The idea was sound. The execution of it? Not so much. The assignment rotated among the news staff, so most of us had to do one every week or ten days. We called people for interviews at seven o'clock in the morning, sometimes earlier. Imagine your husband or parent died the day before. You're grieving and worrying about funeral arrangements and other issues. And now some impudent reporter is waking you up with questions about the departed. Some people were kind and helpful, pleased that Mom or Dad was getting a nice send-off in the local paper. Others regarded it as an intrusion. All the reporters hated those super obits. I finally figured out the secret to them: I didn't call the widow or widower or any other immediate family member. Instead, I scanned the paid obits for one that listed the pallbearers, usually good friends of the deceased who could talk about their friend without becoming emotional. After a few months of super obits and, as I recall, a few complaints from emotional readers, Stan dropped the feature.

Writing obituaries, I had learned in Monroe, is a minefield. It's one of the few times a person will ever be the subject of a newspaper story. Family members will treasure the obituary. In those days, most of them were printed for free as news stories. Today, newspapers charge hundreds, sometimes thousands, of dollars to run them. If you make a mistake writing about an event in someone's life, it can be traumatic. Decades later, I still regret the minor error I made in an obituary about the father of two friends from college. (I think I misspelled his middle name.) I learned that accuracy is always important but never more so than when you are dealing with the intimate details of a person's life or reputation. That is how it should be.

Journalists make mistakes, as does everyone. But not everyone makes his or her mistakes on the front page of the local paper. And not everyone has incorrect details about his life printed in the paper. I never wanted to get things wrong. I tried not to and always marveled that many people would not phone me to correct the record when they saw some inaccuracy of mine. Several times during my years as a reporter, I would encounter someone who would tell me something like, "You know that story you wrote two months ago about that new road? You got the mileage wrong. It's not ten miles long. It's twenty." By the time I learned this, I had written "ten miles" three more times. I always wanted to know about my mistakes as soon as possible so I could correct the record and avoid repeating the wrong information. I think most reporters feel the same.

Another mistake still bothers me. It happened after Shreveport gadfly Larry Napoleon "Boogaloo" Cooper announced his candidacy for lieutenant governor in 1983 against Bobby Freeman, Jimmy Fitzmorris, and others. Cooper was a quirky, dapper African American civil rights activist with a distinctive flat-top haircut. When he filed to run for the office, I pulled out the phonebook and found a *Larry N. Cooper* listed. I copied down the address and wrote my story, identifying "Boogaloo," the lieutenant governor candidate, as the person living at that location. The next morning, the other Larry N. Cooper called the newsroom and demanded to speak to me. The Cooper who lived at the address in my story was not nicknamed "Boogaloo," and he was not running for lieutenant governor. Embarrassed, I had to tell my editors we would need a correction. That was another lesson I learned about not taking lazy shortcuts to get information.

Boogaloo lost that race, and he hated how I covered him the following year. When he signed up to run against Senator Bennett Johnston in 1984, I told readers Cooper was "an unsuccessful candidate for lieutenant governor." Boogaloo was incensed. Although he finished a distant fourth in a four-man field with 2.99 percent, he still won almost 45,000 votes. To him, I suppose, that seemed like a great success. I passed him along to an editor, Mary Durusau, who had a wicked sense of humor and a unique way with disgruntled readers. She listened to him for what seemed like five minutes—he was no doubt shouting at her—before finally ending the conversation with, "Well, Boog, I think what Bob meant was that you didn't win." A few weeks later, when I covered a press conference by Cooper at a local church, he didn't care for my impertinent line of questioning. He refused to answer me. "Get out!" he bellowed, pointing to the door, after I persisted. So, I got up and stalked out. I was pleased that this ended the press conference, as the three or four other reporters in attendance also walked out in solidarity with me.

I enjoyed Shreveport, but I longed to see if I could make it in a larger market as a journalist. In November 1984, Edwin Edwards—almost a year into his third term—prepared to defend himself against an expected federal indictment. He hired a well-regarded defense attorney, William Jeffress, to represent him. In anticipation of the indictment and subsequent federal trial, Stan sent me to Washington to interview Jeffress for a profile. I resolved to make the most of the trip and mailed a resume to Kathy Gest, managing editor of *Congressional Quarterly*, a first-rate weekly publication that covered Congress, particularly the intricacies of legislation. I got the interview, but I was not ready for such a job.[2] I also called Daryl Owen, Bennett Johnston's chief of staff, asking if I could interview him for a profile about a Shreveport native working in a powerful position in DC. He welcomed me over. After I finished the interview, Daryl asked, "Did you know Rafael Bermudez is leaving Russell Long's office? Russell's looking for a new press secretary. Would you be interested in something like that?" A little stunned, I said yes. Daryl arranged an interview for me the next day with Karen Stall, Long's legislative director. The conversation went well and, two or three weeks later, Long and his chief of staff, Kris Kirkpatrick, came to Shreveport-Bossier. I met them for coffee in the restaurant of the Bossier Hilton.

Long asked what I thought was an odd question as he began the interview: "How much do you make at the *Journal?*" I was making $18,000 a year. I rounded it up to $20,000, embarrassed that I made so little. Long said he wanted more young people around him. He was sixty-six and had served in the Senate for thirty-six years. My role, if I got the job, would be to work in Washington for about a year and then move to Baton Rouge in 1986 to help with his reelection campaign.

At the time, I gave little thought to Long's political affiliation. It wasn't as if I would be working for a liberal, like Ted Kennedy, so his membership in the Democratic Party caused me no concern. At that stage of my life, I would have probably entertained a job offer from a Republican. It was not so much that I was a committed Republican—I had switched my voter registration to independent when I moved to Shreveport—but that I was a conservative-leaning agnostic, comfortable with voting for politicians of either party. And Long was among the most conservative Democrats in the Senate. The closest thing to a liberal Democrat in the Louisiana delegation those days was Lindy Boggs, who represented Orleans Parish in the House. There was one Republican in the delegation, Robert Livingston, whose House district encompassed suburban New Orleans and part of the north shore of Lake Pontchartrain.

Still, I wasn't sure I would get the position. I knew nothing about working on Capitol Hill. I only knew a little more about what a

Interviewing US Senator Russell Long in Monroe in 1982. Left to right: Long's press secretary, Rafael Bermudez; me; state Senator Lawson Swearingen; Long.

congressional press secretary did. Looking back on it now, I marvel that Long even considered someone so inexperienced. But mercifully, he did. Shortly after Thanksgiving 1984, Kris called and offered me the job. He wanted me in Washington by the second week of January. What I didn't realize at the time was that working for Long would be the bridge in my gradual conversion from conservative to moderate and, eventually, to liberal.

7

SENATOR LONG WANTS TO SEE YOU

On my first day working for Russell Long, in mid-January 1985, I rode the Metro's red line from my rented townhouse at Dupont Circle to Union Station. The day was bright, clear, and cold as I stepped from the subway and leaned into the biting wind that swirled through the plaza facing the Capitol. Looking up the slight hill, I could see the Russell Senate Office Building, where I would work for the next two years. I was bursting with excitement and optimism for the adventure that awaited.

And then a pigeon swooped overhead and relieved himself on my overcoat. I'm not superstitious, but I did spend most of the five-minute trek to my new office wondering if this sudden turn of events was an ominous warning about dark days ahead.

For the first week, I oriented myself to the job in my new, exciting city. I still knew little about the work of a press secretary. Thank God for Ava Angelle, Long's deputy press secretary, a young woman from Breaux Bridge who had assisted Rafael Bermudez. Ava knew how everything worked, including how to distribute a press release, find the Senate Press Gallery, or respond to an interview request. I had a steep learning curve. A few weeks before moving to Washington, I had flown down to Baton Rouge to meet with several Long staffers. I spent most of the day with Rafael and Dan Borné, another former Long aide. Over lunch, both men regaled me with stories about Long's endearing quirks, including his affection for fast food and canned soup. Rafael offered sound advice about responding to Long's questions. "He's going to ask you for advice about something that you will know nothing about," he warned. "Don't be surprised by that and if he takes your advice seriously." That would happen more than once over the coming years. Rafael also revealed the secret to sharing a meal with Russell Long. "When you're with him, don't order anything that you can't eat in a few minutes," he advised, pointing out that Long could inhale a hamburger and fries before I unwrapped mine. I soon learned this was no exaggeration.

I was on staff for a week but had not yet seen Long, as he and his wife, Carolyn, were out of town during a weeklong Senate recess before Reagan's inauguration. I hoped to attend the outdoor ceremonies on the US Capitol's west side, but a massive snowstorm swept through the region the night before. Temperatures plummeted. The high that day was seven degrees, with a wind chill of minus twenty-five. It was impossible to hold the ceremony out of doors. Reagan took his oath in the Capitol Rotunda. Even the inaugural parade was canceled.

The night before, Long's distant cousin, Representative Gillis Long, died of a heart attack, just seventeen days into his eighth term. A powerful Democrat who represented central Louisiana and chaired the House Democratic Caucus, Gillis was close to Russell, who had supported him when he ran for governor in 1963 and lost to John McKeithen.[1] When I got to the office on Monday morning, Long's secretary, Dot Svendson, called to tell me the senator wanted a tribute about Gillis that he could deliver on the Senate floor.

I had never written such a statement, but at least I knew how to write on deadline. So, I banged out 200 words for a boss I hadn't yet seen, about a man I never met. "The Bible says we know a man by the fruits he bears," I wrote. "Those of us who knew Gillis can attest that his was an abundant, vigorous life. His fourteen years as a member of Congress were active and productive. Today, my family mourns the loss of a very dear friend and relative. But this occasion should be more than a time to mourn. We can and should make it a time to thank God for blessing our lives with such a wonderful and able instrument of his goodness."

After I finished and did some editing, I walked down the marble-floored hallway to Long's office on the second floor of the Russell Senate Office Building. I gave him the draft and sat beside his desk as he studied my words. If he made any substantive changes, I don't recall them. After a few minutes, he said, "This is good. I'm going to go to the floor. Come with me." We rode over to the Capitol on the dedicated subway and took the senators-only elevator to the second floor. As Long headed for the Senate floor, I dashed up to the staff gallery in time to see my new boss read my words into the *Congressional Record*. That was a thrill I have never forgotten. I knew at once I would love this new line of work.

I thought I knew lots about Long, but I knew nothing about his vivacious wife of fifteen years. The former Carolyn Bason had been the personal secretary to Senator Sam Ervin, from her home state of North Carolina, when she met Russell Long in 1969. Russell had been informally separated from his first wife, Katherine, for years. Katherine lived in Baton Rouge, where she raised their two daughters, while Russell spent most of his time in Washington. By the late sixties, Long was a lonely senator with a severe drinking problem who needed the calming influence of a woman like Carolyn. After his divorce from Katherine—she and Russell would remain friends until their deaths three months apart in 2003—Russell married Carolyn. Her influence on him was immediate. He sobered up and reestablished himself as a legislative leader in the Senate.

Where Russell was a little shy and retiring, Carolyn was all personality. To talk with her, even for a few minutes, was to come away believing you had met your new best friend. Her facility with names and faces was a valuable commodity in her personal and political partnership with Russell. And a partnership it was, for Carolyn took just as much, if not more, interest in Louisiana politics as Russell. It was not the rare morning that I arrived at my office to a phone message from Carolyn, who had already spied some news story buried in the clippings sent home the night before. She often wanted to make sure I saw it, too, and wondered how I or her husband might respond. Carolyn was protective of Long's personal and political interests in ways that he often wasn't. That happens in many political marriages. She could sometimes be demanding on staff members, but I immediately took a liking to this petite North Carolinian with a pronounced Southern drawl. When not taking one of us to task and prodding us to better protect and promote her husband, she loved to laugh, delighted in whatever gossipy political tidbit you could offer, and cared about the staff members who worked for Long.

IT WAS THE morning of Monday, February 25, 1985, and I had been working for Long only six weeks. My office was just off the Russell Building's rotunda. From my desk I had a postcard-like scene of the US Capitol. I was just beginning to figure out how things worked around the place. I had found the barbershop in the basement of the Russell Building, staffed by a team of authentic Italian barbers. I discovered where to find a good lunch—usually the large cafeteria in the Dirksen Senate Office Building basement. I was still agog at the famous senators I ran into as I walked around the building. Down our hallway—some called it "Confederate Row"—were the offices of Long, Republican Strom Thurmond of South Carolina, and Democrat John Stennis of Mississippi. The only non-Southerner on our wing was Malcolm Wallop, an affable Republican from Wyoming. Altogether, our section of the building had 108 years of service in the Senate. It was like a living Southern political history museum. Long, Stennis, and Thurmond all signed the 1956 Southern Manifesto and voted against the Civil Rights Act of 1964. Confederate Row also looked a little like a nursing home. Stennis, then eighty-three, was confined to a wheelchair after having his left leg amputated the year before. Thurmond, with his ancient, orange-tinted

In my office in the Russell Senate Office Building in 1985, where I worked as press secretary to Senator Russell Long. I had a stunning view of the US Capitol.

hair, was a year younger than Stennis and was showing his advanced age. His staff wouldn't allow him to wander off to the Senate floor without supervision. Little did I know that Thurmond would still serve in the Senate fifteen years later. At sixty-six, Long was the youngster of the three. Wallop, at fifty-one, was virtually a child.

Late that morning, my phone rang. It was Dot Svendson. "Senator Long wants to see you." I hurried down to his office, where I found Long and Kris Kirkpatrick, who was in DC that week. Long motioned me to a chair next to Kris on the side of his large wooden desk. He was smiling.

"Bob, I've decided that I'm not going to run for reelection," he said in a matter-of-fact tone.

My mind raced. I assumed Long's smile was betraying a joke. I thought he and Kris might be checking to see if I had the gumption to argue with him. I did. I began trying talking him out of it.

"Senator, do you really want to—."

Kris placed his hand on my arm, as if to say, "Stop. This is not a prank." I realized Long was not joking when he said, "I want you to arrange a press conference for me so I can make the announcement." I assumed he meant the following day.

"When do you want to do it?" I asked.

His answer stunned me. "Make it for three and we'll do it right here in my office." It was then about noon.

I later realized Long had been dropping hints for weeks about not running for an eighth Senate term. In late January, at a private reception in Shreveport, former US Representative Joe D. Waggonner had introduced Long to the gathering and made a cryptic comment to the effect that he thought Long might not run again. I hadn't picked up on it. After the speeches, Kris approached me with a worried look. "What did Joe just say?" I'd heard nothing unusual. But Joe somehow knew that his friend was having doubts about seeking another term.

A few weeks later, Long attended a retreat for Senate Democrats running for reelection in 1986. He was stunned when the consultant hired by the Democratic Senatorial Campaign Committee instructed each senator, "Take out your calendar right now and mark off one week between now and election day. That's the only time off you'll have." That seemed outrageous to Long. If the second-most senior member of the Senate, who was also the senior Democrat on the Senate Finance Committee, had to work that hard to win reelection, he wasn't sure he still wanted the job. Republican US Representative Henson Moore of Baton Rouge was already making plans to challenge him. Unlike Long's last six races, this one would not be a cakewalk. By Monday morning, he and Carolyn made up their minds. He was retiring.

After getting my orders to call the press conference, I rushed back to my office and began making phone calls to alert the Louisiana press corps and others in the Senate Press Gallery. Thankfully, Long wrote his statement over the weekend, so I didn't have to produce any words for him. I was stunned by the reaction to my calls. I hadn't realized that Long almost never held a Washington press conference. That fact alone told reporters that something momentous was afoot. As the word spread, my phone began ringing. Everyone wanted to know what was happening. A few reporters figured it out, suspecting that the only reason someone like Long would call a last-minute press conference was if he were retiring. Shortly before three o'clock, I began ushering the press into Long's office. By the time he sat down at his desk to read his statement, the room was packed with television and print reporters. "At some point I think the good Lord permits you to live a long life and if the people are good enough to you a senator ought to consider at what point he ought to retire," Long said. "And that's my decision. It's been my life for thirty-six years, and I love this body, but after thirty-six years here I've decided that that is enough."

Long took a few questions from the reporters, including one that I recorded in my journal later that night. "Senator, how many TV cameras were there when you announced for the Senate the first time?"

Long paused, then grinned. "Well," he said, "there wasn't any television when I announced."

A few minutes after Long finished his press conference, Senator Ted Kennedy of Massachusetts burst into our reception room. He was red-faced and breathless. "I need to see Russell right away," he told the receptionist. He was ushered into Long's office, where he spent the next twenty or thirty minutes trying to persuade his old colleague to change his mind. It never occurred to me that someone like Kennedy, the liberal lion of the Senate, would hold such affection for a Southern conservative like Long. The two men could not have been more different in philosophy and style. Adding to my confusion was the fact I knew Kennedy had defeated Long for Senate majority whip in 1969. In the ensuing years, however, they became friends. Like most colleagues who came to know Long, Kennedy grew to appreciate him for his humor, good sense, and innate ability to sniff out and consummate a legislative deal, all qualities that many of Kennedy's colleagues would ascribe to him.

The next day, I received a kind note from Kennedy's press secretary—a former Texas journalist named Bob Mann—who urged me not to despair over Long's retirement. "In essence," he wrote, "you're still gonna have a lot of fun. And two years is more notice than I ever got [as] a newspaperman or political operative." Only a month earlier, the *Washington Post* had published a small item about the novelty of two senators with press secretaries with the same name: "To correct any possible confusion: Sen. Russell Long has a new press secretary, Bob Mann. He has not hired away Sen. Edward Kennedy's press secretary Bob Mann. There are two Bob Manns and they aren't related, but they are both from Texas."

Over the next two years, I would often get phone calls at my home, sometimes late at night, from national reporters looking for a quote from Kennedy who mistook me for "the other Bob Mann."

AFTER THE DUST settled from his announcement, Long confessed to me one day, "I'm concerned that you might be unhappy with me for hiring you for this job and then announcing my retirement a few weeks after you started."

I laughed. "Not at all," I told him, as I thought, "I would do this job for free, if that were my only way to get a job here."

I had only met Russell Long a few times before I went to work for him. When I saw and interviewed him in Louisiana, I thought he always seemed a little befuddled. He sometimes stuttered and mumbled. His sentences were often punctuated with long pauses. If you didn't know him well, it was easy to conclude this was a man past his prime. I would soon learn that was very wrong.

During dozens of trips to Louisiana, and in talking with him in his office in Washington, I quickly saw that Long's mind was as fertile and active as that of anyone I would ever meet. Nowhere did that become clearer than riding with him along the backroads of Louisiana. Car rides from event to event in Louisiana were not spent returning phone calls—none of us had a cell phone—but in conversation. Usually, it was just four of us: Long, riding shotgun, as Kyle France drove and Kris and I sat in the backseat. As we sped along, Long would hold forth for hours about his latest idea for reforming the tax code or an innovative approach to some other legislation. As I rode around listening to Long think aloud about policy, I realized that about a third of his ideas were eccentric and another third were unworkable. The other third, however, were brilliant, the product of his many years of deep thought about policy, particularly the US tax code. Sometimes, however, he would fulminate about something more prosaic. His pet peeve was dirty gas station restrooms. If he ever ran for governor, Long informed us, he would propose a law requiring filling stations and convenience stores to keep their restrooms clean. One day, he floated the idea of creating an army of state bathroom inspectors. I've always thought this was not a terrible idea.

Traveling with Long was an amusing adventure. When he wasn't sharing ideas for tax policy or rehearsing a speech or interview, he regaled us with tales about growing up the son and nephew of Louisiana's two most famous politicians. As he was a master storyteller, many situations reminded him of joke. His storehouse of funny anecdotes was inexhaustible.

He also seemed to lack sweat glands. As we rode around in the hot Louisiana summers, he would crank the air conditioning down or, sometimes, off. The rest of us wilted and swooned. Often still wearing his suitcoat, Long seemed perfectly comfortable. Part of this resulted from his morbid fear of catching cold and his stubborn belief that one could get sick by going back and forth from a warm environment to a cold one. Long might leave a chilly Washington wearing two or three pairs of socks and long underwear. As soon as he arrived at the airport in Louisiana, he would duck into the restroom and shed his spare socks and long underwear, now ready for the warmer Southern climate. To ward off colds and a sore throat, he sucked on honey-lemon cough drops. He often pushed a dollar bill into my hand and sent me off looking for a new supply of lozenges.

Not as energetic as he once was, the sixty-six-year-old Long needed a nap many afternoons around two or three. When in Washington, he would sneak away to his spacious, ornate hideaway—just steps from the Senate floor—remove his suit and shirt, and put on pajamas. Then, he would stretch out on his sofa for an hour's nap. When on the road, we might book a room at a Holiday Inn for an hour. The senator would catch a quick nap, while Kris, Kyle, and I killed some time returning phone calls or drank coffee in the lobby.

Everyone who traveled with Long was subjected to his crash course in packing. He even drew up a four-page memo, "How to Pack a Bag," which he gave to me and others. It included tips on traveling light and how to pack several suits in his hard-shell luggage without getting them wrinkled. This involved the skillful and strategic use of hat pins and tissue paper. One of Long's tricks was to pack only two or three pairs of socks for the week and wash them out in the hotel sink at night. His memo also contained Long's own design for a more functional suitcase.

When I went to work for him, I knew he was a powerful member of the Senate, but I quickly realized I did not understand the source of much of Long's power. Sure, he was the former majority whip and served for years as chairman of the Senate Finance Committee and was now its senior Democrat. He had forgotten more about tax law than most members ever learned. He was a legend in Louisiana and Washington, the second-most senior member of the Senate. The *Wall Street Journal* once called him "the fourth branch of government." Jimmy Carter, who found himself on the losing end of many fights with Long, had lamented about him: "I was very pleased to be elected, because I thought it was time a Southerner had a chance to run the government. When I got here, I found out one already was."

All of this and more explained Long's political power. It was not, however, useful in figuring out his political influence. I soon learned that Long was so effective in Washington because almost all members of both parties liked him. He had an endless supply of jokes, many of them about his uncle Earl, that he would uncork just as a debate became testy. Long knew when to use humor to defuse a difficult situation. By the time the laughter stopped, his adversaries often forgot what they were mad about.

One of my favorite stories about his humor-as-tactical-weapon happened sometime in the 1970s when he had tried to persuade the Senate Finance Committee to approve a minor tax break for importers of Mardi Gras beads. Some members of the committee objected. Instead of getting his back up, Long reached for a story. A Louisiana man once got into a poker game in a bar in east Texas. Holding a full house, he claimed the hefty pot as he slapped down his cards in victory. But another player, whose hand was a complete bust, raked in the chips. The Texas player explained that in this part of the state a complete bust was called "a phloogie" and he pointed to a sign on the wall that read, *A Phloogie Beats Anything.* The man from Louisiana kept playing and soon he had a worthless hand of cards. He bet everything he had, assuming he, too, had a phloogie. As he began scooping up the chips, the other player stopped him again, this time pointing to another sign on the wall: *Only One Phloogie to the Night.*

When the laughter died down, Long explained that the tax provision he wanted was "just a phloogie for Louisiana—a little onetime thing." In the hysterical laughter that followed, no one could remember to oppose Long's request. One of Long's Republican colleagues from Oregon, Senator Bob Packwood, later told me about the episode: "I think he would have gotten it anyway, but you so much appreciated the humor that you were inclined to give it *for* the humor."

His colleagues knew that Long was brilliant—I knew only a few politicians with a sharper mind and quicker wit—but they also knew he was honest, hardworking, and always willing to cooperate to make a deal. And his colleagues loved him for his generosity of spirit. Years later, when I was working on my biography of Long, I interviewed Senator John Danforth, a Republican from Missouri. Long often told me how much he liked Danforth, although it perplexed him that his Missouri colleague, an ordained Episcopal priest, could not quote the Bible as fluidly as he could. When I spoke to Danforth about Long, he recalled a day early in his tenure on the Senate Finance Committee. Danforth said he was stunned to hear Long, the chairman from the other party, call on him during a bill markup. "I was seated way on the far end," Danforth told me. "And Long was inviting me, the most junior member of the committee, to share my thoughts on the bill." Long did not view his colleagues through the lens of their party affiliation. He saw them as potential partners, and I discovered that he worked hard to make the Finance Committee a bipartisan panel. I was struck that Republican members of the committee I interviewed—including Bob Dole and Bob Packwood—were often the most effusive in their praise for him. When Long ran for reelection in 1980, Dole even cut a television spot for him.

On my first trip back to Louisiana with Long in 1985, we passed through Shreveport, where I saw Joe Waggonner, who had first suspected Long wouldn't run for reelection. Joe represented northwest Louisiana in Congress for almost twenty years before retiring in 1978. He and Long were the same age and had remained close friends. And Joe gave me some of the best political counsel a new staffer could receive. "Russell is sixty-six years old," he said in his measured baritone. "You're not going to change him. He's set in his ways, so don't try to make him into something he's not." This was brilliant advice. First, Joe recognized that, at twenty-

With former Congressman Joe D. Waggonner in 1986. Joe represented northwest Louisiana in Congress for decades.

six years, I thought I was smarter than I was and knew more about politics than I really did. And he understood that a veteran politician in his mid-sixties, like Russell Long, was not likely to change much. Working with Long to maximize his strengths, not eliminate his weaknesses, was sound advice and a lesson I applied when working for other politicians: don't force them to change their ways to adapt to the cameras or audiences. Identify their strengths and adapt the cameras and audiences to them. Put them in situations where their gifts are most likely to shine.

FOR MUCH OF Long's Senate career, his constituents, friends, and colleagues grew accustomed to hearing his uncle Earl jokes. Russell was sixteen in 1935 when an assassin killed his father, Senator Huey P. Long. He worshipped his dad but had not known him that well, as Huey was often gone, either on the campaign trail, running state government in Baton Rouge, or off in Washington after his election to the Senate. With his father gone, Huey's brother, Earl, became Russell's surrogate father. Russell campaigned for Earl in the governor's race of 1947. After Earl took office, he hired Russell as his executive counsel. Less than a year later, with Earl's support, Russell won a special election to fill the unexpired term of Senator John Overton, who died in the spring of 1948.

Russell had a thousand Uncle Earl jokes but, as many observers noticed, he rarely talked publicly about his father. Maybe it was his reluctance to mine the pain from losing his dad so suddenly and violently. Whatever the case, this changed in the late spring of 1985, as the fiftieth anniversary of Huey Long's death approached.

Speaking about his father—and defending him—seemed to invigorate Long. I suspect he also knew that 1985 might be the last time Huey Long and his record would receive wide national press attention. I'm certain he knew the year would also be his last and best chance to influence how history would view his dad. In the late spring, Long told me he wanted my help in writing a speech that he planned to give on the Senate floor on the fiftieth anniversary of his father's death on September 10, 1985. A few days before this, he would also go to the Louisiana State Library in Baton Rouge to deliver a speech about Huey and then lay a wreath at his tomb, below the giant statue of Long on the grounds of the State Capitol. While he seemed to want me to come up with a first draft, I knew I couldn't begin to put words in Russell Long's mouth about his father. I had read T. Harry Williams' Pulitzer Prize-winning biography, *Huey Long*, but I knew I couldn't compose words for Long that would be so intimate and personal. I offered a compromise. "Why don't I interview you about your father," I suggested. "I can record the interviews, get them transcribed, and then turn them into a speech text that you and I can edit." Long agreed. For the next month or two, we found an hour or so every week for my interviews. Sometimes, we would meet in his hideaway or his Watergate apartment.

One weekend in early June, I drove to Long's weekend home in the Shenandoah mountains. He and Carolyn were still out playing golf when I arrived at their home atop Rattlesnake Mountain. I sat in my car reading his father's memoir, *Every Man a King*, while I waited for them to return. Finally, they appeared and within thirty minutes Long and I were sitting in roughhewn rocking chairs on his front porch. I soaked up the breathtaking view of the valley below as he regaled me with stories about his dad. He spoke at a furious pace that afternoon, devoting most of his time to rebutting the attacks of Huey's enemies. Mostly, he talked about the 1929 impeachment proceedings.

After about ninety minutes of reminiscing, Long and Carolyn were ready to leave for dinner with friends at the famous Inn at Little Washington in nearby Washington, Virginia. Knowing I would be invited to join them, I had brought a sport coat but had neglected to wear a tie. Carolyn thought I should wear one of Senator Long's ties and quickly produced a specimen from his closet. Unfortunately, she chose one of Long's favorite new ties. He had worn it several times over the past two weeks. It was a wide, patterned monstrosity of silver, bright blue, gold, and orange. It was hideous, an assault on the eyes. Almost everyone in the office, including me, had joked about its unsightly qualities, especially after he had worn it during a recent appearance on PBS's "McNeil-Lehrer News Hour." I swallowed hard, put it on, and wore it that night to dinner. "It was such an ugly tie," I told my journal later. "I was very self-conscious about it."

Four days later, I went to Long's Watergate apartment to review what transcripts I had produced so far, but I suspected he would also want to talk about his father. I was right. Shortly after we began, Long told me why he had decided to enter politics after his father's death. "I saw all these people [in his father's political organization] who were left," he told me, "and there was no idealism in it anymore." Sometimes our Huey Long sessions got derailed by other events. This would be one of those times. After about thirty minutes of talk about Huey, Long remembered he wanted to call Ronald Reagan's attorney general, Edwin Meese, to lobby on behalf of Louisiana getting one of the new judgeships created for the Fifth Circuit Court of Appeals. He grabbed the phone and was speaking with Meese within a couple of minutes. These were the moments I thanked God for my role as a fly on the wall.

"I only want one thing from you, General," Long shouted into the phone. "Justice!"

Then, Long lit into Texas and explained why the Lone Star State did not deserve another judge on the court. "Texas hogs everything up," he said, adding, "Lyndon Johnson used to kid me about my SUFT program: Save Us from Texas. When he became president, I said, 'Now, Mr. President, you're now president and you've got a commitment to all the states, not just Texas.'" Long ended the call by telling Meese he had no interest in naming Louisiana's new appeals court judge. Unspoken was the fact that Long wasn't giving up much. As he was a member of the party out of power, the White House would never have consulted him on judicial appointments.

Finally, after a half-dozen of these interview sessions, I massaged the transcripts into a speech that was Russell Long's defense of his father's record and a loving tribute to the dad he barely knew. For an opening rhetoric flourish, I suggested he begin by quoting his father's famous campaign speech under the Evangeline Oak in St. Martin Parish, in which Huey echoed Longfellow's celebrated poem about unrequited love: "Where are the roads and highways that you sent your money to build, that are not nearer now than ever before? Where are the institutions to care for the sick and disabled? Evangeline wept bitter tears in her disappointment, but it lasted only through one lifetime. Your tears in this country, around this oak, have lasted for generations. Give me the chance to dry the eyes of those who still weep here." Long agreed and then began, in his own words:

It has been fifty-eight years since my father stood in the shade of that beautiful oak in St. Martin Parish and asked Louisiana's citizens to trust him with their hopes and aspirations. His words were not the empty, demagogic promises so often made by politicians of that day. They were the sincere words of a man who was on the verge of taking Louisiana by storm and would soon assure himself a place as the most outstanding and successful governor in our nation's history. . . .

He promised the people roads where there was mostly dirt and mud. He kept that promise, building thousands of miles of concrete, asphalt, and gravel roads in just a few short years. He promised better schools and educational opportunities for a population that was largely illiterate. He kept that promise and built an educational system which for the first time gave opportunities for learning to all children, not just the privileged few. . . .

In matters of my father's life, I am a prejudiced man. He is my hero, the one person in this world who has inspired me above all others. . . . This view is one that also sees Huey Long as a mortal man, not perfect by any means, with weaknesses like everyone. However, I strongly believe that what motivated my father was his love for mankind and his belief that every man and woman deserved the opportunity to enjoy a good life. . . . I hope that he would be proud of me today, for I have tried to champion the causes of those who need a friend in government and to work to build a system which encourages everyone to enjoy a meaningful place in our economic system.

Sunday, September 8, was the fiftieth anniversary of the day in 1935 that Long's father was shot in a first-floor hallway of the State Capitol, across the street from where Russell would speak at the State Library. That morning, as we drove from his farmhouse to downtown Baton Rouge, Long was quiet. Rain began pouring as soon as we pulled up to the building. We waited in the car for about ten minutes, and when the rain abated, we dashed through the backdoor. Inside, Long gave his emotional speech, much the same text he would deliver in the Senate two days later, on the anniversary of his father's death. His remarks lasted about thirty minutes. He closed with a poignant quote from his father: "Then no tear-dimmed eyes of a small child will be lifted into the saddened face of a father or mother unable to give it the necessities required by its soul and body for life; then the powerful will be rebuked in the sight of man for holding that which they cannot consume, but which is craved to sustain humanity; the food of the land will feed, the raiment clothe and the houses shelter all the people; the powerful will be elated through the wellbeing of all, rather than through their greed."

Done, he stepped from the podium and many in the audience followed him to his father's grave where, in the light rain, he laid a wreath. Standing next to his brother, Palmer, he prayed silently at his father's grave for a few moments and then made his way back to his car, retracing almost the exact steps he had taken fifty years earlier, as a sixteen-year-old boy walking behind his father's casket. As our car pulled away, we all congratulated him on the speech. He said nothing for about thirty seconds, then finally he broke the silence. "That was for Dad," he said. "I owed him that."

In January 1986, Long agreed to speak about his father again at another major event, this time at the National Press Club, site of the premiere of a PBS documentary about Huey Long directed by Ken Burns. In August 1985, Burns had sent his co-producer, Richard Kilberg, to Washington to give Long a sneak peek at the film. Kris Kirkpatrick and I watched the film with him one morning in a small viewing room in the Senate Recording Studio in the Capitol basement. "I was surprised at how emotional I felt after it was over," I wrote that night in my journal. "I've spent the last two months laboring on this project [Long's speech] and I didn't realize how wrapped up in it I had become." There were some difficult scenes in the film. Betty Carter, widow of crusading anti-Long newspaper editor Hodding Carter, spoke about how she did not grieve Long's demise. "There wasn't a Saturday night we didn't talk about killing Huey Long," Carter said. That night, I wrote: "Hard stuff for me to hear. Even more difficult and painful for RBL. He showed no emotion afterwards."

Later, in Long's Capitol hideaway, Kris and I had talked with him about the film and whether he should speak at a New Orleans screening in September. He asked my opinion of the documentary. "I thought it was very balanced," I said. "Just like the T. Harry Williams book. If it just told one side and all favorable, it would not have any credibility." But Long hated the film. He thought Burns had cast his father as a corrupt politician. And he was particularly annoyed that Burns had featured comments critical of his father by Cecil Morgan, an anti-Long former state senator. "I've always said that while there was no conspiracy and specific plan to assassinate Huey Long," Morgan remarked in the film, "I think the thing had to happen."

By the January premiere, Long was ready to speak about the documentary, especially Morgan's comments. "They failed to adequately identify Cecil Morgan," Long told the National Press Club crowd after the showing. "Mr. Morgan was that charming, articulate, well-bred gentleman whom they identified as a 'former legislator.' I think it unfair to identify Mr. Morgan minus his principal claim to fame." Long was just warming up. "After he did his best trying to keep Huey from giving the children schoolbooks and after he did his best trying to impeach Huey, Mr. Morgan moved along to a place where his talents were more fully appreciated. He became general counsel for Standard Oil of New Jersey." As everyone in the room knew from watching the film, Huey Long's attacks on Standard Oil—including his efforts to tax the corporation to pay for building roads, bridges, and improving Louisiana schools— incurred the oil giant's wrath and retribution. "Too tough" was how Long summed up the documentary for the Press Club audience.

Many of the stories he told about his father were passed along to Russell Long by his mother, his uncle Earl, or friends and associates of Huey. Long's stories about Earl, however, came mostly from personal experience. He was not opposed to embellishing those Uncle Earl tales to please a crowd, but the true stories were often funny enough. One night in the winter of 1985, I caught up with Long at Washington's National Airport for a flight back to New Orleans. Snow was already beginning to pile up when we arrived at our gate. By the time we boarded the plane, a blizzard was setting in. The airline allowed us onboard, but the FAA soon shut down the runway until the snowplows could reopen it. In the meantime, ground crews started de-icing our plane. They would hose us down two or three times. We sat on the tarmac for almost two hours before we began our flight to New Orleans. And I made the most of the time.

"Tell me stories about your uncle Earl," I begged. Long was happy to comply as I prodded him for details and prompted him to tell more tales. He regaled me for hours.

Finally, about the time he seemed to exhaust his store of Uncle Earl stories, he turned to me and asked, "Did *you* ever know Uncle Earl?"

I chuckled. "No, Senator, I didn't. I was only about two years old when he died."

That innocent question summed up Russell Long's way of dealing with his staff. He was almost oblivious to our ages. If he hired you, he assumed you knew what you were doing. At the very least, he would listen to your views. I was all of twenty-seven but he treated me and others who worked for him with complete respect. Sometimes, I went overboard with my advice. When that happened, he had a kind way of putting me in my place. One day, I was in his office urging him to do something. I cannot recall the issue, but I remember I was pressing the matter with more certainty than was appropriate. At first, he humored me, this kid who assumed he knew better than a thirty-seven-year veteran of the US Senate. Finally, he smirked and stopped me.

"How old are you?" he asked.

"Twenty-seven," I said.

He rocked back in his chair and fiddled with a pencil as he pondered my answer for a second or two, and then he responded, "I sure wish I had as many years ahead of me as you do." I wasn't sure, but I think I had been put in my place. Whatever we were debating, I dropped the subject.

In all my years around Russell Long, I never saw him act rudely to anyone. It did not seem in his nature. He was usually in a good mood and often eager to tell a funny story. He blanched at the sight of another senator mistreating a staff member. I was with him one day in the anteroom behind the Senate Finance Committee hearing room in the Dirksen Building when Senator Daniel Patrick Moynihan, a New York Democrat, began berating a staff member in front of Long, me, and a half-dozen others. It was a humiliating experience for any young staffer to be chewed out in front of a crowd. Long glanced at me and whispered, "Let's go." When we reached the hallway and started back to his office, Long leaned into me and draped an arm over my shoulder as we walked. He said nothing, but I took the gesture to be his way of reminding me, "I don't treat my staff like what you and I just saw."

The closest Long ever came to insulting me happened one Sunday afternoon in 1986, when I met him at Washington National Airport for a flight back to New Orleans. He was heading home on personal business and so was I. So, technically, I was not staffing him. We would go our separate ways when we arrived in Louisiana. Long was of a generation who never traveled in anything but a suit and tie. That day, he dressed as formally as he would for any day in the Senate. On the other hand, I showed up dressed in jeans and a light jacket, and certainly no necktie. As I settled into my seat next to him in the waiting area, he greeted me warmly, while showing great interest in my attire. Finally, after a minute or two of silence, he leaned over, smiled, and said, "You know, I can't wait until the day when I'm no longer in the Senate and can dress like I don't give a damn. You know, like you're dressed today." All I could do was laugh and wonder if he was really joking. A few years later, I reminded him of the remark and said I believed he might have meant it as a backhanded rebuke. He smiled.

IN THOSE DAYS, I still considered myself a moderate-to-conservative independent, even though I was working for the second-most senior member of the Senate. Not long after Long announced his retirement, I naively sent a resume over to the White House, asking to be considered for a speechwriting job in the Reagan administration. I didn't understand why no one responded. Now, I know. It made no sense, even in the relatively bipartisan atmosphere of Washington in those days. Then, as now, one was expected to pick a team and stay with that team for the rest of your career. Moving back and forth from one side to the other was not often done. I would have been suspect and regarded as disloyal by both sides. The environment wasn't as partisan as it is today, but everyone knew which jersey you wore when you went to work in the morning.

Even though I was briefly amenable to working for a Republican, my political philosophy continued to evolve. Working for a Democrat in an office of Democrats—although, no one ever asked about my party registration before I got my job with Long—surely influenced my thinking. My politics were not liberal, but I was more open to other ways of seeing the world. The seeds of my liberalism, I now understand, had been planted years before. I had always admired politicians like Hubert Humphrey and Lyndon Johnson. When I went to college, like many young people away from their parents for the first time, I was introduced to new ideas and different ways of seeing the world. Working as a journalist broadened my mind further, as I interviewed honest, hardworking people who only wanted government to give them a little help, not a handout. And West Monroe Mayor Dave Norris had opened my eyes further with his patient instruction and prodding.

My ideological evolution was gradual, but my party switch was sudden. The budget deficit debates in 1986 finally pushed me into the arms of the Democratic Party. That's when I saw an unflattering side of the Republican Party, especially in how its leaders disparaged those living in poverty. I credit then-Republican Senator Phil Gramm of Texas—who sponsored a program of draconian budget cuts—for opening my eyes. His attacks on government spending to help the down-and-out offended me. Defending his proposed deep spending cuts aimed at the poor, Gramm said in April 1986, "I think they will be easy on the people who do the work and pull the wagon, which is the way it was meant to be." I found his implication—poor people are lazy and do not work—repulsive. A few years earlier, Gramm had asserted, "We're the only nation in the world where all our poor people are fat." Gramm showed me a side of the Republican Party I had not fully recognized before. Maybe I had just not wanted to see it. Whatever the case, I wanted no part of it. I was now a Democrat.

8

I Still Got a Lot of Snap Left in My Garters

I still had so much to learn about being press secretary to a United States senator. I was grateful to apprentice in the office of a senator planning his retirement. It's not that we weren't busy—Long was helping write the huge tax reform bill Ronald Reagan would sign into law in 1986—but it was more that I worked for a boss focused on his approaching retirement. Our press office performed all the normal activities of a Senate office, but at a relaxed pace not gearing up for a reelection campaign. That changed in the late spring and early summer of 1985 as Edwin Edwards went on trial in New Orleans federal court on corruption charges.[1]

The idea of an imprisoned or politically crippled Edwards generated frenetic talk about who would run for governor in 1987, even as the race to replace Long in the Senate heated up. As Louisiana government foundered in the vacuum created by Edwards' absence—he would spend most of 1985 fighting to stay out of prison—a host of pundits, politicos, and interested voters floated the names of possible candidates. The news that Lieutenant Governor Bobby Freeman was also under investigation by a federal grand jury (he was never charged) only fueled speculation about who the next governor might be. Long's name rose to the top. And he did little to tamp down rumors about his candidacy.

The press conjecture sparked something that neither Long nor any of us would have predicted—a flood of letters pleading with him to run. Some reporters thought we were encouraging the correspondence. We weren't. After a while, I and others on the staff mentioned to a few reporters that these letters were pouring in and their stories about it prompted more letters, but the initial letter-writing campaign was spontaneous. By the end of 1985, the *Baton Rouge Advocate* published its annual statewide political poll, which showed Long with a 77 percent favorability, the highest approval for any potential candidate for governor, including Buddy Roemer, Edwin Edwards, and US representatives Billy Tauzin and Bob Livingston. The Long fever grew even stronger in February

1986, when the *Advocate*, published by Charles Manship, Jr., son of Huey Long's arch-nemesis Charles Manship, printed an editorial begging Long to run. "It is our hope for this state that enough Louisianians—including the state's senior U.S. senator—can convince Long that running for governor will be the right choice. Right for him. And certainly right for the state. We hope that he will announce as a candidate at the earliest possible moment." It was then about twenty months before the election. Long was not ready to announce his decision, but that editorial and the continued stream of letters into our office were talking him into the idea.

I was with Long in early March when he tested the waters by traveling the state and listening to people about a governor's campaign. When he spoke to a meeting of the Baton Rouge Chamber of Commerce in late February, a reporter had told him, "Senator [Bennett] Johnston has said he believes you would accept a draft to run for governor." The audience burst into sustained applause. Long smiled, enjoying the affirmation of his hometown audience. When the applause died down, he told them the only thing he was running for "is my freedom" but added, "I know about that other matter, and I'll think about it." That night, in Shreveport, Long had told his audience, "I might feel like getting back in the trenches." Later in the year, as he seemed to inch even closer to running, he began telling people, "I still got a lot of snap left in my garters, as Uncle Earl used to say."

Most thought Long would win, if he ran. Writing for the *Shreveport Times* in early March, reporter John Hill observed: "If the intended purpose of Sen. Russell Long's trip to Louisiana last week was to test the waters for a possible gubernatorial candidacy, then he'll run. And if the venerable senator runs, he'll win, maybe even without a campaign." Long's junior colleague in the Senate, Bennett Johnston, agreed. "If he runs," Johnston told the *Alexandria Daily Town Talk* in August 1986, "it'll be a cake walk, and he'll waltz right in."

Throughout his year of flirting with the governor's race, Long's main source of hesitation was his reluctance to challenge Edwards. If Edwards had announced in early 1986 that he would not seek reelection, Long might have declared his candidacy for governor right then. Edwards, however, was no fool. He knew that the minute he announced his retirement, his political power would dissipate. And he now had no reason to exit the race, as a federal jury acquitted him of corruption charges in the spring of 1986.

That summer, Long decided he and Edwards should quit their dance. We dropped him off at the Governor's Mansion one morning for a private meeting with Edwards, who, after an hour, refused to offer much insight into his thinking about running. The longer Edwards remained in the race, the harder the decision became for Long. Russell Long was a team player. I believed he wanted to be governor to complete the job he thought his father started but never finished. When asked about Huey, he would respond, "History will judge Huey Long, for better or for worse. I loved my father." And he insisted if he ran it would not be to match his father's record. Instead, he said, he hoped "to turn this state around." But the lure of being governor—winning the job his father once held—was powerful.

As the end of his Senate term approached, Long knew he must decide soon. Would he return to Louisiana and launch a governor's campaign, or would he sign on with a Washington law firm as a lobbyist? Through November 1986, I assumed he would run. Most of us on his staff believed that Louisiana needed someone, like him, who understood how to govern, represent the state well on the national and international stages, and remove the stench of corruption that had settled over the Governor's Mansion under Edwards.

Each day, the staff gathered the letters from people begging him to run and sent them to Long's home. In April, the president of the Mid-Continent Oil and Gas Association wrote to Long, saying, "I think you are the only person who can pull this state back together." An elderly constituent from Slidell wrote to him in July: "Please run for governor. We are on Social Security, have a pension that is just a little less than my Social Security, and a part-time job that *may* not last much longer." In September, a supporter from Kenner told Long, "It would be an act of pure service [if you ran for governor]. Your realistic, conservative leadership is badly needed here at home." I'm certain Long and Carolyn read all those letters.

On November 3, 1986—Long's sixty-eighth birthday—I slipped my own two-page memo into the pile and sent it to the Watergate with other letters from that day. "I know you are looking for a sign," I wrote, "and I would suggest that your retirement from the Senate is that sign. For were it not for that decision, made two years ago with no knowledge of this race, you would not be afforded this historic opportunity to give your state the benefit of your years of experience and wisdom. If that's not a sign, I'm not sure what is. It is, at the very least, a dramatic opportunity and one I pray you take." The next day, he told me the memo made Carolyn cry.

On Monday, November 18, I flew with Long and Carolyn to New Orleans. The following day, he would announce whether he would become a candidate for governor. About thirty minutes into the flight, Carolyn wandered back to the economy section, where I sat. "Russell wants you to go up and sit with him," she said, as she took my seat. I went to the first-class cabin and settled in next to Long. He handed me the handwritten statement he planned to deliver. He would not run. The reason was simple, he wrote. "My wife, Carolyn, puts it as concisely and clearly as anyone: 'People should know when to go.'" He had not made the decision lightly. He would say, "It occupied my thoughts for hundreds of hours and many days. It was a matter of a great amount of meditation, prayer, and discussion with my wife and other members of my family." After I finished reading his handwritten speech, I looked up at him and smiled wanly. I had no words.

Long broke the silence. "If the Lord had meant for me to do something else," he said, "I would know by now."

"Well," I responded, "you know how I felt. But I respect your decision."

That night, after dinner in Baton Rouge, Long gathered with his staff and a few close friends around the pool at his modest "farmhouse" on the outskirts of town. He ruminated about his decision to forgo the race. I detected a tinge of regret in his voice. Long was a spiritual man. "I kept waiting for a sign," he said. That sign, at least the one he looked for, never came. As we drove away, leaving him and Carolyn alone under the dark Louisiana sky, I joked to Kyle France, "If a meteor strikes that cow pasture after we leave, we might have a governor's candidate on our hands tomorrow morning." Alas, there were no meteors that night.

As for the possibility that Edwin Edwards would be shipped off to prison, that would have to wait until 2002. But he would not be reelected

With Senator Russell Long and his wife, Carolyn, in 1986.

in 1987. He would run later that year and drop out when Buddy Roemer forced him into a runoff.

OVER THE MANY months Long had considered running for governor, the race to replace him in the Senate raged on. At first, he had been ambivalent about helping Democratic US Representative John Breaux of Crowley in his Senate campaign against Republican US Representative Henson Moore. On at least one occasion, I prodded Long to get more involved in Breaux's campaign.

"Don't you want to help John?" I asked him one day that summer.

"John can take care of himself," Long snapped.

In late September, after Breaux's media consultant began airing a spot of Long attacking Moore—filmed at a New Orleans fundraiser for Breaux in July—one of Bennett Johnston's staffers, Jim Oakes, called me from Louisiana. He wanted to know if we knew anything about it. I didn't, but I called Long at the Watergate and asked him what he knew. "They've done this without my permission," Long said, angrily. "And I want it off the air immediately. I don't even want to see it. I want it off."

After Breaux learned about the contretemps, he phoned Long to apologize. By then, Long had softened and asked to see the spot. It was strong. In it, Long charged that Moore had no accomplishments to his name after ten years in Congress. Finally, Long decided to allow Breaux's campaign to air the spot for another week, which was about how long they had planned to run it. Later, a poll by the *Shreveport Journal* showed that Breaux's statewide numbers shot up at the same time the ad began airing on television.

I've never been sure why Long took so long to get involved on Breaux's behalf. Maybe he wanted Breaux to prove that he could mount a serious, well-funded, credible campaign. Early on, there were plenty of people who thought Breaux didn't stand much of a chance against Moore. Long was one of them. In mid-July, I had brought him a Republican poll someone had leaked that showed Moore comfortably in the lead with 32 percent. Breaux was in third place with 16 percent, behind Attorney General William Guste. "If this is right," Long told me, "then Moore's our next senator."

Long eventually realized he could not remain on the sidelines, especially when it appeared that a Republican might capture his Senate seat. And over time, Breaux proved himself to Long and others. He built a professional and aggressive campaign that Long came to see was worthy of his support. More than anything else, Breaux's patient courtship seemed to pay off. The more Long got to know Breaux, the more he admired him and the energetic, smart way he ran his campaign. Once

Breaux made the runoff with Moore, Long was fully onboard.

One Saturday morning in November, about ten days before the general election, Long tracked me down in Monroe, at the home of my friends Ron and Renee LeLeux. The *Washington Post* published a poll that morning that showed Breaux within striking distance of Moore. Long was so elated that he called to share the news and celebrate. "There's this poll in the *Post* this morning," he sputtered, filling me in on the details. "I think John can win this thing!"

A few days later, I was with Long in Lafayette for a rally with Breaux. The huge, boisterous crowd at the Cajundome revved him up so much that when Long took the stage, he stunned us all with his pungent attacks on Moore, ridiculing his lack of legislative accomplishment. "I don't know anyone in Washington that likes Henson Moore!" Long bellowed, perhaps getting a bit carried away. After a few years of watching Breaux in the Senate, Long later told me, "If I had known John was going to be such a good senator, I would have retired earlier." Until he died, Long would be one of Breaux's biggest fans.

As Long's retirement day approached, the accolades about his thirty-eight years in the Senate poured in. Every journalist in Washington and Louisiana wanted an interview. NBC News did an extensive retrospective about him, as did other major news organizations. The only one Long rebuffed was the most popular show on television at the time, "60 Minutes," which airs Sunday nights on CBS. When I went to see him about the request, I was excited about the opportunity of working with the show's producers and whichever correspondent CBS would assign to the story. Long shot me down.

"I'm not doing that," he said, explaining that the show had once produced a piece on him and his oil wealth. CBS hired an airplane or helicopter to fly over his modest, Baton Rouge farmhouse, describing it, he remembered, as a palatial home. "Don't just tell them no. Tell them, 'Russell Long said go to hell.'"

I swallowed hard and told him I would, but when I called the producer back to give him the news, I couldn't do it. I knew that Long was reacting emotionally and he would think better of the command in a few hours. Moreover, I hoped to work in Washington for many years. The last thing I needed in my next job was a reputation for being difficult to work with. I told them Long was too busy to participate in the story and thanked them for their interest.

In the back of my mind was also the chiding I once received from Kris Kirkpatrick for quoting Long verbatim in a statement after Ronald Reagan nominated William Rehnquist for chief justice in 1986. When I caught up with Long in the lobby off the Senate chamber earlier that afternoon, he dictated a statement to me in which he not only supported Reagan's choice but averred that the president had a right to propose anyone he wanted for the job, including "a housewife." To Kris's horror, I issued the statement without trying to persuade Long to soften the language. As a former reporter, I considered it a fantastic quote for the press in a state that worshipped Reagan. After Kris explained my misjudgment, I would not make a similar mistake again.

As the end of Long's Senate days approached, I needed a new job. I loved working in Washington and in the Senate. We were all thrilled when Breaux beat Henson Moore by five points and deprived Republicans of a seat they counted as secure from almost the first day. Like Long, I had not always been confident Breaux could defeat Moore. Reagan was enormously popular in Louisiana. He visited the state several times that fall to campaign for Moore. Other than Long, Breaux had no one of similar stature to vouch for him. Over the previous two years, I had been around Breaux many times and liked and respected him. I found him down-to-earth, smart, and politically savvy. And unlike many people, Breaux never seemed to doubt he could win.

One morning in late February 1986, Breaux and I sat next to each other for more than two hours on a flight from New Orleans to Washington. As Long rode in first class, Breaux and I talked the whole time. He showed me a new poll that had him *only* nine points behind Henson Moore. Trailing the frontrunner by almost ten points did not discourage him at all. In fact, he explained energetically how he would win the race. By the time we reached Washington, I believed he could win. And when he did, I knew instantly that I wanted to work for him.

My job interview with Breaux occurred on the run one afternoon in mid-November. I met him in the Senator's Dining Room in the Capitol, while he was roaming around the building, meeting with members of the Senate Finance Committee and lobbying for a seat on the powerful panel that Long chaired for so many years. He asked for my insights into a few of the members he was meeting. We got along well, but I assumed he was unsure about hiring me. I was still young. My experience was working for a retiring senator who had not wanted a press operation to set the world on fire. I had been aggressive about getting Long into more news stories than he wanted. Many times, in fact, I realized he was probably talking with a reporter to indulge me. Breaux surely knew, as an incoming freshman, he would need someone assertive and who could get him news coverage from day one. I knew I could be that person, but I wasn't sure if Breaux knew that. I went to Long and told him I had applied for the job and hoped he might put in a good word about me. A few days later, Long asked to see me in his office. "I just met with John and gave you the $10,000 selling job," Long said.

I also wrote a five-page memo to Breaux in which I outlined the various ways I proposed to establish and energize his press operations. "I know that you plan to have a strong, aggressive press operation and I think you should have that," I wrote in the conclusion after I spelled out the eight points I thought he should consider in setting up his press shop. "I also know you are concerned with the fact that Russell Long's style is so different from yours that I might have difficulty making such an adjustment. The only thing I can tell you in answer to that is to point you to those polls which clearly show Russell Long as the most popular man in Louisiana, who could have been elected governor, or re-elected senator, had he run. The type of media coverage that he received over the past year or so does not come by accident." I don't know if my memo and this closing argument had much sway over Breaux. The truth was that my work as Long's press secretary contributed little to his popularity in Louisiana. Long's thirty-eight-year record and his legendary name accounted for 99 percent of it. I was a bystander who hadn't screwed up too much.

Still, weeks went by and I heard nothing from Breaux. In the meantime, I planned a week away in Paris. I asked Breaux's office to call Karen Stall, Long's chief of staff, if they had any news for me while I was gone. In 1986, carrying a cell phone to Europe was unheard of, and I had no email address to check. Four or five days into the trip, I found a payphone on a street somewhere, stuffed a fistful of French coins into the slot, and called our DC office. "They've offered you the job," Karen told me. I asked her to tell them I accepted.

I still had one more memorable experience in Russell Long's office. On the morning of Saturday, January 3, 1987, I went to work for him for the last time. He would become a former senator at noon, as Breaux became the state's new junior senator at the same moment (the swearing-in ceremony would happen on the following Monday). Russell and Carolyn wanted to spend his last hours as a senator in his Russell Senate Office Building office, and I wanted to be with him as well. I arrived late that morning and joined a half-dozen staffers who were still around and wanted the same experience. We sat in the office as an introspective, slightly melancholy Long reminisced about his many years in Washington. When the clock struck noon, he was no longer a US senator. He and Carolyn stood up and unceremoniously walked out the door, into the marble-floored hallway, and towards their waiting car. We said our goodbyes and watched as they ambled down the hall. Then, Long stopped. He realized he still had his office key. As he fished the key out of his pocket and removed it from his keychain, Long paused for a moment. He stared at the key for a second and did something uncharacteristically sentimental. He kissed it. And then he handed it to Karen Stall. As he walked away into retirement, I went next door to the Dirksen Senate Office Building, where Breaux's temporary quarters would be.

I began the next chapter of my life with as much trepidation as enthusiasm. That night, I confessed my fears to my diary: "I am not at all sure this job will work. [Breaux's chief of staff] has made me many promises, but I basically don't trust him to keep them. Some, I will make an issue out of; others only prod to get what had been promised. I've been promised that press has top priority. We'll see."

9

He Checked a Bag

In the late 1980s, people often asked me about the difference between working for Russell Long and John Breaux. The answer was easy. With Long, I spent the better part of two years working for a senator who was retiring and closing his office. It's true that for almost a year Long entertained running for governor, but we were never putting together such a campaign. We were mostly helping a sixty-eight-year-old senator navigate towards the end of his political career. Breaux, on the other hand, was new to the Senate and hungry for press coverage.

If Long's office was like a going out-of-business sale, Breaux's first year in the Senate was like the launch of a Silicon Valley startup—creative and relentlessly aggressive. There was no reporter whose call Breaux would not return. And while Long was best acquainted with the national reporters who covered tax policies, Breaux's practice—in his first two terms, especially—was to call Louisiana reporters first.

While the energy in Breaux's office was greater than Long's, it was also more relaxed than any Senate office I ever knew. In our early days, before Breaux got his permanent quarters in the newer Hart Senate Office Building, we occupied space on the ground floor of the Dirksen Building. The Senate divided our office into two sections along two hallways, bracketing a section of rooms occupied by Senator Don Riegel, a stolid Democrat from Michigan. Every evening around six, the Breaux office—as it had for years on the House side—would relax for a happy hour. Some uptight Riegel staffers must have thought we were crazy, but we were Louisiana people accustomed to having a little fun. As he would for every day of the seventeen years I would work for him, Breaux set the tone. He was funny, informal, and kind and caring to everyone on his staff.

Not that Russell Long was formal and indifferent. He was funny and engaging in his own way and always treated us well. But with Long, you always knew you were with the son of Huey Long and the second-most senior member of the Senate. He was a legend whom you would never call "Russell." Almost everyone on staff referred to Long, out of his presence, as "RBL." Breaux was "John" to most of his staffers. His wife, Lois, also wanted staffers to use her first name. When there was a staff party, whether in the office or at someone's house, Breaux wanted to be in the middle of it. If someone not familiar with Washington or Louisiana politics would have dropped into one of our many informal get-togethers in those days, she might have had difficulty picking out the US senator in the room. Breaux had been a staffer to Edwin Edwards. Edwards had expected Lois, as an extension of her husband's duties, to work for the Edwards organization, too—only without pay. I think John and Lois were so kind and courteous to their staff because they had been in our shoes. They knew the challenges and travails of serving a politician. Perhaps that's why they rarely asked—and never expected—personal favors and errands from the staff. Breaux could be demanding or upbraid us when we screwed up, but such times were rare. To his credit, nothing irritated

John Breaux was as unassuming as any member of the US Senate. If you'd dropped in on any party of Breaux's staffers, you might not have recognized the senator in the room. I'm with Breaux (center) and staff member Kyle France (left) in 1992.

him more than arriving late to an event. When he got angry, it usually passed quickly. We always knew, instantly, when Breaux was irate: his lips narrowed, almost disappeared, as he talked. When that happened, you knew he was serious. But in all my years working for Breaux, he only chewed me out two or three times, and "chewed out" is not the best way to describe the experience. It was more like, "Look, that was the wrong way to handle that situation. Try not to do it again."

Breaux was also remarkably self-effacing. Prone to the occasional malaprop or mixed metaphor—I once heard him tell a friend on the phone, "I was walking on thin eggs"—he laughed whenever someone would point out a verbal miscue. Often, after we were settled inside the car after one of his speaking engagements, Breaux would turn around to say to us, "All right, tell me what you were laughing about in the back of the room." He would guffaw as we gave him a rundown of his verbal bloopers.

When traveling around Louisiana with Long, we would usually go to dinner with friends in whatever town we were visiting and then head back to the hotel. Russell and Carolyn were usually tucked into their beds by ten. The Long travel schedule was not leisurely, but it was not brutal. I soon discovered that a Breaux schedule was a different animal. Long liked to pack a suitcase, which he dutifully checked at the airport. When we landed in New Orleans, we would head to baggage claim and wait for our bags to appear. I assumed everyone did this. The first time I traveled with Breaux, I checked my bag. I immediately noted that Breaux did not. He brought a garment bag and a small duffle onto the plane so he could hit the ground running in New Orleans. On that first arrival with him in Louisiana, he looked at me with a mixture of horror and disgust when I told him we needed to stop in baggage claim to retrieve my suitcase. When Martin Walke, Breaux's state director, caught up with us, Breaux greeted him by pointing disdainfully to me and saying, "He checked a bag." I felt as if I committed a crime. I never made that mistake again.

Baggage on these trips would be the bane of my existence. A few years later, on one of his trips to Louisiana, some staffers and I met Breaux at the airport in Alexandria, in central Louisiana. This time, the airline had forced him to check his luggage. And because he almost never checked anything, we forgot to fetch his bag as it plopped onto the conveyer in baggage claim. After a long day of meetings and events in Alexandria and Lake Charles, it came time to transfer his belongings to the car of another staffer, who would drive him to Lafayette for the night. But when I went to our van to retrieve the bag, it was missing. "I know it's here somewhere," I said, rooting around in the vehicle as panic swept over me. But it wasn't. After a few minutes of retracing our steps, I reached a shocking conclusion: "We never got his bag in Alexandria! It's still in the airport."

Alexandria was almost two hours away. It was then around nine o'clock. One quick-thinking staffer roused Elton Pody, the former mayor of Ruston who was then running the Alexandria Chamber of Commerce. Like the loyal supporter and friend he was, Elton was happy to rush to the airport, find Breaux's bag, and drive it halfway to Lafayette. We would meet him somewhere on the side of the highway to retrieve it.

It fell to me, however, to deliver the bad news to Breaux. I found him in the bathroom of the arena where that night's event had just concluded.

"Well, I have some good news and bad news," I said, trying to be as upbeat as possible. "It's about your bag."

"Oh?"

"First, the good news," I said. "We know *exactly* where it is."

"Well, that's good," Breaux said. "Where is it?"

"That's the bad news," I said. "It's still in Alexandria. None of us got it off the belt in baggage claim when you arrived this morning."

Breaux's response was typical. He did not get angry. He simply asked, "Well, what's your plan for getting it?"

When I told him about Elton's heroics and that he would have the bag in about two hours, he just answered, "Okay." No shouting, pouting, or histrionics. He would have been within his rights to berate and punish me. After all, what did he pay me for if not to make sure I performed the simplest tasks?

Perhaps Breaux was so understanding because he knew he was so prone to lose things himself. Over the years, I lost count of the number of times we dismantled the campaign's van searching for a cell phone, a charger, a pen, a briefing book, reading glasses, or something else that Breaux had mislaid. After a while, I learned to always be the last person to leave his hotel room before checkout. "Just a minute!" I would shout, as he headed for the front desk. I would stalk the room like Sherlock Holmes, looking under the bed, pawing through the sofa cushions, and peeking into the shower. I was amazed by how many times I found something he had abandoned.

MY FIRST TRIP with Breaux in 1987 had challenged my stamina. At the end of the first or second day of this trip, we ended up in New Iberia, where he gave a speech to the local Chamber of Commerce's annual banquet. The event was at a Holiday Inn, where we stayed that night. After the banquet, I headed back to my room, as I had always done when working for Long. Along the way, I noticed a gaggle of Breaux's friends parading down the hall to his room, where he then hosted all of us for an impromptu "after-party" for an hour or two.

At every stop we made in my seventeen years working for him, Breaux offered a masterclass in how to work a room. There was rarely time for a proper meal, as that meant less time for him to move from table to table to shake hands with each person. One of us would usually fetch him a glass of wine but, beyond that, he often consumed nothing during the event. On the way to the next stop or the hotel, we would swing through a McDonald's or Popeyes drive-thru, so he could grab a quick meal. Long did not disdain meeting people. He enjoyed the politicking, too. But for Breaux, campaigning—meeting new people, getting to know them better—was like oxygen. He seemed to thrive on every minute of it.

From his first week in the Senate, Breaux wanted to talk about wetland erosion in Louisiana. In those days, the topic was gaining traction, but not enough for Breaux. He had represented Louisiana's Seventh District—southwest Louisiana, from Lafayette to Lake Charles—in Congress for fourteen years. An avid hunter and fisher since his youth, he witnessed the slow disappearance of the wetlands and marshes of coastal Louisiana. In the House, he chaired the Fish and Wildlife Subcommittee of the House Committee on Natural Resources, which gave him special insight into the problem. In the years before his Senate race, he began speaking more about it. He pushed legislation that required the US Army Corps of Engineers to create, protect, and enhance wetlands when working on navigation and flood control projects. Breaux's legislation—the Emergency Wetlands Resources Act of 1986—established the Bayou Sauvage National Wildlife Refuge outside New Orleans. That bill made 19,000 acres of wetlands accessible to the public, which Breaux called "a model environmental education center for the nation." In those days, it was rare to find an audience in north Louisiana concerned about the disappearing coast. When he ran for the Senate, Breaux thought voters needed to know and care more about the issue, and he began talking about it in campaign speeches and other appearances. And he talked it up to his colleagues, especially those who represented states whose rivers and streams drained into the Mississippi River. Breaux thought those states, because Louisiana built levees to prevent flooding from the water drained from their states, should bear some responsibility for Louisiana's wetlands loss.

In my first month on his staff, I worked with the Senate Recording Studio to produce a fifteen-minute documentary of sorts, with a long interview of Breaux and graphics showing Louisiana's dramatic, shocking wetlands loss. I sent it to television stations all over the country. I never knew just how many stations used anything from the video, but it was the beginning of our efforts to help people in other states understand the crisis.

In his first year in the Senate, Breaux hit on an idea for dealing with wetlands erosion and, by 1990, he got legislation passed to create the first federal trust fund to finance restoration projects. The provision, which

Breaux inserted into a deficit reduction bill, directed that federal Highway Trust Fund revenues derived from taxes on gasoline used for lawnmowers, chainsaws, tractors, and other small engines go towards rebuilding wetlands around the country. In its first year, the bill generated about $35 million. That wasn't much, but it was the first time the federal government took responsibility for restoring wetlands in Louisiana and other states.

That Breaux got the bill passed was a testament to his ability to broker bipartisan compromise. If there was ever a senator who believed in the need to work with members of the opposite party, it was Breaux. Today, that impulse or philosophy has fallen into disfavor. A member of Congress willing to work with colleagues from the opposite party is regarded suspiciously by his or her own colleagues and is usually considered a turncoat. It's easy to forget that it wasn't always that way. When Breaux came to the Senate in 1987, there were still a dozen or more members who, like him, wanted to work across party lines. Louisiana's other senator, Bennett Johnston, was one. Others included Joseph Lieberman of Connecticut, Susan Collins of Maine, Lloyd Bentsen of Texas, John McCain of Arizona, John Chafee of Rhode Island, Howell Heflin of Alabama, and David Pryor of Arkansas. Many of them were Southern Democrats, like Breaux, whose home-state politics forced them to hew closely to the middle. Others, like Chafee, were Republicans representing more liberal states who also stuck to the middle to stay in office. Breaux was sincere in his centrism. He was not reflexively conservative or liberal. He listened to his colleagues, worked hard at becoming friends with them, and never let his politics become personal.

One morning, I wandered into Breaux's office in the Hart Building to find him reading the newspaper and watching one of the morning news shows. He often got to the Senate before dawn to play tennis with a colleague or friend. He was usually the first person in the office and, if you wanted some private time with him, I discovered it was good to show up early and hang out in his office while he perused and highlighted the morning paper. He highlighted *everything*. He must have gone through two yellow highlighters a week. On this morning, Breaux looked up and threw down his pen, visibly angry about something a colleague said in the *Washington Post* that he thought sounded overly partisan. That brief outburst stuck with me, because I saw that his centrism was not calculated but heartfelt. He believed that his job was to get something done, pass some bills, and make progress—even if incremental—on the issue of the day.

But that's not the only reason he spent so much time with President George H. W. Bush. It was not the rare weekend morning when he was at the White House playing tennis with Bush, whom he knew well from their House days. The two men seemed to like each other. But it didn't hurt Breaux with his Senate colleagues that he was a Democrat who knew Bush well enough to sell him on a difficult compromise. And I'm sure Bush understood that, in Breaux, he had a friend in the Democratic caucus who could explain him and his positions in a fair, dispassionate way.

Breaux's close friendship with Bush, however, didn't mean that he always supported his friend. In March 1989, I drove Breaux to the White House for a difficult Oval Office meeting during which he told Bush he could not support his controversial nominee for Defense secretary, former Texas Senator John Tower. Breaux knew the prickly Tower well enough from his House days to dislike him. That was one strike against him, but I doubt Breaux would have voted against his nomination on personal dislike alone. Breaux also believed published reports that Tower had a serious drinking problem. Maybe that would not have been an issue for someone serving as Agriculture secretary. But running the Pentagon? "This nominee represents a risk that I cannot in good conscience take," Breaux said from the Senate floor after his meeting with Bush.

Despite their parting of ways over Tower, whose nomination failed, Breaux and Bush remained friends. Breaux not only liked Bush; he knew he would get a lot less done for his state if he were constantly at odds with the president. He instinctively looked for ways to cooperate with the White House. During Bill Clinton's time as president, Breaux would play the same role—this time as the liaison between Clinton and Senate Republican leader Trent Lott, Breaux's former neighbor and closest friend in the Senate.

Speaking of Lott, his office and ours were on friendly terms despite our political differences. Lott was a conservative Republican who was good friends with my boss. I didn't agree with him on much, but in the late 1980s it didn't seem odd to be friendly with his staffers. Our offices were so close that my brother, Paul, who worked for the Senate Energy Committee, spent enough time with the Breaux staff that he met his first wife, then a Lott staffer.

And it wasn't strange in those days for Senate staffers to have warm friendships with or date—or even marry—a staffer who worked for someone of the opposite party. For a time, I dated the deputy press secretary to Republican Senator John Danforth of Missouri. When I attended functions with Danforth staffers, no one seemed to think it was strange that my girlfriend brought a Democrat along. And the same applied when I brought her to gatherings of Breaux staffers. Shortly after I got to Washington, I joined the US Senate Press Secretaries Association and, in 1990, became president of the group. We met three or four times a year and, in the fall, about two dozen of us would make a weekend trip to New York for some business combined with pleasure. It was always a good mix of Republicans and Democrats on this excursion and at our meetings. We never talked about partisan politics, and I never saw or heard about a political argument breaking out.

Not all his Democratic colleagues appreciated Breaux's bipartisan ways. One night I was with Breaux outside the Capitol when Ted Kennedy called him after he noted that Breaux voted with the Republicans on what Kennedy regarded as a key vote for the Democratic side. I listened to Breaux's side of the conversation as Kennedy lit into him for his apostasy. Breaux didn't do much talking, but when he hung up, it was clear Kennedy struck a nerve. "Kennedy doesn't get how difficult it is for a Democrat to win elections in Louisiana," he grumbled. He wanted Kennedy to understand that elections back home were not like contests between a Kennedy and former KKK leader David Duke. In such a contest, we all knew that Duke would have won. Instead, Democrats in Louisiana won office statewide by capturing 95 percent of the Black vote while losing *only* 60 percent of the White vote. Breaux tried to get Kennedy to visit Louisiana and see things for himself, but the Massachusetts senator never found the time until years later when he married Victoria Reggie, a woman from Breaux's hometown of Crowley. Kennedy didn't spend much time in Louisiana even then, but he was there more often than before and, I assume, saw some of what Breaux tried to tell him. To my knowledge, he never chewed out Breaux again over a vote.[1]

It wasn't Breaux's centrism but his campaigning ability, his skill in recruiting candidates and raising money, that won him his first big leadership role in the Senate. In 1988, his Democratic colleagues elected him the chair of the Democratic Senatorial Campaign Committee. In the 1990 midterm elections, Democrats not only held their majority in the Senate but picked up one seat to increase their numbers to fifty-six. Breaux's centrism would be the key to his election in 1991 as chair of the Democratic Leadership Council (DLC), a group of moderate Democrats formed in 1985 to pull the party back towards the center after the 1984 Democratic nominee, former Vice President Walter Mondale, lost badly to President Ronald Reagan. In taking over the DLC, Breaux was replacing his good friend and centrist ally Bill Clinton, who led the group in the years after Dukakis's defeat.

I watched Breaux's easy friendship with Clinton for years. They were from neighboring states, cared about many of the same issues, and, while Breaux was more conservative than Clinton, believed that their party lost elections because it failed to communicate its values to the American people. Breaux and Clinton wanted to take moderate positions on many issues, but they also felt that their party was not as liberal as Republicans made it out to be. The so-called party of fiscal responsibility drove up the national debt while accusing Democrats of wasting taxpayer money. A few years later, when Clinton became president, he would demonstrate that Republicans talked a good game on that issue while he and his fellow Democrats generated the first budget surplus in decades—a surplus that Clinton's successor, George W. Bush, would squander. As Clinton moved towards running for president, the DLC leadership was the perfect platform for him to catch the eyes of many Democratic activists who were tired of losing elections. He began dropping by our Senate office to see Breaux. I wasn't in those meetings, but I know that Breaux was an early political advisor and, once Clinton was in the White House, became one of his closest allies in the Senate.

WORKING FOR BREAUX was quite different from working for Long, but it was just as exhilarating. And sometimes, it was mundane and exciting all at once. Before I moved to Washington, I had watched the occasional congressional hearing on C-SPAN and always noticed the smartly dressed staffers seated behind senators. Sometimes, a member would lean back and consult his or her aide. I assumed those conversations were weighty and serious. "Senator," I imagined the clever staff person whispering, "ask the assistant secretary why his statement says his department spent $15.5 billion on price supports for corn last year when the department's budget clearly shows it was only $10.2 billion."

My thrilling opportunity to be one of those clever staffers came in 1988, when Breaux chaired a series of hearings for the Nuclear Regulation Subcommittee of the Senate's Committee on Environment and Public Works. In January and February of that year, he convened hearings on his legislation to abolish the Nuclear Regulatory Commission, which he believed had failed to police the nuclear power industry. As his press secretary, I found myself sitting behind him on the dais. The cavernous hearing room in the Dirksen Senate Office Building was full of lobbyists and reporters. Klieg lights bathed the room in a glow that enhanced the importance and gravity of the issue being considered. From my perch behind the center of the dais, I spotted a couple of attractive women, likely industry lobbyists, who I was sure found irresistible the influential aide who sat just behind the powerful subcommittee chair.

About fifteen minutes into the hearing, my moment of glory arrived when Breaux rocked back in his chair and summoned me with a crook of his finger. As I leaned forward, I imagined that the pretty young women were even more impressed with my influence and proximity to power. I assumed they wondered who I was and how they might meet me. I drew close to Breaux and cocked my ear to receive his question.

"Can you get me some coffee?" he asked.

Deflated, I got up, skulked to the anteroom, prepared his drink—with creamer and one sugar—and delivered it to him as I imagined the thoughts going through the minds of the women: "Oh, he's just the coffee boy."

Despite the occasional coffee-fetching indignity, I kept my sense of wonder about the Senate and the remarkable people who worked there. Almost every day, I ran into Ohio Senator John Glenn, whose office was down the hall from ours in the Hart Senate Office Building. Glenn never knew my name, but I saw him often enough over several years that we greeted each other with familiarity. He was unfailingly polite. That would always be the best part of the job for me: the chance to work around legendary members of Congress and have a tiny hand in governing the country. As a young person who grew up fascinated by politics and government, I viewed my work not as a job but a big, thrilling adventure. Early in my days in Washington, I usually rode the Metro to and from my house in Dupont Circle. I would sometimes encounter Senator William Proxmire. The Wisconsin Democrat was a renowned maverick who relentlessly attacked what he considered wasteful spending. Every month, he would announce the new recipient of his "Golden Fleece Award." The first time I saw Proxmire, I struck up a conversation with him. He had become friends with Louisiana Representative Buddy Roemer and wanted to talk about him. Everywhere I went, I ran into members of Congress or Cabinet members. Arkansas Senator David Pryor lived directly across the street from me. On any day, you might see a presidential motorcade roaring up or down Pennsylvania or Connecticut avenues. And I never knew where I might see someone famous or important—at the Capitol Hill Safeway, the Hawk and Dove, or the Kennedy Center.

One Saturday June 1989, I went with my friends Jim Oakes and John Copes to what was then the Professional Golf Association's annual DC-area tournament—the Kemper Open in Potomac, Maryland. A lobbyist for a defense contractor Jim knew provided us tickets to a hospitality tent, where we could enjoy some excellent food and drinks before we began following the players. As we prepared to shove off, I noticed an older gentleman wearing a baseball cap and dark-blue windbreaker. He joined our group. The lobbyist who introduced him said, "You all know Warren." I did not, in fact, know Warren, but since everyone else in the group seemed to, I shook his hand and offered him a hearty, "Hi, Warren." We began our walk, and I chatted with Warren as we shuffled from hole to hole. Every time I got a good look at him, however, I had an odd feeling we *had* met somewhere before. But I could not put my finger on the circumstances of our acquaintance. It all became clear about forty-five minutes into our walk, when someone passed by and recognized my new friend, "Warren."

With good friends at a Baltimore Orioles game in 1989. Left to right: Me, Diane Copes, Vickie Tiner, Stan Tiner, and Jim Oakes.

"Hi, Senator Hatch," the person said.

And it hit me, as the blood drained from my face. My new buddy, "Warren," was the junior senator from Utah—Orrin Hatch.

Thankfully, I had less-embarrassing encounters with other members of the Senate. Sometimes it was after the annual State of the Union Address in early February. This was usually a fun evening, because it brought out almost every member of Congress, most of the Cabinet, and the Supreme Court. It was always a working night for press secretaries, who leapt into action as soon as the speech was over. We returned phone calls from reporters back home who wanted our bosses' reactions. One way to satisfy the craving of local television stations for comment was a "cattle-call" setup in a basement room in the Capitol. During the speech, staffers would watch from a holding room on the House side. One year, it was the room where Harry Truman played poker with Speaker Sam Rayburn when he got the call to rush to the White House after FDR died. When I worked for Breaux, as soon as the speech was done he would find me in that room and we would get in line. Once we reached the front, a videographer would hand me a microphone and I would conduct a brief "interview" for the home audience. Usually, it was something penetrating like, "Senator, your reaction to the president's speech tonight?" And then

Breaux would talk for two or three minutes and we would move on.

After one State of the Union night in the late 1980s, Breaux and I were standing in line, waiting for the "interview," when I noticed in front of us was Senator Claiborne Pell, an elderly, veteran Democrat from Rhode Island. As Pell inched closer to the cameras, I noticed that he was looking around nervously. It occurred to me that his press secretary was missing. If so, he couldn't do the interview. I tapped him on the shoulder.

"Excuse me, Senator," I said, introducing myself. "I see your press secretary hasn't made it yet. Would you like me to do the interview with you?"

Relieved, he accepted. When I put the mic in his face and asked him for his reaction to the speech, Pell responded as one might expect from a well-bred, patrician New Englander. "It was a peppy speech," he said in his upper-crust accent. I suppressed a giggle and remember nothing else he said. Pell was famous for having sponsored the legislation that created higher education Pell Grants, which helped fund my college education. I have always regretted I didn't thank him for how his work changed my life. Who knows what I would have ended up doing without a college degree? One thing I know: without the college education that this patrician Rhode Islander's bill helped fund, I would not have been in the US Capitol basement, following the State of the Union, standing in a line with Claiborne Pell and John Breaux.

10

TURN THAT RECORDER OFF

A friend in Shreveport who left journalism for politics once told me: "Once you go back to journalism, you won't know the answers, but you will know all the right questions." I believed that and had taken the job with Russell Long intending to return to journalism one day soon. However, I had made only $18,000 working for the *Shreveport Journal* and my salary more than doubled when I went to Washington. I knew that it would be a financial sacrifice if I returned to journalism.

But I still wanted to write about politics, and I always dreamed of producing a book. I just wasn't sure about what or whom. I had no credibility as an author. No one would award me a book contract based on my few years working in small-town journalism. I needed something more. That meant writing a book about someone famous who would cooperate with me and give me access to his or her life. It didn't take long to realize that the most famous person I knew was Russell Long. After a few months, I finally screwed up my courage and went to ask Long what he thought about me writing a book about him. I sat in his law office one morning in 1988 and made my pitch.

"Look," I said, "someone will eventually write a book about you. You want it to be someone you know and trust. I think that person is me."

That argument seemed to resonate with Long. After all, we worked well together on the speech about his father in 1985. He knew what it was like to be interviewed by me. My one stipulation was that I wanted editorial independence. It would be an authorized biography, not an autobiography that I would ghostwrite for him. We didn't discuss it until several years later, but I wanted to show him the finished work to ensure I made no factual errors. But I was not offering him editorial control. He listened politely and said he wanted time to think about it. After a few weeks, he said yes. He would cooperate on the book.

At the time I thought—and still do—that Long agreed to go along with this project because he doubted it would ever come to fruition. It wasn't that hard to cooperate with someone who would probably never finish the book he was writing about you. But true to his word, Long was generous with his time over the next three years. We met eighteen times from October 1988 until January 1992 for interviews that lasted around two hours each, as I asked him methodically about his life and career. Early on, he gave me a letter to hand to his friends and colleagues that attested to his approval of my work and his desire that they cooperate with me. That letter, and a few phone calls by Long, would open many doors in the coming years. I'd sit down for interviews with former colleagues, staff members, and friends of Long's, as well as his wife, Carolyn, and his first wife, Katherine.

The interviews with some of Long's former colleagues were the most interesting. The day I went to former Arkansas Senator J. William Fulbright's office on Pennsylvania Avenue, I was thrilled to meet the legendary former chair of the Senate Foreign Relations Committee who challenged Lyndon Johnson by opposing the Vietnam War. Like Long, he also voted against the civil rights laws. I admired Fulbright's educated, nuanced approach to American foreign policy and had just finished reading his 1989 book, *The Price of Empire*, which he wrote with his former committee aide Seth Tillman, whom I would interview for a subsequent book. When I sat down with Fulbright, I knew that he was gruff and direct and, as he would soon demonstrate, immune to flattery. Hoping to butter him up a bit, I said, "Senator, I just finished reading your book, *The Price of Empire.*" Fulbright's eyes narrowed and he leaned in a bit, before spitting out, "Well, why the hell would you do that?"

When I interviewed Strom Thurmond, I was stunned to find that his secretary situated her desk not outside his office in the Russell Senate Office Building but *inside* his office. The eighty-six-year-old Thurmond could not be left alone for one moment. He needed constant care and attention, not unlike a toddler. Regardless, he was kind enough to meet me and answer my questions. By this age, however, his answers were rote and unreflective. Time had prompted no reassessment of his strident opposition to civil rights. To every question, Thurmond responded with what sounded like a preprogrammed answer. I remember thinking it was like talking to a tape recorder: to my questions, he would push a button and a well-rehearsed answer would spew forth. Spending time with this legend and observing him up close was far more interesting than anything he told me. Ten years later, when my wife and I took our then-toddlers to Washington to see where I once worked, we sat next to Thurmond in one of the Senate dining rooms. It surprised me to see that the same devoted staffer/minder still worked for him. Only now, besides escorting him everywhere, she also shouted into his ear, repeating the words spoken by visitors, so the senator could carry on a conversation.

During the four years I worked on the Long book, I had a day job (the Senate) and a night job (researching and writing a book). When I told Breaux about the book, he was wholehearted in his support. Not every senator would have celebrated a staffer writing a book on the side. I knew that Lyndon Johnson, when he was majority leader, became incensed when he learned that one of his staffers was moonlighting as a novelist. Politicians are notorious for demanding complete loyalty from staff members and that often means dictating what they do on their time off. Breaux was never like that. That's not to say that he wouldn't call me early in the morning if something caught his eye in the newspaper or he needed me to do something for him. That came with the job and I never minded it, although I had to climb out of the shower more than once to take a morning phone call. But Breaux loved the fact that his press secretary was writing a book on Long. As we traveled around Louisiana, Breaux almost always introduced his staff to audiences. Invariably in those years, when he got to me, he would say, "And my press secretary, Bob Mann, who is writing a book on Russell Long." I think he enjoyed bragging that he had staffers engaged in intellectual pursuits, like book writing. To his credit, Breaux always supported staff members in DC who attended law school at Georgetown University's Capitol Hill campus while they worked for him. My book also solidified Breaux's connection to Long and what he meant to Louisiana and emphasized how much affection he had for his predecessor.

To say that John Breaux and Russell Long admired each other was an understatement. Breaux always brightened considerably when he was around Long. He loved hearing his stories, and I suspect that Long occasionally gave him some good advice about navigating the Senate Finance Committee. And Breaux also celebrated that—in Carol Speer, Kyle France, and me—he had three former Long staffers working for him. One of the treasured photographs hanging on my LSU office wall is of Breaux, Long, Kyle, and me eating together in the Senators Dining Room after Breaux ran into Long one day in a Capitol hallway. He invited him to lunch and then quickly summoned Kyle and me to join them.

With Breaux's backing, I set about trying to figure out how to write my book. Long not only agreed to interviews, but he gave me exclusive access to his papers, which he donated to LSU's Hill Memorial Library and were still being processed. I spent many weeks in Baton Rouge combing through the dusty, decades-old files. And after getting microfilmed copies of virtually every news story written about Long during his Senate career, I read each one and made notes on three-by-five index cards. Most evenings after work, I rushed home to my Capitol Hill townhouse—826

Constitution Avenue, NE—wolfed down a quick meal, and headed to the congressional staff reading room in the Madison Building of the Library of Congress. The room had a large microfilm machine on which I could read the stories and make copies when necessary. I probably went a full year during which I spent three or four evenings a week reading news stories in that room.

In almost every way, Long was obliging. The one time he was not concerned my digging into the period of his life in the 1960s when he admitted he had been drinking heavily. During that time, he had become progressively more erratic. By 1969, his alcohol abuse exasperated his colleagues enough that they voted him out of his whip position and gave the job to Ted Kennedy. To hear his conduct described by others, it sounded like the classic description of an alcoholic. And yet, I often had dinner with Long since 1985, during which he would always consume a cocktail or two. We would go to lunch sometimes to talk about the book and he would have a glass of wine. I never saw him drink to excess. He appeared in control of his drinking, which I then understood to be impossible for a true alcoholic.

So, I began asking a few of his close friends and relatives about this. One of them was his cousin, Bill Heard Wright, a Baton Rouge insurance executive. When I asked Bill one day if he thought Long was an alcoholic, he said he didn't think so. I thought nothing more of the conversation until I went to see Long at his office a few weeks later.

"So, I hear you are asking people if I'm an alcoholic," Long said bluntly, as we sat down to talk.

I gulped and probably turned red, but rallied to reply, "Yes, I am. So, are you?"

Long paused for a second or two and said, "Turn that recorder off," which I did. For the next two hours, he recounted every story he could remember about his bad, embarrassing behavior during his hard-drinking days. Some stories were doozies. Finally, he was done and allowed me to turn the recorder on. I never could persuade him to answer the question directly, but I believe he wanted me to see what he overcame with the help of Carolyn, whom he married in 1969. "She saved my life," he told me several times, meaning that her influence was crucial to his learning how to control his drinking. Today, based on what I know about his drinking problem, I think I understand that Long may have been one of those rare alcoholics who overcame his urge to binge and returned to drinking in moderation.

In early November 1991, my girlfriend and future wife, Cindy, and I went to a dinner in suburban Washington that Carolyn threw for Long's seventy-third birthday. Afterwards, as we were walking to our respective cars, Long pulled me aside and asked how the writing was going. He wanted to see what I'd produced so far, as he knew that my deadline for submitting the book to my publisher was fast approaching. He also knew that, by the terms of my contract, I would need his written permission to use quotes from our interviews in the book. That was one bit of leverage he could use if he didn't approve of what I wrote about him. I promised him I would send him a copy of the manuscript, which I did a few weeks later.

A few weeks after that, he invited me to his office. There, he told me he objected to my discussion of his drinking problem. While I used none of the stories he told me during our off-the-record session, I did not shrink from writing about his drinking and the political damage it inflicted. He asked me to consider removing that from the book.

"Senator," I explained, "this book tells your story in a way that I think will help people see more clearly all the positive contributions you've made to Louisiana and the nation. But people know you had a drinking problem. If I don't write about it, then what does that do to my credibility? If I ignore the negative stuff, why would anyone believe the positive stuff?" And then, I added what I thought was the argument that would appeal most to him: "Not to mention that this is a story about your redemption and your having overcome adversity. That's a story people need to hear."

He was not convinced but agreed to think it over. In the meantime, I suggested that he and I appoint his former press secretary, Rafael Bermudez, as an arbiter of this and other disputes that might arise as he read the manuscript. Rafael reluctantly agreed to play this role. Lucky for him, it never came to that. For whatever reason, Long dropped his opposition to my description of his drinking. Strangely, looking back over the book, I'm still perplexed he didn't object to my unflattering portrayal of his opposition to the 1964 Civil Rights Act. That part of his career reflected poorly on him in ways that, to me at least, his drinking did not. But he never raised an objection to my criticism of his civil rights record.

For the first two years of the book research, I did not have a contract. I would probably not undertake such a project today without a publisher's contract, but I knew that, as an unproven author, I needed to produce some or all the book and show it to a publisher. I was prepared to write the entire thing "on spec." Thankfully, that didn't happen. My good friend Sally Lee knew about my book and shared my work with a friend from her college days, Tim Wells, who had published an excellent book about the Iranian hostage crisis, *444 Days: The Hostages Remember.* One day, Tim called and asked if he could come visit me at my office. A few days later, he dropped by and we talked about my project. He offered some writing advice. But more important, he had a literary agent in New York. "You need an agent," Tim advised. "I'm going to send your stuff to Clyde."

He meant Clyde Taylor, a literary agent with a powerful firm, Curtis Brown Ltd. Clyde once was the head of a big New York publishing house and he now represented authors, helping negotiate their contracts and get them the best terms and the most money possible for their work. A few weeks later, Clyde called and offered to represent me.

It was the beginning of a great friendship. Clyde negotiated three book deals for me until his sudden death in 2002. We spoke by phone every few weeks and usually it was to talk politics, not books. He always wanted to hear the latest gossip from DC and scarfed up whatever news I had about the latest Capitol Hill drama. Clyde was a courtly North Carolina native who found his way to New York, and among his conservative family, he was an oddity. His ex-wife was from Louisiana, which bonded us further. After a while, I regarded him more as a friend than my agent. I miss him still and owe him so much for helping open doors to New York publishers that would have been closed to me without his influence. I also miss talking politics with him. When I say that Clyde lived and breathed politics and was a committed liberal, I am not exaggerating. Upon his death, his family suggested that, instead of sending flowers, friends should donate to the Democratic National Committee. Clyde would have loved that. I was proud to dedicate one of my books to him and his memory.

PARAGON HOUSE WOULD publish my first book, *Legacy to Power: Senator Russell Long of Louisiana*, in the fall of 1992. By then, I had moved to Baton Rouge and was about to be married. It was the only real book party I've ever had, and it was memorable. Some good friends in Baton Rouge arranged an event hosted at Long-View—a house built on Capitol Lake by Earl Long and now owned by lobbyist Randy Haynie. Russell and Carolyn Long attended, as did former Governor Edwin Edwards and a host of friends and other politicos. Wearing a Saints jacket, jeans, and cowboy boots, Edwards introduced me after he told attendees he and Long had spoken once about their "unexpressed, secret desires." Long's, Edwards joked, "was to someday have a book accurately depicting his life. Mine was to someday have a book that did not." When it came his time to speak, Long joked, "Let me say that I'm not getting any royalty out of this book. This is one of the few things I've done that there wasn't anything in it for Russell." Long told the crowd mine was "an honest book" and that "Bob told the story as he knew it, as he understood it."

It was a grand evening. Ted Jones, one of Long's good friends, also hosted a book signing for me at the 116 Club, around the corner from the Hart Senate Office Building in DC. Long and I sat side by side for more than an hour scribbling our names in the books. In almost every case,

Long would sign first, "With profound admiration, Russell Long." That was his inscription, whether he knew the person well or not. He handed the book to me and, for most people in the line, I realized I could not improve much on that message. So, I cosigned the sentiment. I knew that most people were in line for Long's signature, not mine.

What I learned from writing this first book was that researching and writing books is some of the most mentally taxing work a person can do. I read a few books about how to write a book. Good books about great writing are useful, as are books about grammar and usage. But so much of writing a book is finding your way, word by word, page by page, until you have a first draft that you can start knocking into shape. In my mind's eye, I have seen each book as a block of wood that I chipped away at until, after many passes and much detail work, it eventually resembled what I imagined when I started. The first draft, I have learned the hard

Former Senator Russell Long signs copies of my book, Legacy to Power: Senator Russell Long of Louisiana, *at a book party in Baton Rouge in December 1992.*

With former Senator Russell Long and Senator John Breaux at a signing for my Long biography in Washington in late 1992.

way, is not the beginning of the end but—just barely—the end of the beginning.

I've now written eight books and I would like to say that each got a little easier, but I'd be lying. Each is challenging in its own way. There are few shortcuts for research, especially when digging around in archival collections. Writing the first book taught me useful lessons about organizing my research—keeping track of thousands of bits of information gleaned from books, letters, memos, news stories, and interviews—which I continue to refine and never get just right.

But I'm getting ahead of myself, because this chapter should not end with the completion of my Long biography. It must end at another significant juncture that caused me to place the book aside for six months, uproot myself from Washington, and return to Louisiana for what I still consider the most important period of my professional life. In 1990, I decided to come home to help save Louisiana from the threat of David Duke.

11

Racist! Nazi! Bigot! Get Mad!

Like a lot of moderate-to-liberal White Louisianians in the late 1980s, I thought racism was going out of style. There was *some* evidence the South was ready to enter the twentieth century just in time for the twenty-first. It turned out we were too optimistic. Louisiana and the rest of the country got a stark reminder of racism's vitality in 1989, when a neo-Nazi and ex-Ku Klux Klan leader, David Duke, won a Louisiana House seat in Metairie, defeating John Treen, brother of former Republican Governor Dave Treen. A Democrat-turned-Republican, Duke was no newcomer to Louisiana politics. He had been a professional bigot since his college days, when he spewed his racist and anti-Semitic sewage into LSU's Free Speech Alley.

"I'm a National Socialist," Duke had said during his first speech at LSU in the fall of 1969. "You can call me a Nazi if you want to." In the same speech, he claimed that Whites are "the master race." In his biography of Duke, journalist Tyler Bridges wrote that Duke had struggled to make friends at LSU because he "was so filled with anti-Semitic fervor and love for Nazi Germany." By 1974, Duke had become a minor national figure and a hero within the lunatic, racist right. When he went to Boston in September of that year, 2,000 people turned out to hear him speak in the city's predominately Catholic, working-class southside. "Two hundred years ago our ancestors stood up and fought against the tyranny of the British bayonets," Duke told the crowd, to cheers. "The federal government is taking money out of your pockets to finance the production of little Black bastards. The real issue isn't education. The real issue is niggers!"

In the late 1980s, Duke created "the National Association for the Advancement of White People," as if White people in the South had not advanced enough. And he began running for office—as a Democrat. He lost races for the state legislature in 1975 and 1979. In 1988, he ran for the Democratic Party's presidential nomination before switching to the Republican Party later that year and running for the state House in the New Orleans suburb of Metairie. Strangely, although I had lived in Louisiana since the early 1970s, I knew almost nothing about Duke until his election to the state House.

By the time Duke won his seat, he had cleaned up his act—superficially, at least. His appeal was no longer in the blatant racism of his youth (he was thirty-eight in 1988) but in speeches that he littered with racist and anti-Semitic dog whistles, which reassured many Louisiana Whites that he wanted to challenge leaders in Baton Rouge and Washington to shrink the budget and stop wasting money on federal-state programs like food stamps and Aid to Families with Dependent Children (AFDC). Duke's supporters could comfort themselves with the thought it wasn't Black people they wished to punish but the government bureaucrats and liberal politicians who wasted their hard-earned dollars. To anyone paying close attention, it was clear Duke was not only the racist and anti-Semite he always had been; he was also a charlatan of the first order. This became obvious in 2003, when a federal judge sent him to prison for stealing supporters' money and blowing it on a gambling habit. As he had crowed in a 1978 interview: "The media can't resist me. You see, I don't fit the stereotype of a Klansman. I don't have hair cropped so close to my head my ears stick out two or three inches. I'm not chewing tobacco, and I don't have manure on the bottom of my shoes."

In Baton Rouge, fellow legislators ostracized Duke. No matter. He thrived on the animosity of his detractors and he parlayed his House election into national TV appearances (including CNN's "Crossfire," ABC's "Primetime Live," and "The Phil Donahue Show"). From Washington, where I worked as John Breaux's press secretary, the whole thing seemed surreal. I was in Louisiana every four to six weeks and I wondered how I could have missed the rising tide of racism that Duke was riding. No group in DC was more alarmed by Duke's sudden celebrity—and the national and international media that he attracted—than the national Republican Party, whose leaders were embarrassed that their racist "Southern Strategy" from the 1970s might be back in vogue. It was as if you had an uncle who had humiliated the family for decades with his lunacy, and just as you thought he was dying of old age, he rallied and began babbling even louder. Duke was the crazy uncle or, maybe, more a chip off the old block of the party's racist forebears—leaders who'd been using racial appeals throughout the South and elsewhere since passage of the Civil Rights Act of 1964 pushed White voters in the region away from the Democratic Party of Lyndon Johnson and Hubert Humphrey.

If he remained in the House, Duke would have been mostly a Republican problem. Some Louisiana Democrats didn't mind that, because it allowed us to point out what had long been obvious—the GOP talked a good game, but it was still a comfortable home for racists and neo-Nazis. But on December 4, 1989, the threat to Louisiana became more real when Duke announced he would challenge US Senator J. Bennett Johnston in his bid for a fourth term in the Senate. As chairman of the Senate Energy and Natural Resources Committee and a senior member of the Appropriations Committee, Johnston was among the most powerful Democrats in Washington. In his early days as a Shreveport lawyer, he had espoused some segregationist views, but like Russell Long and a host of White Democrats in the South, he put that behind him by the time he ran against Edwin Edwards for governor in 1971 and lost the Democratic Party primary by 4,488 votes. Edwards beat Dave Treen in the February 1972 general election and Johnston began running against US Senator Allen Ellender, an elderly lawmaker and Huey Long crony who had served in the Senate since 1937. Ellender was ancient, but Johnston was no shoo-in. That changed when the senior senator died on July 27. With the name recognition from his near miss in the governor's election, Johnston cruised to the Democratic Party's nomination for the now-vacant seat and waltzed into office in the general election. From the Senate Appropriations Committee, Johnston dedicated himself to bringing home as much bacon as possible. This included presiding over construction of the massive Red River Waterway project and road, bridge, and flood control projects. He also became the most effective defender of Louisiana's military installations, including the Army's Fort Polk, near my former Leesville home, and Barksdale Air Force Base, in Bossier City, across the Red River from Shreveport.

When I was the political writer for the *Shreveport Journal,* I ran into Johnston often, and from the first time I met him, I liked him. He was friendly and soft spoken in a way that did not scream "politician." Like Breaux, he was a trim, athletic man addicted to tennis. He was also addicted to Tabasco, which he squirted on everything he ate. I once saw him sprinkle a bowl of vanilla ice cream with the hot sauce. Johnston was not a bad politician, but I never got the sense that political ambition was his main motivation. He was ambitious, to be sure, but he seemed to be one of those members of Congress who enjoyed debating and making policy—in Johnston's case, energy policy—and who regarded campaigning and fundraising as a necessary evil.

If there was ever a Louisiana politician who should have been safe from a challenge, it was an effective, moderate Democrat like Johnston. Even so, there was evidence to the contrary. In 1978, ultraconservative Democrat Baton Rouge state Representative Woody Jenkins captured 40 percent of the vote against Johnston in the state's open primary, instituted at

Edwin Edwards' urging in 1975. Two years later, Jenkins won 39 percent against Russell Long. At least 40 percent of the electorate was willing to vote for an ultraconservative. Despite that, the next time Johnston appeared on the ballot—in 1984—he won an impressive 86 percent of the vote, which made his reelection in 1990 seem secure.

But the times were changing. The national Democratic Party's most recognizable faces were now Northern liberals—leaders like Walter Mondale, Ted Kennedy, Thomas "Tip" O'Neill, and Michael Dukakis. The only prominent national leader in the Democratic Party from the South in those days would have been Jimmy Carter, whom most White Southerners regarded as a failure. Then, there was Ronald Reagan, who won the White House against Carter in 1980 and captured the hearts of many Democratic voters, who would switch their party affiliation to the GOP. This was the headwind Johnston faced in early 1990 as he went into his race against Duke.

But he and many Democrats in Louisiana and DC did not understand the political climate. I know I did not. Like Johnston and others, I looked at the early polls, which showed Johnston with a big lead, and concluded he would win the election in a walk. I also did not believe that the people of my state would further tarnish Louisiana's already poor reputation by sending a former Klan leader to the US Senate. But there were warning signs that my judgment was misguided. Johnston's pollster, Geoff Garin, conducted a survey in June 1989 that showed, by an 81 to 16 percent margin, voters thought the state was headed in the wrong direction. And 44 percent of voters said they wanted someone new to replace Johnston. Faced with that and other evidence of the evolving political climate, by early 1990 Johnston and his staff were taking the Duke threat more seriously. Not that any prominent Democrat or major pollster thought Duke could win a Senate race, but the race attracted three other well-known Republican elected officials who also wanted their party's nomination: Secretary of State Fox McKeithen (son of former Governor John McKeithen), Metairie state Representative Quentin Dastugue, and New Orleans state Senator Ben Bagert. After Bagert won the state Republican Party's endorsement at its convention in January 1990, Duke vowed to run anyway in Louisiana's open primary. At first, this might have seemed a positive sign, as Duke and Bagert were bound to split the Republican vote while Johnston hoped to have the Democratic field to himself. But the risk was that Duke might win all the racist Republicans, allowing Bagert to peel off just enough moderate Republicans to force Johnston into a runoff. If that happened, blood would be in the water and anything could happen in the general election. Johnston had to win without a runoff.

Early in 1990, Jim Oakes, my former Capitol Hill roommate who was managing Johnston's reelection effort, asked if I would take leave from Breaux's DC office to work as the campaign's press secretary. I was eager to return home and help beat a neo-Nazi. And Breaux was happy to lend me to Johnston, thinking he was doing his colleague a favor and giving me some campaign experience that might come in handy when he was up for reelection in 1992. In April, I loaded up my red Geo Tracker and headed to Baton Rouge and Johnston's headquarters in a rented space on College Drive, between Perkins Road and Interstate 10. It was great to be back in Baton Rouge after five years in Washington.

I had loved living in DC. On weekends, during breaks from working on my Long book, I often rode my bike down the National Mall past the Washington Monument and the Lincoln Memorial. Sometimes, I would turn north and pedal through the steep hills of Rock Creek Park, which jutted up the length of the District starting just north of the Kennedy Center. Other days, I would turn south and cruise along the Potomac River path to Old Town Alexandria, and sometimes all the way to George Washington's home at Mount Vernon. During the late spring and summer, I played on the joint Breaux-Johnston softball team. We often faced other congressional office staffs in games on the Mall. During the workday, on calmer weeks, I would sometimes steal away to the Senate Library, a mostly secret space tucked into the third floor of the Capitol,

In March 2007, I interviewed two of my former bosses, former Senators J. Bennett Johnston (left) and John Breaux (right), for Louisiana Public Broadcasting's coverage of the McLeod Lecture series at McNeese State University in Lake Charles. (Photo courtesy of Louisiana Public Broadcasting)

not far from the Senate visitors' gallery. The reading room features a breathtaking view of the Mall and the Washington Monument. In the days before pagers and cellphones, I could sneak into the library, settle into a comfortable, green leather club chair, and read unbothered for an hour. I also enjoyed prowling the bookstores of Washington, especially at Dupont Circle, where I was a regular customer at Second Story Books and Kramerbooks.

As much fun as it was, living on Capitol Hill was stressful. Street crime was a constant worry. Jim once had his car stolen from its parking spot in front of our house. One day, I came home to find my front door kicked in by burglars. Muggings were common up and down my street. Parking on the Hill was challenging. Sometimes, there was an open spot in front of my townhouse, but I was often forced to park a block or two away. That meant that grocery shopping was a problem, especially in bad weather. Just getting to the store was a struggle. There were shops and stores in the Capitol Hill vicinity, but they did not offer the wide selection I could find back home. I often drove thirty minutes or more to larger stores across the Potomac in Alexandria, Virginia. And prices in DC were high.

I also missed ready access to Southern food—chicken fried steak, black-eyed peas, butter beans, and cornbread. After a few months in Washington, Jim discovered a restaurant in suburban Virginia called "Po Folks" that served such cuisine. It was a long trek, but we made the forty-five-minute drive at least once a week to get our fix of "home cooking." On Capitol Hill, a dumpy tavern, the Tune Inn, served a good plate of hamburger steak, mashed potatoes, and green beans. We ate there often. In Baton Rouge, however, I knew I could get such food at two dozen places within a five-mile radius of the campaign headquarters.

On the warm Friday evening of May 11, some of us on Johnston's Baton Rouge campaign staff wanted to take the measure of our opposition. So, we piled in a car and drove forty minutes north to Jackson, Louisiana—a town of 3,800 in East Feliciana Parish—to the Lions Club meeting hall, where Duke was holding a rally. The room was electric and full of White men and women, most of them in blue jeans and work clothes and all eager to hear Duke's racist-coded message dressed up as economic populism. "I'm not a racist," Duke would tell this crowd and others as part of his standard stump speech. "I believe in equal rights for everybody. But the time has come for equal rights in this country, even for White people." He demanded drug testing for welfare recipients who have children out of wedlock. The crowd surely understood him to mean "shiftless Black people." He also wanted the death penalty for those who sold illegal drugs, another dog whistle that his audience no doubt heard as "Black pushers in the hood." The crowd loved it. They whooped and hollered. And when it was over, Duke—as he did at almost every rally across the state for months—lingered to talk to his fans, take pictures, and sign autographs.

We stayed, too, waiting our turn to introduce ourselves to the notorious Klansman. We shook his hand and then someone said, "We are all working on Bennett Johnston's campaign." To my surprise, Duke didn't recoil. He smiled and welcomed us to the contest. In that brief encounter and a few others that I had with Duke that year, I got a glimpse of his appeal. He may have been angry and strident in his youth, but he had learned to react to hostility with coolness and composure. When hecklers yelled at Duke, he responded calmly. His words and the sentiments behind them might have been abhorrent, but he was almost never the one screaming. To the casual observer, Duke seemed reasonable by comparison.[1] After that encounter in Jackson, we suspected our opponent might be more of a challenge to Johnston than we imagined.

There was also the question of whether we could believe the polls. Geoff Garin produced a survey in April 1990 that showed Johnston crushing Duke by thirty-six points, with Bagert in third place, pulling 13 percent. But there was good reason to wonder if our lead was not that large. Everywhere Duke went, he was drawing large crowds. In Crowley, in April, he attracted 600 people. We would have struggled to draw a third of that on a good day. Most worrisome was the suspicion that in the polls conducted by Garin and others, some voters were hesitant to admit they were supporting a former Klan leader. They might not tell a pollster Duke was their candidate, but when they drew that curtain on election day, we suspected some of them—no one knew how many—would pull the lever for Duke.

Johnston was one of the kindest, most sincere people I've known in politics. While he was not among the Senate's great orators, he wasn't a bad speaker. He just seemed to expect that people would be moved by his passionate discussion of the appropriations process and the billions he was bringing home to Louisiana. This wasn't the red meat many voters wanted in the late 1990s, but it was what Johnston knew was important to the state's economic future. Given our current politics, it's admirable that he wasn't eager to become a cheap demagogue for votes and thought Louisiana's people cared about public works and defense projects. Like so many veteran lawmakers, Johnston delivered speeches that were a little wonkish. He was great at discussing the intricacies of energy policy or describing the funding he secured for this or that project. He was not so adept at telling voters why he thought the proposal or project was vital to their daily lives. One day that summer, I sat in a Shreveport TV studio and watched as a reporter interviewed him. When the topic turned to abortion policy, Johnston explained how he had voted on various amendments and bills that addressed the issue. I realized he was not sharing how he felt about abortion itself. An anti-abortion viewer might have given him credit for voting against abortion but could still be left wondering how much Johnston believed it.

While Duke was setting the woods on fire, Johnston sometimes seemed to phone it in. Voters needed to see his passion, not just hear about his record. At one point, at an event in Houma, Johnston told a gathering of supporters, "I may not be much, but the other side is pretty bad." That prompted Johnston campaign staffer Ross Atkins to coin this little ditty: "J. Bennett, United States Senate, might as well keep him in it." Johnston was not accustomed to the type of race in which he found himself in 1990. Even the challenge from Woody Jenkins in 1978 never posed an existential threat to his political career. Until midsummer, Johnston may never have considered he might lose to a racist like Duke. Acknowledging Duke and attacking him seemed, for a long time, the wrong strategy. Incumbents often ignore their challengers, knowing that to call them out by name or to debate them elevates them in a way that millions in television advertising could not. As the summer went on, and Duke grew more popular, we knew Johnston could not afford to ignore Duke. We had to take him on.

No one saw this better than one of Johnston's adult sons, Bennett III, who was traveling with us on the campaign RV for a few days. When we arrived in Farmerville one morning, young Bennett slipped his dad a piece of paper on which he had scribbled in block letters: "Racist! Nazi! Bigot! Get mad!" That seemed to do the trick, giving Johnston a jolt of energy. When his time came to speak, Johnston fired away at Duke. "The National Association for the Advancement of White People is the Klan without the bedsheets," Johnston roared, echoing a line I once heard from Russell Long about the White Citizens Council. "Did you all read about the sex book he wrote?" (This was a self-help sex manual for women Duke published in 1976.) "If I had done one-tenth of what David Duke has done—one-tenth!—why, they'd ride me out of town on a rail! Why, this man has celebrated Adolf Hitler's birthday every year!" At last, this was the Bennett Johnston the situation called for—cognizant of the danger to his state and his political career and willing to fight for both. At the next stop, my tape recorder was running to capture Johnston's fiery language. I phoned some radio stations in Baton Rouge and New Orleans and fed them audio of the speech.

Johnston's attacks on Duke were good and powerful but not the knockout punch for which we'd hoped. For weeks, we debated what to do with video that our media consultant, John Franzen, obtained of Duke at a nighttime cross burning. The thirty-second ad that Franzen created showed Duke shouting, "White power!" and snapping a Nazi salute while standing before the burning cross. "There's no more truly representative symbol of the White race than the fiery cross," Duke said in the footage. "White victory!" When I first saw the spot, I thought it was a kill shot. I was certain it would take out Duke.

But it didn't. After the spot began running, Duke's numbers slumped from 29 percent to 23 percent. But only a week later, the guy with the Nazi salute rebounded to 27 percent in Garin's poll. Could it be we had done Duke a favor by reminding racist White voters he was the true-blue White supremacist they were looking to send to Washington to shake up things? Could it be that racism, anti-Semitism, and misogyny were features of Duke's candidacy, not bugs? It now appears the attacks on Duke by Johnston and our allies—including the Louisiana Coalition Against Racism and Nazism, led by Tulane's Lance Hill and the Reverend James Stovall, a kind, principled Methodist minister—did not hurt Duke as much as any of us imagined. Duke was well known. We weren't telling voters anything about him they didn't know. It wasn't so much that we had to show voters Duke was a racist but that we needed to explain how electing him would damage the state's reputation. In this sense, Duke was like Alabama's Roy Moore, a far-right ex-judge and alleged pedophile who almost won a US Senate seat in 2017. Many voters in Louisiana then seemed fine with an odious character representing them in Washington. It was only when they realized how much Duke's and Moore's election would harm their states' reputation and economy did enough of them pull back.

What may have saved Louisiana from the eternal embarrassment of sending a Hitler-loving racist to Washington was that Bagert, two days before the election, dropped out and averted the possibility of a runoff between Duke and Johnston. Bagert's pollster, Kellyanne Fitzpatrick—later with the married named Conway and a top aide to Donald Trump—called Jim Oakes to give him the news. When we got the word on our way to Bossier City that afternoon, our caravan pulled to the side of the highway. We all poured out of the RV and the cars and celebrated for a few minutes. As we whooped it up on the roadside, Duke was in Baton Rouge getting the same news. Duke once thought he could force a runoff with Johnston. And maybe he could have. Whatever the case, he now realized that this campaign, at least, was over. As a last-ditch effort, Duke stormed around the state for two days claiming that Bagert withdrew only after Johnston promised to retire Bagert's $150,000 campaign debt. The charge was ridiculous and no one in the media gave it any credibility.

On the morning of election day, Saturday, October 6, I flew with

Johnston and his wife, Mary, on a private plane from New Orleans to Shreveport so they could vote. As we settled in for the forty-minute flight, Johnston was in a good mood. He knew he would win a fourth term later that night. Pulling out a yellow legal pad, he calculated what he thought his numbers might be, based on Garin's latest polling. The last survey showed Johnston with 55 percent of the vote and about 20 percent still undecided. Johnston gave himself 55 percent of those undecideds and sat back, confident that he would win reelection with about 65 percent of the vote. To me, this also seemed reasonable. He had won reelection six years earlier with 86 percent. Duke was more popular than whoever challenged him last time, so winning "only" 65 percent seemed like a fair and wise calculation.

What election night taught all of us, however, was that in a contest with a well-known incumbent, the great majority of undecideds have already decided they will not vote for the incumbent. They are only trying to decide whether to vote for the challenger or not at all. In this case, Johnston and the staff were stunned when the results started trickling in. Duke was exceeding everyone's expectations. For much of the evening, I camped in the New Orleans Hilton ballroom, deflecting questions from the press about why Johnston wasn't running away with the election. For more than an hour, I pleaded with the staff upstairs in Johnston's suite, "Let's get him down here and declare victory." But Johnston and those around him—including me, I must admit—were shell-shocked. Sure, Johnston would win reelection with 54 percent of the vote, but this meant Duke polled an astounding 43.5 percent. Two minor candidates would split the remaining two points.

Johnston finally came downstairs. He declared victory and thanked the voters and his staff and supporters. We should have been celebrating, but it felt like a defeat—not for us as much as Louisiana. Almost 60 percent of the state's White voters, we would later discover, voted for Duke. The former Klan leader would carry twenty-five of the state's sixty-four parishes. Johnston won almost all the state's Black vote, which we expected for obvious reasons, but I never expected so many White voters to support a racist like Duke. And Duke would not view the election returns as a defeat but as a springboard to the Louisiana governor's race the following year. I had misjudged the racial evolution of my state. Soon, one of those signs would be within my own family.

12

But, Baby, He's a Democrat!

In 1988, Jim Oakes told me about an interesting and pretty young woman he met in New Orleans. He had been with Bennett Johnston and former Johnston aide Tommy Hudson at a wine bar on St. Charles Avenue one night when Johnston approached the table where Cindy Horaist and several of her friends were sitting. He asked if they could borrow a chair. She and her friends obliged. Johnston noticed Cindy right away and mentioned that one of his aides might enjoy meeting her. He introduced her to Jim and persuaded Cindy to write down her phone number. Before long, Jim and Cindy were fast friends, bonding over their love of every kind of sport, especially professional football. Cindy was a Lafayette native and LSU graduate who worked as a hygienist in the office of the New Orleans Saints' dentist, King McGoey. She knew all the players and coaches well. When Jim would come to town, he and Cindy would attend a Saints game or some other sporting event.

I laughed when Jim told me he had become friends with a woman who had written a letter to the *Daily Advertiser* in Lafayette in October 1986, complaining that John Breaux had held his primary election-night party in New Orleans, not Lafayette. "I feel [he] could have selected a location in the area which would have allowed his longtime loyal supporters to attend," Cindy had written. "I hope this is not any indication that, if elected, he would forget about his friends in Acadiana."

Cindy would sometimes phone our house in DC to speak to Jim. When she found out he wasn't home, she never gave me the impression she was eager to end the call. Instead, we'd talk for a few minutes. I noticed that she always made the effort to ask about my day. But I still didn't know how to spell her unusual last name. Once I wrote a note for Jim that said, "Cindy Oray called." In early November 1988, she came to DC to attend a Saints-Redskins game with Jim. He wanted me to meet her. I remember my first impressions of her: beautiful and friendly. At first, I assumed that she and Jim were dating. (They were mostly just good friends who bonded over football and other sports.) We went out to eat that night and I didn't see her again until the spring of 1990, when Jim and I moved to Baton Rouge to run the Johnston campaign.

About one weekend a month, Cindy would drive to Lafayette to see her parents. And she would usually drop by the headquarters to visit Jim. Several times, however, Jim was out or in some meeting, so she wandered into my office. One day, she showed up with a delicious pear pie she had baked for us. We talked for more than an hour. I found her just as beautiful and enchanting as the first time we met, but she often would mention her friendships with various Saints players. I assumed she would never be interested in a skinny, nerdy congressional aide who spent nights and weekends holed up in the Library of Congress.

Cindy, however, liked me enough to arrange a date with one of her friends. The friend was great, but I was growing attracted to Cindy. One weekend a few weeks before the election, I was in New Orleans and had Saturday night off. I called to see if she would join me for dinner. I did not think of it as a date—at least, at first. She was Jim's friend and now mine. It started out as a platonic evening. By the end of dinner at the now-defunct Chart House on Jackson Square, it began to feel like a date. And by the time we finished our Pimm's Cups at the Napoleon House, it was definitely a date. On Sunday afternoon, when I got back to Baton Rouge, I confessed to Jim that I was falling for his good friend. It seemed like the honorable thing to do, especially if you suspect you might have discovered a soulmate.

"Look," I told him, "if you aren't serious about Cindy, I want to date her." Jim liked Cindy, but he had recently met the person who would become his wife. He assured me he and Cindy were just friends. I had the green light! And I began finding every reason possible for campaign business in New Orleans in those last few weeks before election day.

By mid-November, I returned to Washington and was adjusting to a new life that featured a great job in DC and a girlfriend in New Orleans. For the next year and a half, Cindy and I made time to speak by phone at least once a day—and often twice. My job with Breaux took me back to Louisiana every six weeks, so I usually flew in early or stayed a few days after each trip to spend time with her. When I wasn't planning to visit Louisiana for more than a month, she would come to Washington for a long weekend. I know some relationships like ours don't survive the distance, but we made it work by never losing contact—for even a day— and ensuring we saw each other as often as possible. That my job allowed me to travel home frequently was a huge help.

In April 1992, on a porch swing at the St. Francisville Inn in West Feliciana Parish, I proposed to Cindy. We were married in Lafayette on

December 18. At the time of our wedding, we had never been together more than five days in a row. We were then and now compatible in almost every way. It also helped that we viewed politics the same way. Although she was a registered Republican, she had drifted away from the party for many of the same reasons I did. David Duke's rise pushed her even farther away. By the time we started dating, she was a moderate-to-liberal voter. But like many in Louisiana, who never worry about party registration much (we don't have closed party primaries, so it doesn't usually matter), she had not changed hers. For our first wedding anniversary in December 1993, she gave me a photocopy of her change-of-registration form. She had become a Democrat.

With my future wife, Cindy Horaist, in 1992 in Washington, DC.

Not much of this pleased her very conservative Republican father. The first time she brought me to Lafayette to meet her parents—Alfred and Gerry Horaist—Cindy was nervous about how her dad would react to a liberal Democrat who worked in politics. It didn't matter that I had worked for Russell Long, John Breaux, and Bennett Johnston—three of the most conservative Democrats in the country. I was still a Democrat and, therefore, more than a little suspect. Here's just one example of how he viewed me. In 1991, Cindy called her father to ask if she could miss a car payment that month—she had borrowed the money from him—and instead fly to Washington to see me.

"Why do you want to spend the money to go see him?" my future father-in-law asked.

"Because I love him, Dad," she replied.

"But, baby," he pleaded, "he's a Democrat!"

It was Al's curse that all three of his children became committed Democrats. Cindy's brother, David, worked as a volunteer in Mary Landrieu's US Senate campaigns. Their older sister, Jan, is a Democrat married to Michael Skinner, whom President Bill Clinton appointed as US attorney for the Western District of Louisiana in 1993. Mike later served as chair of the Louisiana Democratic Party.

Despite our political differences—and we had some heated discussions over the years—I came to love this generous, kind man who raised three remarkable children and was a devoted grandfather to my son and daughter. In his later years, we didn't talk politics as much as we had in the beginning. What was the purpose? I would never change his mind and he would never change mine. Besides, with grandkids running about the house, there were more important things to discuss. When Al died in 2016, I cried. He was a good man with whom I disagreed about much. But we focused—like so many people in divided political families—on what united us: our love for his daughter and my children. My father-in-law taught me much about how friendships can survive political disagreements. My political beliefs are important to me because it's not just about who wins and loses; it's also about who can attend college, who can find a job, who can get the healthcare they need, and who can get the help they need to raise a family. These are often life-and-death decisions. But those conflicts don't have to—and shouldn't—stand in the way of friendship and family bonds. If you work hard enough with most people you can always find some common value to focus on and use that to build a warm, trusting relationship. I'm blessed to have had such a relationship with my father-in-law and dozens of close friends in Baton Rouge and elsewhere who do not share my political views.

WITH THE JOHNSTON campaign over, I went back to finishing my biography on Russell Long, which I had put on the shelf for six months. I had just a few months until it was due to my publisher. I hoped it would do well and might lead to the opportunity to write other books. I never expected that my years of devotion to producing this modest tome would change my life in such a wonderful way.

My first book, *Legacy to Power: Senator Russell Long of Louisiana*, came out in November 1992, just a few weeks before Cindy and I married. It received good reviews in newspapers all over Louisiana and elsewhere. It sold well, too. And I soon learned that with one book under my belt, the job of selling another one was easier. Many people who sign a book contract never finish the work. That's because writing a book seems romantic and sometimes sounds much easier than it is. When I began the Long book, I thought it would take about a year—six months of research and six months of writing. It took about three years of research and more than a year of writing to produce the first draft. It was the hardest mental work I had ever done. But now that I had proved I could take a book from concept to completion, publishers might bet on my next project.

At lunch in New York with the editor of my publishing house, Paragon House, I wondered aloud about what kind of book I could tackle next. He asked, "What would you like to write about? What story hasn't been told that you could tell?" While I had written about Long's involvement in the civil rights bills of the 1960s, I did not think of writing about civil rights until that moment. But I replied, "I'd like to write about how the Senate debated and passed the civil rights laws."

The topic, until then, had not been fully explored: how the civil rights movement in the streets translated into legislative action in the halls of Congress. I settled on telling the story through the lens of three major figures in the US Senate during that period—Lyndon Johnson, the majority leader, vice president, and president who pushed for passage of the 1964 Civil Rights Act and the 1965 Voting Rights Act; Senator Richard Russell of Georgia, the cagey Democrat who led the Southern forces arrayed against the civil rights bills from the 1940s through the 1960s; and Senator Hubert Humphrey of Minnesota, the idealistic LSU graduate who fought for civil rights beginning at the 1948 Democratic National Convention, through the 1950s, and into the early 1960s and who, as Democratic whip, managed the 1964 bill on the Senate floor.

Paragon House had paid me a modest advance for my Long book, which I used to buy Cindy's engagement ring in 1992. With Clyde Taylor's skillful representation, several houses competed for my civil rights book. We settled on Harcourt Brace, a venerable publishing firm in New York.

I received a handsome advance, some of which I used for a down payment on our first house. The rest financed my research, including travel to dig through the papers of Johnson, Russell, Humphrey, and others.

Around the same time, I persuaded Breaux to let me move back to Louisiana and open a Baton Rouge office for him, where I would handle the Louisiana press and help schedule and manage his Louisiana travels. One motivation for the move in August 1992 was that Cindy was not keen to relocate to Washington. If I insisted that it was the only place I could be successful, I know she would have moved to DC. After eight years in Washington, however, I was ready to return home. I loved Washington, but I missed the quieter, easier life that Louisiana afforded. More than anything, I thought starting a new life—and having children with Cindy—would be better in Louisiana.

So that summer, we bought a house in Baton Rouge and I came home to help with Breaux's reelection campaign that year, a walk against token opposition. Breaux's state director, Norma Jane Sabiston, was a good friend with whom I worked in Washington on Breaux's staff. Since Breaux faced little opposition, the two of us were the only campaign staff he needed. Cindy remained in New Orleans to plan our wedding, coming to Baton Rouge on weekends. We bought more house than we needed, so I invited Norma Jane, who lived in New Orleans, to stay with me during the week to eliminate her commute. I'm sure our new neighbors were puzzled by the new guy in the neighborhood. During the week, he shared a house with a woman who disappeared on Friday, just in time for the arrival of a different woman.

After the campaign and my wedding were over, I settled down to working in our new offices on the twentieth floor of One American Place in downtown Baton Rouge. Out of my office window, I enjoyed a bird's-eye view of the Louisiana Capitol. The best aspect of my new role was that Breaux allowed me to work only three days a week for him, giving me two days at home for writing my next book. When I proposed the arrangement, I volunteered to take a sizable cut in pay to account for my reduced workload. Because the cost of living in Baton Rouge was so much lower than in Washington, I would never feel a serious loss of income.

Baton Rouge in 1992 was a sleepy town with none of the character or panache of its boisterous downriver neighbor, New Orleans. It offered little in the way of cultural attractions—unless one favored that monument to the "glory" of slavery, the antebellum plantation home. Dozens of them dotted the landscape along the Mississippi River from Natchez, Mississippi, to New Orleans. There were few good restaurants in Baton Rouge, although plenty of diners offered the kind of Southern cooking I had missed during my days in DC. There were precious few movie theaters and just a couple of decent bookstores. During our first years of married life in Baton Rouge, an exciting Friday night out on the town consisted of dinner at some nondescript chain restaurant followed by a trip to the local Barnes & Noble bookstore or the city's lone Home Depot.

Baton Rouge was a "family" town. By that, I mean it was—and still is—a decent city with cohesive neighborhoods, hundreds of churches, dozens of playgrounds, and other well-maintained recreation centers. The parish had robust and well-funded library and parks systems. It was not a bad place to raise a family, if you overlooked the city's crumbling schools, persistent poverty, profound segregation, and inadequate health services for the poor. In those days—and still today—Baton Rouge had three important centers of gravity: state government, the petrochemical industry, and LSU football. And not necessarily in that order. State government and nearby chemical plants and oil refineries paid the bills, while LSU football—and, sometimes, basketball and baseball—provided the entertainment. What went on in the classroom on the other side of campus was irrelevant to most fans.

With a decent, well-appointed home office, I treasured the chance to devote myself to a book—at least for two days a week—which was a significant change in routine from the first project. In Washington, I had worked full-time in the Senate and then spent nights and weekends on research and writing. I had little social life beyond occasional weekend golf outings with my friends. But now, I wanted to spend as much time with Cindy as possible. And Breaux supported this arrangement. Many other politicians would have balked at such a crazy deal, but he thought it was a great idea. He could not have been happier for me and, except for agreeing that I would drop the book during the weeks he was in Louisiana, he gave me free rein to split my time between him and writing.

Besides diving into various archives, I tracked down retired senators, former congressional staff members, and others of the civil rights era who were still alive. I also interviewed former aides to Presidents Kennedy and Johnson, including Harris Wofford, Clark Clifford, Theodore Hesburgh, Harry McPherson, Nicholas Katzenbach, Burke Marshall, and George Reedy. I spoke with several former Humphrey staffers.

I enjoyed interviewing retired senators, but my most interesting encounters were with two former White House aides. Harry McPherson was a Texas lawyer who came to Washington to work for Johnson in the 1950s and stayed on with him through his vice presidency and presidency. McPherson played several roles for Johnson over the years, including writing speeches. When I called Harry, he welcomed me to his K Street law office. He was not only generous with his time and his memories; he volunteered to call former Johnson aides and others and urge them to talk with me. Harry's book about his time working for Johnson in the Senate, *A Political Education*, remains one of the best political memoirs ever written. His sketches of dozens of senators during the 1950s—some call it the Senate's Golden Era—are priceless. His prose was elegant.

I also had a memorable encounter with Harris Wofford, who was John F. Kennedy's top White House civil rights assistant. Wofford was the aide who had urged then-candidate Kennedy, in 1960, to phone Coretta Scott King when her husband, Martin, had been jailed in Georgia. News of that simple phone call swayed enough Black votes to Kennedy to help him win the White House. By the time I caught up with him, Wofford was a US senator from Pennsylvania. His surprise election in 1991 was the first successful statewide campaign for Louisiana's James Carville, who would manage Bill Clinton's presidential campaign the following year. Wofford agreed to talk and invited me to his office one cold winter evening. After we began talking, the Senate chamber signaled a vote. (Every office had a clock equipped with a buzzer and series of lights so no member would miss a roll call.) Wofford needed to rush to the floor for a vote on some amendment. Instead of dismissing me and inviting me back another time, he brought me along. We hopped in his car and drove to the base of the Senate steps. Wofford dashed inside to vote and then returned. With my tape recorder running, we sat in his car for more than an hour as he reminisced about his days working for Kennedy and his efforts to persuade the young president to take a risk on pushing harder for a civil rights bill.

I loved the research as much as the writing, for the chance to talk with people like Wofford and McPherson about their roles in making American history. But I have always enjoyed the challenge of taking complex issues and legislation and making them digestible and understandable to the average reader. For *The Walls of Jericho: Lyndon Johnson, Richard Russell, Hubert Humphrey and the Struggle for Civil Rights*, I focused on the stories of the main characters to make the legislation come alive. More so than any book I've written, *Jericho* had a story and a narrative energy to it that made it easy to write. The whole saga pulled me along in a way that I've always hoped to recreate. Maybe a writer only gets one book like that in a lifetime. If so, I'm happy that mine came in my early thirties, because the reviews and the reaction to *Jericho* changed my professional life and opened doors to me that allowed me to write other books and led to my rewarding third career in academia. Breaux loved the book, too, taking a copy to the White House one day and presenting it to President Clinton, who wrote me a lovely letter of thanks.[1]

I was fortunate the book came out when many newspapers were still devoting significant space to reviews. The book got favorable write-ups in the *New York Times, Atlanta Constitution, Philadelphia Inquirer, Austin American-Statesman,* and others. George F. Will devoted one of his syndicated columns to it ("a gripping account of the 1964 and 1965 acts"). The most satisfying, however, was Michael Pakenham's review in the *Baltimore Sun* in May 1996: "I am strained to think of a book that is the match of that one for richness of anecdotal detail in tracing the technical developments through the Congress, especially in the Senate, in a way coherent to general readers." This was so rewarding because it was precisely my goal in writing the book. "It is not particularly literary," he added, "but the message, the story, cumulatively, is borne by such a tide of morality that it begins to sing and then gradually rises to the eloquence of a mighty choir."

The success of *The Walls of Jericho* led to a few exciting appearances. The best was a speech the University of Georgia invited me to give about Richard Russell's civil rights record at an event marking his hundredth birthday. That the university and his family members wanted me to speak reflected well on them. Russell's civil rights record was deplorable. He was a great legislator with many worthy accomplishments, but he was also a racist who helped enable the oppression of Black Americans for several decades. I said as much to the crowd at UGA. What else could I do but be honest about his strengths and weaknesses as I saw them? Afterwards, several of his nieces and nephews approached me to say I had accurately described their uncle. They loved and admired him and were proud of his long service to Georgia—he served as governor in his thirties before his election to the Senate—but they could not deny his racist views. I've often wondered how I would have responded if I heard someone condemn the racism of someone I loved.

The book also led to opportunities to talk about Hubert Humphrey, whom I admired since my childhood. During my research I had not thought to contact Humphrey's sister, Frances Howard, who once worked for Eleanor Roosevelt. It was an embarrassing oversight that she overlooked when she invited me to lunch in her Washington apartment one Sunday in the fall of 1996. I spent a delightful afternoon listening to stories about her remarkable brother. A few years later, a filmmaker from St. Paul, Minnesota, Mick Caoutte, contacted me for a PBS documentary he was making about Humphrey's life, especially his role in the Civil Rights Act. Mick came to Baton Rouge and interviewed me for several hours. When the film premiered in St. Paul, he honored me with an invitation to speak about Humphrey before it showed. Mick and I became friends in the years since and he's shown the Humphrey film and his next—a superb documentary about Thurgood Marshall—to my LSU students. In 2015, LSU Press asked me to write a new foreword to

Humphrey's 1940 LSU master's thesis, *The Political Philosophy of the New Deal*, which they first published in 1970. For a person who worshiped Humphrey from childhood, I was enormously proud to see my name with his on the cover of a book.

BESIDES WRITING MY books, I continued representing Breaux to the Louisiana press and, sometimes, took a leave of absence to work in statewide campaigns. In 1995, I left Breaux's staff for six months to serve as communications director for the Louisiana Democratic Party. James Brady, who would later become a federal judge in Baton Rouge, was party chair and Jim Nickel, my former Breaux colleague (and now godfather to both of my children), was the party's executive director. Our goal that year was to elect a Democrat as governor and, to us, that meant keeping former Republican Governor Buddy Roemer from winning his comeback effort. Roemer, who switched from Democrat to Republican near the end of his term, had campaigned for reelection in 1991 and finished an embarrassing third behind Edwin Edwards and David Duke. Edwards won the wild runoff election that attracted national and international attention. Bumper stickers that said, "Vote for the Crook, It's Important," cropped up everywhere. Edwards saved the state from a former Klan leader, but his fourth term as governor was a disappointment. In June 1994, Edwards announced he would retire from politics, which threw the next year's governor's race wide open. In the wake of that decision, Roemer announced he would make another run at the Governor's Mansion.

The other prominent Republican in the race was Franklin state Senator Mike Foster, who switched parties on the day he qualified for the race. The Democrats included Baton Rouge US Representative Cleo Fields, the only major Black candidate; Lieutenant Governor Melinda Schwegmann; state Treasurer Mary Landrieu; state Representative Robert Adley of Bossier Parish; and Baton Rouge attorney Phil Preis. With so many Democrats in the running, the state party would remain neutral until one of them made the runoff. Assuming a Democrat-Republican runoff, the Democratic Party would only promote its candidate for the final month of the campaign. Until then, we focused on taking out the Republican who seemed most likely to pose a strong challenge in the fall.

And to all of us, that was Roemer. Brady and Nickel hired an opposition research firm from North Carolina to investigate every aspect of the former governor's public life. The firm did a thorough job and produced a series of reports that filled a dozen Black binders. For months, my job was to comb through those books, find juicy tidbits about Roemer, and try to persuade local reporters to write stories about them. We had more information about Roemer than we could ever persuade the press to cover. So, we created

With my friend and longtime Breaux staffer Jim Nickel in 1992. At the time, Jim was executive director of the Louisiana Democratic Party. To my children, he is "Uncle Jim" and their godfather.

a weekly newsletter called *The Buddy System*, aimed at spreading some fresh bit of dirt about the former governor. Every week, I would scour the opposition research and conjure a new tale of scandal involving Roemer. These were the days before social media. Many reporters still did not use email. No one had a BlackBerry. It would be another twelve years before Steve Jobs would unveil the iPhone. This newsletter went out by fax each week. It took several hours for the computer's fax program to push it out to all the reporters and newsrooms on our list.

I had some success getting the press to read what I fed them about Roemer, but they usually ignored us. Still, we regarded Roemer as the Republican most likely to make a runoff—and we wanted to eliminate him. That was before I recognized that political campaigns brought out my most competitive and ugly side—a win-at-all-costs mentality that sometimes short-circuited my better judgment. That is where my mind was on July 15, 1995, when I agreed to speak to a statewide gathering of the Young Democrats of Louisiana in the House chamber of the State Capitol. I did not notice a reporter for the *Sunday Advocate*, Doug Myers, who sat in the back of the room hoping for something interesting and newsworthy. I did not know until the next morning's paper that my appearance provided the news for which he hoped.

My phone rang around six o'clock that morning. It was Nickel. "Have you seen today's paper?" he asked in a whisper. I hadn't. "Go get it and call me back." So, I trotted to the end of the driveway, threw open the Sunday paper, and saw at the bottom of the front page my blistering attack on Roemer. The headline read: "Democratic official blasts Roemer as 'racist.'" The story quoted me saying, "You can't tell the difference between Buddy Roemer's rhetoric and David Duke's rhetoric." About a television commercial in which the candidate proposed bringing back chain gangs for convicted criminals, I observed that Roemer wanted to "bring back the inhumanity and the degradation of chain gangs to deal with our state's crime problem." Knowing that most in the audience would remember that Roemer's father and brother had been convicted of federal crimes (an appeals court later overturned his father's conviction), I added: "We say to Buddy Roemer, 'Why don't you work on cutting the crime rate in your own family and then deal with the crime rate in the state?'" Myers did not quote me saying this, but I also referred to Roemer and his relatives as "the Roemer crime family." The story quoted me further about Roemer: "This is the person, you may recall, when he was in the governor's mansion who played high-stakes poker in the mansion on a regular basis. This is the person who signed the bill that brought us riverboat casinos, and this is the person who now says the gambling he brought to the state is a blight on Louisiana. I don't know what your definition of hypocrisy is, but I think that's a pretty good one."

I was not the only speaker to attack Roemer that day. Mary Landrieu, already a candidate for governor, said, "Roemer is the father of gambling in Louisiana and he's going to have to account for that as he runs for office." US Representative Bill Jefferson of New Orleans, who was thinking about running for governor—he later declined—criticized Roemer for "general hardheadedness and his lack of desire" to work with the state legislature. Unfortunately, my words were the strongest and most quotable of the day.

Seeing my harsh language in the paper rattled me. I wasn't a full-time campaigner. When this election was over, I planned to go back to work for Breaux. I worried that he might find my partisan attack on his former congressional colleague so ugly and toxic that I would not be welcome back on staff. Instead, Breaux seemed to be unfazed by the whole thing. A few days later he showed the story to President Clinton, who was not among Roemer's fans. My job was safe.

For years, I wore the episode as a badge of honor. I thought I had told the truth about Roemer, given it to him with both barrels, and covered myself in glory. I never heard from Roemer or any of his people about the attack—Roemer's campaign declined an offer to comment on my remarks at the time—but it couldn't have been pleasant to see yourself described as a racist in the local paper. About six years later, however, I ran into the former governor at a local bookstore. "Bob, Bob!" I heard him call in his distinctive, nasally, north Louisiana twang. I knew that it was Roemer before I saw his face. Thankfully, he was grinning as approached. "I just read your Vietnam War book," he said. "It was excellent." We had a brief, friendly conversation. I left a bit unnerved and thought, "Why was Buddy Roemer being so nice to me?" For several years, I had observed him sitting in the balcony on Sunday mornings at First United Methodist Church, where Cindy and I attended since 1994. For the longest time, we didn't speak or, if so, only in passing. But Buddy's new friendliness was unsettling.

I thought about it quite often over the next few weeks, until the moment I realized I had to release whatever bitterness and anger I harbored towards him. He had overlooked my insults, so why couldn't I find it within my heart to move on, too? I'm not sure what prompted me to do it, but I started praying for him. Every day, I'd just say a brief prayer: "God bless Buddy Roemer." And before long, I had softened towards him. Now, whenever I saw him at church, I sought him out. We'd have a pleasant visit. When I went to work for Governor Kathleen Blanco in 2004, I ran into him at a reception at the massive, ornate Highland Road home of business executive James Bernhard. Buddy was kind, effusive, and full of helpful advice about the tough job ahead. I was grateful.

Other than seeing him at church on Sundays, I would not spend much time with Buddy over the next few years. In the fall of 2008, now on the LSU faculty, I was teaching an Honors College course on the presidential election between Barack Obama and Roemer's friend, Arizona Senator John McCain. I called Roemer and asked if he would speak to my class and give students his insight into McCain's politics and personality. He readily agreed.

As I stood up that morning in my classroom in the Journalism Building to introduce him to my twenty students, I realized it was time to deal with the animosity that caused me to make a fool out of myself in 1995. It was also time to apply one of the lessons I had finally learned from my first, bruising political fight in Vernon Parish in 1978: let go of resentment. It had taken time, but I eventually understood that harboring anger will rot your insides. It will poison your soul. In the years since that turbulent summer in Leesville, I had also learned the art of apologizing to those I wronged. And I learned about offering forgiveness.

"Before I introduce Governor Roemer to you," I told my students, "I want to tell you about a time many years ago that I campaigned against him and let my partisan and personal feelings get the best of me. I said some awful things about this man. I was unkind and rude. What I said still embarrasses me. We can disagree with each other in politics without getting personal. We can acknowledge that the other person has another idea for fixing the problems we both want to solve. We don't have to make it personal. I made it personal about Buddy Roemer and I want to tell him in front of you all that I'm sorry for what I said. I hope you'll forgive me, Governor." With that, I yielded the floor. Roemer was gracious and kind and returned four years later to speak to another group of students when I taught the same class during the 2012 election.

A few years after that, I was happy to sit next to Roemer at a forum hosted by the Public Affairs Research Council of Louisiana (PAR). While the purpose of my remarks was to critique then-Governor Bobby Jindal's deplorable record, I made it a point to contrast favorably Roemer's record with Jindal's. A half-dozen times that morning, I said, "Governor Roemer had a good proposal." By that time, I realized that much of what Roemer tried to do—including fiscal and ethics reforms and enhanced environmental laws—had been wise. "This man was way ahead of his time," I said in praising him. "He had good ideas that many people, me included, are now beginning finally to recognize."

Say what you will about Roemer—and I have good friends who are still disdainful and skeptical of him—he tried to make Louisiana a better state. That he couldn't do it was often a failure of tactics and strategy, not policy. He has his faults, but so do I. He was and is a decent person and I'm happy I came around to seeing that. As I write these words (in the summer of 2019) in the coffee shop of a Baton Rouge bookstore, Roemer is sitting three tables away, reading a newspaper, and is nearly hidden from my view by a large stack of books he has collected for purchase. We just had a friendly chat, as we often do these days.

Perhaps it was our efforts to sabotage Roemer's 1995 campaign that caused his candidacy to fade. More likely, however, it was that Mike Foster, a little-known but wealthy sixty-five-year-old businessman and state senator from Franklin, ran a fantastic campaign guided by Baton Rouge media consultant Roy Fletcher. For a while, we all laughed at the seemingly amateurish ads Fletcher placed for Foster in weekly newspapers around the state. They were text-heavy screeds under a picture of the bald, rotund, mustachioed Foster. Under Foster's picture in some ads, the campaign added, "Not Just Another Pretty Face." In one newspaper ad in mid-October, Foster attacked Roemer, his chief Republican opponent: "Mike Foster takes *no* gambling money [emphasis Foster], and Roemer knows it. In fact, while Governor Buddy Roemer took thousands of dollars from gambling interests, then refused to veto the video poker bill and allowed it to become law. (Mike voted against video poker) [*sic*] The record shows it and Roemer knows it!"

Ads like these ran in papers for months, augmented by Fletcher's television commercials that portrayed the wealthy Foster—his grandfather Murphy J. Foster was governor of Louisiana from 1892 to 1900 and a US senator from 1901 to 1913—as an outsider and average working man. One spot that ran over and over featured a welder who, at the end of the commercial, threw up his mask to reveal he was the candidate. An avid sportsman, former oilfield roughneck, and man of simple tastes, Foster knew how to weld. But he also lived in a mansion that was larger and better appointed than the official governor's residence to which he aspired. No matter, Foster's good-old-boy image and good-government message captured the public's imagination. After four years of a corrupt and lethargic Edwin Edwards administration, the public craved something better. With his business background and direct, plainspoken manner, Foster embodied everything a majority of Louisiana wanted in a governor. The *Ville Platte Gazette*, one in a chain of Louisiana newspapers that carried the same editorial, summed up this sentiment in early October: "If you want someone who can relate to the working man and woman, Mike may be your man. He has been a welder's helper, a roustabout, a roughneck, a relief derrick man, and a warehouseman . . . Foster is the only chance for change we have."

Foster led the field of candidates with 26 percent and went into the runoff with Baton Rouge US Representative Cleo Fields, the first African American candidate to make a statewide runoff in the state's history. Fields had won 95 percent of the Black vote but got almost none of the White vote. His presence in the race, and his ability to scoop up most of the Black votes, was more than enough to pull votes away from Landrieu and deny her a runoff spot. Who knows if Landrieu could have won, but Fields was never going to win. After the 1995 governor's race, I went back to Breaux's staff, finished work on my civil rights history, and prepared to write my third book. Before I could get started, however, another campaign called.

13

You're Supposed to Keep Him Out of Trouble

When J. Bennett Johnston announced his retirement from the US Senate in early 1995, John Breaux was eager to ensure that he had a good partner—a Democratic partner—in Washington. He settled upon Mary Landrieu as the strongest potential candidate in the upcoming 1996 election and, believing that a crowded field of Democrats would be counterproductive, tried to persuade her to run.

I had been around Landrieu for years, having first met her when I worked for Russell Long and she served in the state House from New Orleans. When I began working for Breaux a few years later, I saw her more often. She always impressed me as an intense, no-nonsense person, not a typical joke-telling, back-slapping politician. Landrieu and a few other women who served in the House, including Lafayette's Kathleen Blanco, came to Baton Rouge not to get along but to shake up the place. The dominant male power structure did not always welcome their hard-driving ways, but the new women legislators injected a new level of professionalism and seriousness into state politics.[1] Landrieu—whose father, Moon, had been New Orleans' mayor and a member of President Jimmy Carter's cabinet—rose through the ranks, winning the state treasurer's race in 1987 and serving two terms in that job before she ran for governor in 1995.

At first, Landrieu said she wasn't interested in another statewide race. "I'm leaning against it at this point, but have not closed the door," she told a reporter in late December. Breaux, however, suspected her refusal to run was a product of her exhaustion and disappointment after a bruising campaign. She agreed to meet with him to discuss it. On a Sunday night that winter, some friends lent us their Baton Rouge home. They brought in a light dinner and then left Landrieu and her husband, Frank Snellings, alone with Breaux, Norma Jane Sabiston—Breaux's state director—and me. After dinner, we moved to the living room, where Breaux made his pitch. At first, Landrieu was adamant: she was too tired for another campaign. Breaux was just as adamant: sleep on it for a while and let the exhaustion of the governor's race fade before you decide, because you can win this race.

Landrieu agreed to think about it. A few weeks later, at a Democratic retreat in Hilton Head, South Carolina, President Bill Clinton pulled her aside and urged her to run. Bennett Johnston did, too. In February, a statewide poll showed her leading the field of potential Senate candidates, offering her more encouragement that the race was winnable.

In trying to pave the way for her candidacy, Breaux called himself Landrieu's "John the Baptist." While he could not convince Attorney General Richard Ieyoub that Landrieu stood the better chance of winning, he helped persuade US Representatives Cleo Fields and Bill Jefferson to forgo the race, which would have split the Democratic vote further. In late March 1996, to our delight, Landrieu finally decided to run. It would be a crowded race of fifteen candidates that included Ieyoub; perennial Senate candidate Woody Jenkins, now a Republican; David Duke; and Republican US Representative Jimmy Hayes of Lafayette, a former Democrat who had succeeded Breaux in the US House and switched to the GOP in 1995. Although it was an open secret that Breaux favored Landrieu, he remained neutral until the primary election that fall winnowed the field to Jenkins—this would be Woody's third US Senate race since 1978—and Landrieu.

Breaux was all in for Landrieu and committed as much time as possible to campaigning and raising money for her. He also allowed me another leave of absence to return to the state Democratic Party to help her from there. It was a fierce campaign and we were still struggling to unite Democrats around Landrieu after the hurt feelings from the previous year's governor's race. Landrieu did not endorse Cleo Fields in that race and, in return, he gave her only a perfunctory endorsement in her race. Ieyoub was also not happy, believing that Breaux had favored Landrieu over him. Breaux liked Ieyoub and would have supported him if he made the runoff with Jenkins, but he believed that Landrieu—having just assembled a strong statewide organization and having run a solid race—stood the better chance of winning.

One benefit of the campaign for me was the opportunity to spend time with Landrieu's husband, Frank Snellings, an old friend from my Monroe days. During the fall campaign we would meet once or twice a week for lunch or coffee. Hanging out with Frank was fun, but it also got me in trouble with Mary after the first statewide televised debate between her and Jenkins on October 28. The morning of the debate, Frank wandered into the state party's office on Third Street in downtown Baton Rouge. I mentioned to him that party Chair Jim Nickel and I would stage a press conference the next day to charge Jenkins with misusing donations from a charitable organization—the Friends of America—that he formed and was housed at his television station's offices next to his large antebellum home on North Foster Drive. The organization was supposed to contribute humanitarian relief to Nicaraguan refugees, but Jenkins paid himself a handsome salary to run it. Our idea was to hold the event across the street from Jenkins' property so that the television station would provide the backdrop for our attacks on him.

I was preparing to scout out the site for the event when Frank offered to drive me. We hopped into his Suburban and drove towards Jenkins' home. After I spoke to the nearby property owners, getting their permission to conduct our press conference in their parking lot, Frank drove us across the street to Jenkins' house. To my surprise, he pulled his car into the driveway and drove around in front of the adjacent television station. I never knew what possessed him, but we were back on the street and driving to the office within twenty seconds. Little did we know that someone in the house or at the station spotted us and asked the Baton Rouge Police Department or the State Police to run Frank's license number.

That night, I was with Landrieu's staff in New Orleans and sat on some low bleachers in the studio, two rows behind Frank. The debate went well. I thought Landrieu scored some good points on Jenkins. Towards the end of the broadcast, however, Jenkins turned to her and asked her why her husband drove onto his family's estate earlier that day. I could feel the blood drain from my face. I looked at Frank. He didn't move. "He came on our property at our home today in his vehicle," Jenkins said. "Drove through our property. Came up to our door. It was very embarrassing. Our children didn't know what to think. I'd like an explanation of that. That's something I'm very concerned about."

Landrieu was dumbfounded and said she did not know what Jenkins was talking about. She was telling the truth. Frank did not tell her about turning around on Woody's driveway because it was so unremarkable. We did not drive past the house but the television station. We did not get out of the car. Frank did not even stop his car. Given that Jenkins lived next door to a television station, it could not have been unusual for visitors and employees to drive and park next to his home. Whatever the case, Landrieu was livid, first at Frank, and then at me. "You're supposed to keep him out of trouble," she barked in the parking lot as we left the station. I was not aware this was part of my job, but how could I argue with her? Frank and I were both embarrassed and chastened. The next day's Associated Press story mentioned the brouhaha and noted that I was in the car with the candidate's husband. Regardless, Nickel and I went ahead with our press conference across from Woody's property.

Cargate soon blew over and Landrieu won her Senate seat by only 5,788 votes out of 1.7 million cast. She took office in January 1997, but Jenkins contested the election, suggesting that Landrieu stole votes. After a lengthy inquiry, the Republican-controlled Senate Rules and Administration Committee found in October 1997 that there was no evidence "to prove that fraud or irregularities affected the outcome of the election" and "it has never been alleged, and no evidence has been uncovered, that Senator Landrieu was involved in any fraudulent election activities."

Mary forgave Frank and me for trespassing on Jenkins' property and we laughed about it—but not for a while. As for Woody, I've seen him and spoken with him a half-dozen times over the past twenty-plus years. The whole thing must not have worried him much. He never mentioned it to me.

THE SUCCESS OF *The Walls of Jericho* gave me the freedom to tackle another big subject. For this next book, I hoped to build upon my growing expertise in Senate history by writing about the next major issue the body addressed—the Vietnam War. Once again, Clyde Taylor worked his magic and got me a generous advance, this time from Basic Books. And Breaux agreed to my outrageous request to take another cut in pay to work only two days in the office for him and three days at home. I started my work immediately, doing the usual archival research and interviews of former senators and their aides. This time, with the help of LBJ's former aide Harry McPherson, I scored an interview with former Senate Majority Leader Mike Mansfield. By the time I met him, Mansfield was in his nineties and losing some of his mental acuity. He remembered most events, but some of his answers started out in 1965 and ended up in 1975. I got a few good tidbits from him but mainly was thrilled with the chance to spend an hour talking with the longest-serving Senate majority leader.

Most helpful was former Senator George McGovern, who granted me several interviews over the course of my research. McGovern was a major character in the story, having expressed early doubts about Kennedy's Vietnam policies in 1962. But he voted for the fateful 1964 Gulf of Tonkin Resolution, which gave Johnson carte blanche in Vietnam and led to the disastrous escalation of the war in 1965. My friend Douglas Brinkley, then a history professor at Tulane University in New Orleans, knew of my new book and invited me to Washington in April 1997 to take part in a daylong symposium marking McGovern's seventy-fifth birthday. Doug asked me to speak about McGovern's Vietnam War record. I had already interviewed McGovern once by phone and studied him enough to be troubled by his silent period during that era. After raising doubts in

1962, McGovern did not rise again to oppose the war until January 1965. I thought that needed to be addressed at the symposium.

With McGovern sitting in the front row in an auditorium at the National Archives building on Pennsylvania Avenue, I listened as legendary historian and former Kennedy White House aide Arthur Schlesinger introduced me. I was new to such symposia and unaware that my fellow presenters would be praising McGovern's record (and it mostly deserved praise). I approached my speech only as a historian. And after researching McGovern, and interviewing him at length, I arrived at several major conclusions, which included that his opposition to the Vietnam War in the late 1960s and early 1970s was heroic. I even read from his remarkable "this chamber reeks of blood" speech that the South Dakota senator delivered to a stunned Senate in September 1970. "Every senator in this chamber is partly responsible for sending fifty thousand young Americans to an early grave," McGovern had said. "This chamber reeks of blood. Every senator here is partly responsible for that human wreckage at Walter Reed and Bethesda Naval [hospitals] and all across our land—young men without legs, or arms, or faces, or hopes."

When I finished reading from his speech, the audience applauded McGovern. As I told the group, most of McGovern's Vietnam record was laudatory. His principled and vociferous opposition to the war hastened its end. But there was another side to McGovern's record that also required attention—his stunning and troubling silence on the war throughout the momentous year of 1964 and much of 1965, as Johnson escalated the conflict. By the time he began speaking out again, as he did powerfully in 1966 and beyond, there was not much he could do. I referred to McGovern's "complicity" in my remarks at the National Archives. It must have been jarring to McGovern's ears. I learned later from a friend that when I uttered that word, one former McGovern staffer began cursing me under his breath.

As the group walked across Pennsylvania Avenue for a luncheon, an older man sidled up to me. "Man, that was one bold talk you just gave in there," he said. "That room was filled with McGovern's biggest fans and you gave them the hard truth. That was brave." I thanked the man and introduced myself. "Bob Mann," I said, extending my hand. He responded, "Dan Ellsberg." It was then it hit me. If the protagonist of the Pentagon Papers regarded me as brave, I had really rocked the boat.

I realize that my words were offensive to the many McGovern friends and colleagues in the room, so much so that columnist Jules Witcover devoted his syndicated column the following week to my remarks and suggested that my use of the word "complicit" was too strong. He was correct. It is not a word I would use today in criticizing McGovern. He wasn't complicit; he was just mistaken about Johnson's willingness to listen to wise and blunt advice on Vietnam.

But if most of the people were offended by my words, there was at least one who didn't seem concerned at all. He was George McGovern. He was lovely and gracious to me in our encounters throughout the rest of the day. His quote to Witcover, when asked about my language, was that "complicit" was "a bit too strong." Several months later, with some trepidation, I called McGovern to ask for another interview. To my surprise, he agreed, and we spent several hours talking in his office about the war. After the interview, we talked for another thirty minutes about his passion for finding solutions to poverty, his interest in Middle East politics, and the tragic death of his daughter Teresa. Never once did he raise the matter of my unfortunate choice of words. He was gracious and kind to a fault.

A GRAND DELUSION: America's Descent into Vietnam was my longest book, clocking in at more than eight hundred pages. It was an exhaustive political history of the war that I hope showed readers why and how American leaders blundered us into Vietnam in the early 1960s and kept us there long after they knew that the cause was hopeless. For this book, I dived deep into a half-dozen archival collections and interviewed former President Gerald Ford and a host of former senators, including Bob Dole, Gaylord Nelson, and Mark Hatfield. I spoke to former Senate aides and White House officials, including George Reedy, LBJ's press secretary. Former Senator J. William Fulbright, who spearheaded the Senate opposition to the war beginning in the mid-1960s, was a central character in the book and I not only combed through his papers at the University of Arkansas; I interviewed as many of his former aides as I could find.

I am always a bit surprised by how eager people are to tell their stories to historians writing about the momentous times in which they lived. No one personified that more than Norvill Jones, who was Fulbright's staff director on the Foreign Relations Committee in the late sixties and early seventies. When Daniel Ellsberg began shopping the Pentagon Papers around in late 1969, he did not go first to the *New York Times* but to Fulbright and George McGovern. In my interview with Jones I learned that when some documents arrived at the Foreign Relations Committee, Fulbright refused them, aware of their explosive nature and how the White House's fury at their having been leaked to Congress might play with the public. Fulbright—wisely, perhaps—told Jones to advise Ellsberg to go elsewhere with his documents. When I interviewed Jones in July 1997, he mentioned that he had documents among his private papers that added significant context to that aspect of the story. "Could I get a copy of them?" I asked. "Sure," he replied. A few days later, I received an envelope full of original documents. He told me to photocopy them and send them back, which I did, grateful for his blind trust in a writer he never met.

That was, perhaps, the most difficult book I will ever write, if only because I was making final edits to the manuscript a few weeks before Cindy gave birth in June 1999 to our twin boy and girl, Robert and Avery. Overwhelmed with two infants and my new job as Breaux's state director, I begged my editor at Basic Books to give me an extra six months to finish the book, which he did. Cindy, who owned and managed a decorator fabric business in Baton Rouge for the first seven years of our marriage, decided a few months later that being a mom was the full-time job she wanted. She sold her building, liquidated her inventory, and spent seven happy years at home with our children until they started school, and in 2006 she became executive director of the Louisiana Prison Chapel Foundation. For the next ten years, with the help of an active board, she raised millions of dollars and presided over the construction of about a dozen chapels in state prisons.

Avery and Robert were almost three when Cindy and I took them to Washington the first time to meet Senator John Breaux in his office.

When *A Grand Delusion* finally came out in January 2001, the reviews gratified me. The *Denver Post* review said I "permanently altered the landscape of serious scholarly debate on the one topic that draws passionate scholarly attention." *Kirkus Reviews* noted my Senate staff experience and observed that I combined my "insider's understanding of the era's political climate with a keen talent for narrative history to produce an insightful analysis of the American experience in Indochina." *Library Journal* called it "a gripping tale, well told and voluminously documented." In the *Los Angeles Times*, Townsend Hoopes, who was Lyndon Johnson's undersecretary of the Air Force from 1967 to 1969, called the book "a considerable achievement" and wrote that it was an "exhaustively comprehensive indictment of the disastrous encounter between the United States and Vietnam." Perhaps most gratifying was the review in *Political Science Quarterly:* "Robert Mann has proved that, in history, there is never a last word. His book offers a vivid and well-written account of Vietnam as it played out in American politics."

In April 2001 news broke that former Democratic Nebraska Senator Bob Kerrey admitted a war crime—killing innocent women and children in a South Vietnam village while he served in Indochina in February 1969. Later that day, my literary agent suggested I write about the story in an op-ed and send it to the *New York Times*. I knew what I wanted to say. Within an hour, I banged out the basics of the column I would send to the *Times* early that afternoon. Within an hour of receiving it, the paper's op-ed editor called to confirm they would run it.

"Mr. Kerrey's disclosure is disturbing, and he should be commended for finally acknowledging the truth," I wrote. "Yet I fear this episode might cause us to spend too much time examining the misconduct and crimes of individual soldiers while ignoring the unconstitutional acts committed by our leaders in Washington in the 1960's and 1970's." While not diminishing the horror of the incident, I noted, "A collective calamity occurred in Washington in the mid-1960's that, in time, led to tragedies like those Mr. Kerrey and others have acknowledged. It was a calamity that might have been avoided if President Lyndon Johnson had been truthful with the American people and if members of Congress were not so eager to forsake their constitutional responsibilities." It began, I wrote, with the 1964 Gulf of Tonkin Resolution and metastasized from there. "Throughout the 1960's, members of Congress—most of them understanding little about Vietnam and our reasons for fighting—supported the American policy, many fearing political retribution if they did not. However, most leaders of both parties in Congress generally knew the futile and reckless nature of our involvement, but did too little to try to stop our headlong rush into Southeast Asia." My main point was this:

It took the deaths of more than 58,000 American soldiers—and between two and three million Vietnamese—and the erosion of public support before Congress finally mustered the "courage" to end a war that it had supported and financed for 10 years.

More than a quarter-century after the war ended, it seems more apparent than ever that our political leaders were culpable in the senseless deaths of Americans and Vietnamese—perhaps more so than Mr. Kerrey and the hundreds of thousands who took up arms. . . .

Bob Kerrey's conduct resulted in the deaths of more than a dozen civilians. Let us not forget that official decisions made in Washington—in the White House and in Congress—resulted in the needless deaths of millions.

In my haste to send the piece to the *Times*, I forgot to run it by Breaux or our DC press secretary. As with all my other writing and commentary that emanated from my books, Breaux was tolerant of a staffer, like me, with a separate career and identity. It did not hurt that Breaux spoke with Kerrey, who liked the piece.

In 2002, as President George W. Bush was pushing the country headlong into what we now know was a needless war against Iraq, I lamented that my Vietnam War book came out a year too early. Among the lessons that this war should have taught American leaders forevermore: humility in foreign interventions, especially inside a country whose culture and history were unknown to us; the need for great skepticism of the White House's argument for war; and the necessity of greater congressional oversight in matters of war. My understanding of the way Lyndon Johnson and his aides lied about the Gulf of Tonkin Resolution to prod Congress into giving him carte blanche in Vietnam made me cautious when—a couple of days after the September 11, 2001, terrorist attacks in New York, Washington, and Pennsylvania—Breaux shared with me the proposed language of a use-of-force resolution the White House provided to House and Senate members. The draft sought to grant the president power to "deter and preempt any future acts of terrorism or aggression against the United States."

That instantly reminded me of the Gulf of Tonkin Resolution, which allowed Johnson "to take all necessary steps, including the use of armed force, to assist any member or protocol state of the Southeast Asia Collective Defense Treaty requesting assistance in defense of its freedom." One could have driven a figurative eighteen-wheeler through the loophole in that language—and Lyndon Johnston did—and I feared the same would be said of the language the White House submitted to Congress.

The month before, upon its thirty-seventh anniversary, I had drafted an op-ed that looked at the legacy of the Gulf of Tonkin Resolution. In the piece, I warned that Congress should not relinquish its war powers to the president in a time of national crisis. I wrote: "If our tragic experience in Vietnam taught us anything, it is that the United States should never again go to war without the informed consent of the Congress and the American public. Part of our country's failure in Vietnam can be attributed to the fact that Americans and their elected representatives were never really included in the critical decisions that led up to our full-scale involvement. The tragedy is that Congress could have participated, but eagerly deferred to the president." I added that, regarding the Gulf of Tonkin Resolution, "while it might appear that those who voted for the resolution on August 7, 1964, were hapless dupes who were swindled by a wily and deceptive president, history suggests another and more troubling conclusion. By that I mean that Congress spent the better part of a decade giving up its war-making powers to the president." The overriding question my piece posed was this: "What is the proper, constitutional relationship between a president and the Congress when our nation considers the deployment of its military forces overseas?" I sent the piece to a few papers, but no one published it.

On the morning of Thursday, September 13, Breaux called me from Washington to discuss the Gulf of Tonkin Resolution and his determination that this crisis not lead Congress to make the same mistake twice. He had read *A Grand Delusion* and come to conclusions like mine. After we hung up, I recalled the op-ed I had written but never placed. I faxed it to him. Breaux read the piece, agreed with it, and took it to the Senate floor, where he asked Majority Leader Tom Daschle and Senator Hillary Clinton to read it. He then told White House officials he objected to the sweeping nature of the proposed use-of-force resolution and it would need to be tightened up to win his approval. An administration official later told Breaux and others they already knew they had a problem and would need to make concessions. After the resolution passed, including specific references to following the War Powers Act, Breaux phoned to tell me that my op-ed made an impact, not only with him, but on the Senate leadership, and that I helped him and others narrow the resolution.

The resolution's final language said: "The President is authorized to use all necessary and appropriate force against those nations, organizations, or persons he determines planned, authorized, committed, or aided the terrorist attacks that occurred on September 11, 2001, or harbored such organizations or persons, in order to prevent any future acts of international terrorism against the United States by such nations, organizations or persons."

MY BOOK WRITING not only gave me a creative outlet that I craved since the day I left journalism in 1985; it also sparked in me a greater desire to enter academia. I knew from the late 1990s that I wanted to be a college professor. But I only had a bachelor's degree in journalism. If I were ever to find a faculty job—in Louisiana or elsewhere—I knew I would need better credentials than that. For a while, I considered working on a PhD in political science at LSU, but enrolling in a graduate program would have meant quitting my job with Breaux and supporting a family on the meager stipend the school would pay me. In 1997, I learned about an external humanities master's program offered by California State University-Dominguez Hills, just outside Los Angeles. On a research trip to the Nixon Library, I visited the CSU-DH campus and was satisfied the program was sound and rigorous. Although parts of the program were online, these were days when email attachments and such were still rare. I would write my papers, put them into large manila envelopes with stamped, return-address envelopes inside, and mail them to my professors at Dominguez Hills. In a week or ten days, the marked-up, graded paper would arrive by return mail. I tailored my program so that, after the core courses, I enrolled mostly in history courses. I took several independent study courses that I and my professors crafted around research into the Vietnam War that I was already doing for my book. And for my thesis, I researched George McGovern's role in the Vietnam War and found room for most of it in my book. The CSU program was perfect for me and my schedule. It has always made me more sympathetic to the struggles of older students—many with children—who are working full-time jobs while trying to earn a degree. Colleges and universities are attracting lots of nontraditional students these days and I'm glad to see my institution, LSU, getting serious about offering online courses and degree programs.

With my master's degree in hand in August 2001, I called my friend John Maxwell Hamilton, dean of LSU's Manship School of Mass Communication. I first met Jack in Washington when he worked for the World Bank. And I had been talking with him for years about my desire to teach. In the fall of 2001, the school signed me up to teach as an adjunct, taking over an elections case-studies course that Sean Reilly, a former state representative who was CEO of Lamar Advertising Company, taught for several years. I led the class, for no pay, at Manship for four consecutive semesters—and loved it. After the first semester was over, I knew I had found my calling. I still had no idea how I might find my way onto a university faculty without a PhD, but I was getting closer.

14

I Really Don't Want to Do Another Campaign

Kathleen Babineaux Blanco was one of the more unusual politicians I'd ever met. While she had been successful at almost everything she tried in Louisiana politics—running for state representative, public service commissioner, and lieutenant governor—she was not the stereotypical political type. Soft-spoken and introverted, in 2002 she might not have impressed anyone new to Louisiana politics as the person most likely to be the state's first female governor. In almost every way, she was just a normal, understated person who did her job well and enjoyed meeting people. She wasn't the best at working a room. She would sometimes spend too much time with just a few people—engaging them in extended, meaningful conversation—unlike some of the grip-and-grin types who could sweep through, shake every hand, and kiss every baby.

Because she was so unassuming, people sometimes underestimated her strength and tenacity. Anyone who knew her well understood this was a mistake. Her spine was pure steel. God had given her a soft voice and forgiving nature, and her anger had a long fuse. But she could raise her voice when necessary and she had a temper that she wasn't afraid to use to shock and awe political opponents, especially when she knew they misjudged her as a meek little lady.

If I ever doubted her fortitude, such notions vanished in January 1997, when her nineteen-year-old son, Ben, died in a tragic industrial accident. A few days later, Blanco mustered the remarkable power to eulogize him. "A mother just has to say goodbye," she told mourners at his funeral that day. In the horrible weeks and months to follow, Blanco almost singlehandedly kept her large family together. She showed them all how to use their pain and grief to strengthen the bonds of their mutual love. And it worked. She and the rest of her family emerged stronger, their faith deeper, and more resilient.

By 2003, I had known the sixty-one-year-old Blanco for years and liked her immensely. When she announced as a gubernatorial candidate, I knew she would make a fine governor, if she could win the race. But I doubted if she could, especially against a crowded field of Democrats, including state Senate President Randy Ewing, former US Representative Claude "Buddy" Leach, and Attorney General Richard Ieyoub. John Breaux had briefly—and seriously—considered announcing his candidacy for governor in early 2002 but opted against it. Immediately after Breaux's announcement, Blanco told reporters, "I'm running." I should have seen there was an opportunity for Blanco in a field with three prominent male candidates, two of whom—Leach and Ieyoub—were from Lake Charles and would carve up the south Louisiana vote. If she played it right, that would leave an opening for Blanco.

What I could not see clearly at the time was that she had all the makings of a successful candidate. As lieutenant governor for eight years, she had trekked to every corner of Louisiana, bolstering the state's tourism marketing efforts and working with mayors and other local officials to promote their cities and towns to tourists. This work generated much goodwill among local officials who not only knew her well when she began running for governor, but liked and respected her for her tenacity and honesty.

Meanwhile, with Governor Mike Foster's backing, his thirty-two-year-old former Health Department secretary, Bobby Jindal, launched a strong run on the Republican side, opposed by fellow Republicans Hunt Downer, the former state House speaker from Houma, and Jay Blossman, a Public Service Commission member from Mandeville. Democrats Ieyoub and Leach spent most of the summer cutting each other up in southwest Louisiana, while Ewing's campaign never caught on. Then, Blossman dropped out, leaving the Republican race to Downer and Jindal. Most of the party's establishment fell behind Foster in supporting Jindal. So did officials in George W. Bush's White House, who had known Jindal when he served briefly as an assistant secretary in Bush's Department of Health and Human Services.

On election day, October 4, Jindal finished first with 32 percent of the vote. Blanco was a distant second at 18 percent. Ieyoub and Leach were not far behind. Had Leach or Ieyoub bowed out before election day, the other might have coalesced southwestern Louisiana and much of the state's Black vote to make the runoff with Jindal. But their competition opened the door for Blanco and she took it. Blanco and Jindal would advance to the November 15 runoff six weeks later.

As the second round began, many believed that Blanco was an underdog, although a quick counting of the votes would have suggested otherwise. The four Democrats together earned 57 percent. If Blanco could unite Democrats, win the endorsement of her former rivals, and persuade Democrats to vote again in November, she could beat Jindal. But few people, me included, thought she stood much of chance. A few days after the primary, Breaux called from Washington.

"I just got off the phone with Kathleen and told her I'd send you over to help during the runoff," he told me.

It was the first I'd heard of the arrangement. "Oh, man, I really don't want to do another campaign," I protested.

"It's just for six weeks and then you'll be back on my staff," he said.

I didn't have much choice. What could I do but be a good soldier and report for duty? Still, it was under some duress. For several years, I told Cindy and some friends that I wanted them to shoot me if I ever agreed to do another campaign. I hated my temperament in the heat of political battle. I was too competitive and aggressive. My instinct was to go for the jugular. I didn't like the bad behavior a campaign unleashed in me and I wanted to keep this dark side buried. Now, I'd have to confront those demons anew.

Within a few days, I reported for duty, joining Kathleen and her aide-de-camp, Rochelle Dugas, in Baton Rouge. My title would be communications director, but I was really a traveling press secretary. I would spend 80 percent of my time on the road with Blanco, while sometimes popping into party offices in Baton Rouge—where Mike Skinner, married to Cindy's sister, Jan, chaired the state organization—or Blanco's headquarters in Lafayette.

On my first day, I climbed into the backseat of Blanco's State Police Suburban for a trip across Interstate 10 to the Lake Charles Richmond Suites hotel for a fundraising dinner. When I heard "fundraiser," I imagined an ordinary political event, much like dozens I had attended over the years. These often featured a dinner of baked chicken, mashed potatoes, and green beans—or a fancier reception with beer, wine, and heavy hors d'oeuvres. This, however, would be a most unusual event. Upon entering the room, I noticed a large, colorful banner strung over the dais, proclaiming the event's host, someone named "Senator Swati." I didn't know every Louisiana state senator, but I knew there was no one in the Louisiana Senate with that name. "Who's Swati?" I asked. Someone told me it was Azam Khan Swati, a wealthy Pakistani business executive with sizable holdings in fuel distribution and real estate in southwest Louisiana and southeast Texas. He was a Texas lawyer who, from 2003 to 2011, would serve in Pakistan's national Senate.

With Blanco running against an Indian-American, someone in the campaign who knew a little about the historical distrust of Pakistanis for Indians had the clever idea to ask Swati to host a fundraiser for Blanco and invite dozens of Pakistanis from around southwest Louisiana. The room was full of wealthy American citizens of Pakistani descent, most of whom owned convenience stores and other small businesses. None wanted an Indian-American governor. I would never have imagined that geopolitics would influence a Louisiana governor's race, but here we were. By the end of the campaign, Blanco would collect over $100,000 from various Pakistanis and their businesses. Since Louisiana election law permits campaign contributions from corporations, most of the checks were from corporate accounts with no Pakistani-sounding name. I never discussed with Blanco the ethics of the campaign's decision to raise money based on the ethnic and cultural rivalry between Indians and Pakistanis, but such a fundraising scheme, while legal, was ill advised. We shouldn't have done it.

The Blanco campaign was a small, shoestring operation, headed by campaign manager Jeff Jenkins, an attorney and former aide in Blanco's lieutenant governor's office. Several staffers from her office or the Department of Tourism and Recreation, which she also headed, took leave to work on the campaign. There was also Ray Teddlie, a brilliant media consultant who had produced Blanco's television spots for years. A reclusive filmmaker who worked out of New Orleans, Teddlie was a gifted political strategist and creative genius. The true campaign manager was the candidate's husband, Raymond—as Kathleen called him—or "Coach," as everyone else knew him. He was vice president for student affairs at the University of Louisiana-Lafayette but had taken leave to work on the campaign.

Coach was a force of nature, a man of large appetites and grand gestures who dabbled in polling and political consulting. He was a political strategist, kingmaker, and—most of all—the guardian and chief architect of his wife's political career. Coach was the true politician in the family, at least as most people understand politicians. He was affable, animated, and committed to his wife's political career. When he wasn't in meetings or attending to university business, he seemed to spend much of his time calling his far-flung network of friends, associates, and former students and players, several of whom worked for his wife. As a former high school and college football coach, he knew how to motivate those around him to do his bidding. In one five-minute conversation with him, it was not unusual to be subjected to a maddening combination of quiet self-pity, gentle wooing, and loud hectoring. I had very few conversations with Coach over the years during which he didn't cover that range of behavior. Like the coach he was, he used whatever worked for the individual he was trying to motivate.

In disposition, Kathleen was the opposite of Coach. She rarely raised her voice. If anyone around her messed up, she was quick to forgive and forget. As I rode around Louisiana with her and Rochelle, bouncing up and down in the backseat of the State Police Suburban, I remembered all the reasons I had admired her and always enjoyed her company. She loved to laugh, even at herself. While she wasn't naïve about politics— she was as quick as anyone to recognize a blowhard or a con artist—she approached her work with openness and a spirit of generosity. As we moved from town to town, I noticed that people were always happy to see her. As one of the most prominent women in Louisiana political history, she was something of an anomaly. Sure, Mary Landrieu was serving in the US Senate but, in Louisiana, state politics mean more to most people. And so, Blanco's presence at events, small and large, also meant more.

And now that she was in a runoff, she was a credible contender to become the state's first woman governor. This drew people to her with even more passion. And she responded in ways that made her even more appealing. By that I mean she was humble, seemingly aware that she bore the dreams, aspirations, and expectations of several generations of Louisiana women. For two hundred years, men had governed Louisiana, and not always very well. For two centuries, no woman had come this close to winning the state's top job. Whether she won or not, everyone knew that Blanco was making history, breaking barriers, and setting new expectations for women and Louisiana government. And as a student of history, I was soon grateful Breaux had forced me into this front-row seat, whatever the campaign's outcome.

Sometimes, the thrills weren't political. One day early in my tenure on the campaign, we headed to the Houma airport for a flight to some event in north Louisiana. For years, I had flown around the state with Breaux. We used a plane rarely, but when we flew it was almost always in a King Air we hired from a Louisiana aircraft company. The King Air was a relatively spacious, two-engine plane that would seat comfortably seven or eight passengers and boasted an airspeed of around 350 miles an hour. When we pulled up to the airport, I scanned the tarmac. I did not see a King Air. Instead, we pulled aside a smaller, single-engine plane with room for only four people, including the pilot—in this case, a pilot named "Boogie." I was skeptical, but Blanco seemed comfortable placing our lives in his hands. She and I pressed ourselves into the slender aircraft, our knees almost touching. And off we went, hurtling through the skies, all at the mercy of some guy named "Boogie." I learned later that this was Darryl "Boogie" DiMaggio, a seasoned pilot who had published a book entitled *Swamp Eagles*, about his passion for flying seaplanes. We were in good hands.

WHILE I DIDN'T think Kathleen had much chance of beating Jindal, this didn't mean I wouldn't work as hard as possible to help her win. To do this, Teddlie, Jenkins, and I had to persuade her and Coach to run Teddlie's spots attacking Jindal. This was complicated by the fact that Jindal, early in the runoff, pledged not to air negative ads against Blanco and challenged her to do the same. She agreed and now worried about the consequences of breaking her promise. Our position was that Blanco agreed not to attack Jindal *personally*. "It's not negative campaigning to criticize his record," I preached more than once. "The essence of political campaigns is comparing your record to your opponent's. Voters are fine with comparing records. They hate personal attacks." She and Coach agreed.

In debates and interviews, Blanco was eager to critique Jindal's record in Washington or during his time in Foster's cabinet. "Bobby," she said in a television debate in late October, "you say you're a problem solver, but we were number ten in childhood immunizations, and at the end of your term [as Foster's health secretary], we were thirty-ninth." Jindal didn't take the criticism well. "Basically," he complained, "they've accused me of hating everything from puppies to kittens." He added, "This is what desperate campaigns do when they fall behind. They start throwing mud and calling names instead of focusing on the issues." Blanco, however, refused to let up her criticism in the press and in debates. Attacking Jindal as unqualified for the various jobs Foster had given him—he had already briefly served as president of the University of Louisiana System—Blanco flung this barb: "The ship of state does not come with training wheels." It may have been the closest she came to a personal attack on Jindal.

Jindal pretended to take the high road, but he was content to allow Foster to attack Blanco on his behalf. This took the form of an ostensible assault on Coach but was, in fact, an effort to question if a woman could run the state without taking direction from her husband. In late October, Foster went on his weekly statewide radio show to suggest that if Blanco were elected, Coach would become "the most powerful man in the state." When asked about Foster's attack, Coach protested, "I've never been involved in her work, and she's never been involved in mine." I'm sure Kathleen rarely, if ever, inserted herself into Coach's job. It was not accurate, however, to suggest that Coach never stuck his nose in her business. In fact, he lived vicariously through her political career. There was no shame in that, but I suppose it was all Coach thought he could say. Perhaps he should have said, instead, "I take an active role in Kathleen's campaigns. What spouse doesn't help when possible? I don't tell her how to run the lieutenant governor's office. She answers to her constituents, not me."

When challenged about his sexist remark, Foster shrugged and protested he "meant no disrespect for anybody." In Foster's defense, the statement about Coach's power and influence came in response to a caller's question. On his own, however, Foster attacked Blanco, trying to associate her with Edwin Edwards. Other than the fact that some Democrats who once supported Edwards' campaigns were now helping Blanco, the two had almost no association or political alliance. Although they would become friends later, Blanco had always opposed the ethically challenged way Edwards ran the state. Jindal disavowed Foster's attacks when it became clear they were undermining his self-styled image as someone who didn't run a negative campaign. "I don't think they were necessary," Jindal finally told reporters. "I don't think they were constructive. I would say to the governor, 'Either stay positive or don't talk about the governor's race.'"

For the first three or four weeks of the runoff, Kathleen and Coach were unsure if they could get away with attacking Jindal's record. As we vacillated, political reporters like John Maginnis realized that Blanco's campaign was foundering. "Stumbling out of the blocks in the runoff," he later wrote in his statewide column, "the Blanco campaign drifted for three weeks as she raised money and struggled to organize her vastly expanded operation. Jindal, seizing momentum, put her on the defensive with his claims she was running a negative campaign against him. Would that she were, thought many Blanco supporters, who were distressed the candidate was not taking the fight to Jindal as he stretched his lead in the polls."

While I wanted Blanco to attack Jindal in TV spots, I wasn't sure if she could survive the potential backlash from running what Jindal and others would label as a "negative campaign." But I was certain she would lose if she refused to go after Jindal's biggest perceived strength—his healthcare expertise. When I joined the campaign, I gave her and Coach a memo spelling out how I thought she should oppose Jindal. I wrote:

Recognize that several of Jindal's perceived strengths can be viewed as weaknesses to be exploited.

A. Intelligence/Ideas/Programs: Here's where Jindal is actually weaker than people think. He is running as much on his ideas as his personality. He is young and relatively inexperienced. He has never held public office. He has never had to lead in the way the governor's job requires. His job will be to persuade the people of the state to vote for him despite these shortcomings because he believes he is the smarter candidate with better ideas. Here's where [Blanco] actually has the advantage, if she will play it.

Instead of trying to debate Jindal on the issues, the goal of this campaign should be to communicate to voters images that demonstrate how much [Blanco] shares their concerns. Jindal may have good ideas, and so does [Blanco]; but [Blanco] understands these issues in ways that Jindal does not—*she cares about these issues more deeply*. And, more importantly, [Blanco] *possesses the values that make it most likely that she will be able to deal effectively with these problems.*

B. Youth/Vigor: Here again, Jindal's youth should be contrasted with images that emphasize and expose [Blanco's] maturity, wisdom, and experience.

We should not be afraid to use fear of the unknown and fear of the known.

In many ways Jindal is a large unknown. He is young and inexperienced. The campaign should exploit this to inject a bit of fear into the electorate and cause them to wonder why they would want to elect a young, inexperienced person when they can vote for someone experienced, wise, and who will run the state with a steady hand.

In ways that Jindal is known (i.e., his public record), this should also be exploited to say that we don't know much about the guy, but what we do know should scare anyone who cares about the health and education of our families.

This advice was not brilliant insight, unique to me. It was what any smart campaign would do—deny the opponent the ability to campaign on his or her strength. If your opponent has built a campaign about his exemplary ethical behavior, you'd better search for personal or financial misconduct in his background. In politics, if you want to campaign as a squeaky-clean politician, you must prove it or be able to withstand the scrutiny. With healthcare, Jindal's record could not withstand scrutiny. His record working for Foster was littered with severe, harmful cuts of health services for poor families. We didn't have to work hard or twist facts to make that case. We only needed to remind people of what they already knew.

For weeks, Jindal aired TV spots attacking not Blanco's record but her decision to run a negative campaign. Blanco had been attacking Jindal in speeches and debates, but she had not yet aired an ad critical of Jindal. No matter; Jindal alleged she did. Those attacks made her and Coach question whether they should start hitting Jindal in television and radio ads. "If we are getting attacked for running a negative campaign," I told them, "we might as well run one."

The most effective way to go after Jindal was clear to anyone who studied his deplorable record as Foster's health secretary. We discovered one of the best summaries of that record in mid-September on the pages of the *Baton Rouge Advocate*, in a letter to the editor by a local physician. The doctor wrote: "Working with uninsured patients, medical education and public health programs, I took interest in Gov. Mike Foster's advertisement printed in The *Sunday Advocate* on Sept. 7 in which he praises Bobby Jindal's record as secretary of the Department of Health and Hospitals and, in particular, Jindal's accomplishment in cutting the DHH budget. For those whose concern about health care goes beyond cutting budgets, the Jindal record is poor." The doctor—who practiced at Baton Rouge's charity hospital, the Earl K. Long Medical Center—reviewed Jindal's record and closed with this broadside: "Bobby Jindal is unquestionably a nice man who is young, well-spoken and intelligent. Yet he failed in his three goals as secretary of DHH. Contrary to what Gov. Foster says, Jindal's record at DHH does not indicate he is capable of the much harder job of governor." This was the first time I ever heard of the letter's author, Dr. Bill Cassidy, who would be elected to the state Senate, US House, and US Senate a few years later. In those days, he was a liberal Democrat who supported Mary Landrieu for reelection in 2002. In 2014, running as a conservative Republican, Cassidy would defeat her.

With the attacks by Cassidy and others in mind, Teddlie prepared several comparison spots. One was a thirty-second talking-head commercial featuring a disabled neurologist, Dr. Evan Howell, who appeared on camera in a wheelchair and launched a strong attack on Jindal's record as Foster's health secretary. His message proved devastating:

> I'm Dr. Evan Howell. I was a staff neurologist at Lallie Kemp Medical Center when Bobby Jindal was head of Health and Hospitals. The cuts he made to healthcare budgets hurt people. Patients were his victims. Many waiting months to see specialists. His decisions were disastrous for people. Mr. Jindal is not politically independent. Voters need to know his real record before they vote. And, by the way, I'm a staunch Republican.

For the rest of the campaign and beyond, Teddlie called him "Dr. Kevorkian," after the Michigan physician, Jack Kevorkian, who spent eight years in prison, beginning in 1999, for his role in about 130 assisted suicides. By the time Blanco and Coach agreed to run the spot, we were almost out of time. But the commercial went right at the heart of Jindal's perceived strength—his supposed healthcare expertise. And the would-be governor was a paper tiger. He could not take a punch. The spot, which started running the last ten days of the campaign, rocked the Jindal campaign back on its heels.

At first, they protested that Blanco was going negative. But having declared that Blanco's spot violated their sacred agreement (it didn't), Jindal couldn't run a similar ad. Instead, he could only play the aggrieved party and hope the attack on him would backfire. I also believe that Jindal's polling did not reveal the damage our spot caused. Two weeks before the election, one prominent poll showed Blanco down by eight points. But the spot was raising serious questions about Jindal's leadership. Too late did Jindal and his pollster realize that the attacks on TV and in direct mail pieces were working. The pieces mailed to Democratic women pointed out Jindal's extreme, no-exceptions position on abortion.

I expected that Jindal had blistering attack spots aimed at Blanco in the can and they would return fire as soon as we started shooting. "We'll soon be taking some pretty heavy incoming fire," I told Coach and Kathleen, still confident that attacking Jindal was our only option. After several days, however, there was no response. Confused, we wondered if Jindal wasn't responding because his polling suggested our spot was having no effect. A few days later, Teddlie added another attack ad to the mix, this one pointing out that, while Jindal laid off state healthcare workers, he accepted a $25,000 pay raise. Still, no Jindal commercials answered our attacks or lodged new allegations about Blanco. Speaking to reporters, Jindal defended himself, but his campaign stayed the course, confident of victory. And perhaps they can be forgiven for believing they had the election in the bag. Through the middle of the campaign's last week, most polling showed Jindal with a small-but-comfortable lead. Blanco never led in a poll since the primary.

In a story about the state of the race a few days before the election, Gannett reporter John Hill had trouble finding any observer who would predict a Blanco win. Pearson Cross, then a political science professor at the University of Louisiana at Monroe, told Hill, "It now appears as if the numbers are firming up and favoring Jindal." Pollster Verne Kennedy, who was running nightly surveys for a group of Republican and Democratic business executives, told Hill that Jindal's strategy of attacking Blanco for being negative paid off, because when her attack spots began airing, "her message wouldn't have the credibility she needed." He added, "Jindal's campaign has run a brilliant strategy."

There was one potential negative attack I knew I would never get Blanco or Coach to make, or allow me to make. A few weeks before election day, I received from an anonymous correspondent an envelope that contained two articles by Jindal, published in a conservative Catholic magazine, the *New Oxford Review*. He wrote one in 1994, the other in 1996. In the 1996 piece, Jindal disparaged Protestantism, bemoaning a "scandalous series of divisions and new denominations" since the Protestant reformation. The 1994 article, however, was stunning. In it, Jindal described in vivid detail having taken part in an exorcism during his time as an undergraduate at Brown University. "Kneeling on the ground, my friends were chanting, 'Satan, I command you to leave this woman,'" Jindal wrote of trying to cast out an evil spirit from his girlfriend's body.

"Others exhorted all 'demons to leave in the name of Christ.'" While he didn't call the intervention an "exorcism," the vivid scene he painted sounded very much like what many people would remember from the 1973 movie *The Exorcist*.

While we couldn't attack Jindal for what many would consider a quirky—if not downright bizarre—religious practice, I thought voters needed to know about this. So, I slipped the two articles to a *Times-Picayune* reporter, Brian Thevenot, assigned to cover our campaign. The problem, Thevenot soon told me, was that "you gave me this stuff so late that my editors think they might influence the race unfairly." He was probably right. Today, with social media and blogs galore, it would have been easy to get the articles into the public eye. In 2003, however, there was no Facebook or Twitter and almost no political blogs that did original reporting. I tried to sell the stories to a few other reporters, but no one would publish them that close to election day.[1]

There was another reason Blanco was doing so well in the campaign's homestretch. In a statewide debate with Jindal, broadcast from WWL-TV in New Orleans on November 12, just days before the election, one moderator asked the two candidates to name the "most defining moment" of their lives. Jindal went first. He said it was "Christ finding me" and boasted about his Christian faith. Then, it was Blanco's turn. But she said nothing. From a private room in the station where I watched the debate on TV, I thought she had frozen and forgot the question. But she was steeling herself for what she knew she had to say. She would talk about the tragic death of her son Ben in 1997. "The most defining moment of my life came," she said, tamping down her emotions, "when I lost a child and found I could survive it. Those are moments when you know you have to have faith. It's hard for me to talk about it."

It still amazes me Blanco could have eulogized Ben at his funeral a few days after his tragic death. I could never have found such strength. But she also believed that Ben was communicating with her from the great beyond, sending comfort in moments when she most needed it. This, she later said, was one of those moments when Ben told her it was okay to talk about his death. It was a raw, honest answer about the most tragic and painful period of Kathleen Blanco's life. After that answer, I knew she had the momentum. Jindal, who had spoken robotically about his faith, looked awkward and phony. It was not his finest moment, but it was Blanco's.

While I could find no way to get Jindal's participation in a quasi-exorcism into the press, I did have a devious idea about getting the threat of a news story about it into Jindal's mind. The day of the final debate on WWL, I suggested to Blanco that she take a copy of his article with her to the television set. "When you sit down at the desk, put the story on top of your papers," I told her. "Make sure he can see it. Of course, you're not going to talk about it or wave it around on television, but Bobby won't know that. It might distract him and throw him off." By the end of the debate, Blanco's performance had been so impressive, I never thought to ask if she had tried my tactic. It didn't seem to matter as much as what she had accomplished with her rhetoric.

His poor debate performance aside, everyone seemed to think Jindal was running a flawless campaign. New Orleans Mayor Ray Nagin, a Democrat, bet on a Jindal victory and crossed party lines in mid-November to endorse the Republican candidate. His letter informing Blanco of the endorsement was dishonest and deceitful. I remember reading it in the front yard of Blanco's Lafayette home while cursing the mayor under my breath. Pollsters and pundits thought Jindal was cruising to victory. Everything seemed to go his way. He appeared to be the inevitable victor. Except he wasn't. Confident of victory or the victim of bad polling—or both—Jindal did not respond to Blanco's blistering attacks on his record until it was too late. "Kathleen Blanco's attack strategy is not working, or at least not working yet, anyway," Jindal's media consultant assured him in a memo leaked to a reporter a few days before the election. "While the current strategy of not counterattacking Blanco seems to be working, we need to stay vigilant in monitoring this."

A few days before the election, Verne Kennedy's surveys showed a turn in public opinion but still gave Jindal a nine-point lead. Kennedy told his subscribers that his overnight surveys suggested the beginning of a shift towards Blanco, but these were just one or two nights' numbers—a smaller sample with a large margin of error. It might have been noise, or it might have been evidence of a sudden turn in public opinion towards Blanco. What we know is that it was the latter. Blanco's spots had hit Jindal's soft underbelly. His numbers were collapsing in the campaign's final days and by the time he and his staff realized it, there was nothing they could do. "Jindal ran a perfect campaign for five weeks," John Maginnis told a national reporter. "But it's a six-week campaign." Blanco won the race with 52 percent to Jindal's 48 percent, capturing the office by 55,000 votes out of 1.4 million cast.

On election night, in the governor-elect's suite at the Lafayette Hilton, I watched the early returns come in as Blanco and her family absorbed the news about her historic victory. Six weeks earlier, I had signed on to the campaign with the expectation she would lose and I'd return to Breaux's staff by Christmas. Now, everything changed. I had not wanted to work for Blanco if she won (I needed just three more years with Breaux to secure my full Senate retirement), but my easy rapport with her and

Coach now made that prospect more appealing. What made working for her even more alluring was the prospect of serving a governor—a chief executive—after years of working for a member of the legislative branch. Still, I had not allowed myself to think about it much, if at all, because of the longshot nature of the campaign. Even through the middle of the final week of the campaign, it seemed unlikely we would win.

In Blanco's suite that night, before she left to go to the ballroom to give her victory speech to several hundred supporters, she and I sat at a dining room table. "I want you to work for me," she said. "You bring a sense of calm to this operation." Given my propensity to treat campaigns as blood sport, that was about the highest compliment anyone could pay me. Maybe, I thought, I had finally conquered my campaign demons.

15

We Had Our Senate President

I knew that state Senator Noble Ellington would not become Senate president the minute he pulled out his legislative guide and began sweating over it. In mid-November 2003, Governor-elect Blanco had composed letters to Ellington, a Democratic state senator from Winnsboro, and Don Hines, his Democratic Senate colleague from Bunkie. Both wanted to be president, a position elected by senators but selected by the governor. For reasons nobody fully understands, the House and Senate always allowed a new governor to pick legislative leaders, often down to the committee chairs.[1] In her letters, Blanco asked Ellington and Hines to tell her whom they proposed to name to committee chairmanships if they became Senate president. She gave me the letters and instructed me to track down both men, watch as they read her request, and return with their answers.

I found Ellington first. He was in his Senate office in the Capitol basement. A smooth-talking, friendly man with a Southern drawl, Ellington was one of the few Democrats in the Senate Blanco and others considered qualified for the president's job. Hines, a diminutive, crusty heart doctor, was the other contender. I wasn't sure Ellington was the strongest candidate for Senate leader, while I worried that the strident, liberal Hines could not unify senators of both parties around Blanco's legislative agenda. But the two men were apparently the best she could find in a body of many minnows and few whales. One person I considered a whale, Baton Rouge Senator Jay Dardenne, was a Republican who had supported Bobby Jindal for governor. A few advisors told Blanco she might want to consider Dardenne as the leader of a "team of rivals," but she shot that down. His vocal support for Jindal was a bridge too far for her and Coach. It would be Ellington or Hines. But who was better? I don't recall if it was she or Coach who devised the test of asking them for their committee chairs, but it was brilliant.

As Ellington squirmed at his desk, hunched over his legislative guidebook and scribbling down names, I sat in a chair across from him and waited. When I left his office about fifteen minutes later, I carried a list of proposed committee chairs, about half of whom had supported Jindal. Next, I went hunting for Hines. I found him in his apartment at the Pentagon Barracks, an ancient building near the Capitol that once served as quarters for Union and Confederate troops. The Barracks housed the Office of the Lieutenant Governor as well as a few dozen senior members of the House and Senate who rented living space from the state. I settled into the sofa across from Hines and handed him the letter. He read it and scowled. "I don't know how I can answer this," he grumbled, handing the paper back to me. "I need to know who she wants me to appoint."

Ding, ding, ding. We had our Senate president. As Hines understood, Blanco wasn't looking for names; she was looking for loyalty. Hines' answer settled the matter. She announced her support for him in late November, along with her endorsement of Joe Salter, a longtime representative from Sabine Parish, to serve as House speaker. A former high school principal, Salter had not been a force in the House before Blanco tapped him, but she trusted him and valued his friendship and his counsel. She also knew that his colleagues admired Joe for his integrity and modesty.

I was now working as the communications director for Blanco's transition. Despite my original desire to go back to Breaux's office as quickly as possible, I got caught up in the emotion of scoring this improbable victory. When Blanco had invited me to join her administration on election night, I had accepted on the spot. Maybe it was my ego. It could have been an inability to say no to a governor asking for my help. It was probably a combination of both. For whatever reason, I was still fully on her team—for now, at least.

Until Blanco's inauguration in mid-January, we would work from temporary space at Louisiana State University. The school's Baton Rouge campus usually provides offices for each incoming governor for modest costs. Within a few days of the election, a few other staff members and I were wandering through a spartan suite of offices on the second floor of Hatcher Hall, a sixty-two-year-old former dormitory the school converted into academic space. The back of the building faced the east side of Tiger Stadium. LSU's Facility Services workers quickly transformed one of the largest rooms—two former dorm rooms with the separating wall knocked out to create one large office—into a suite for Blanco to use for meetings. Members of the fast-growing staff staked out the twenty or so offices on the floor. Mine had a window that faced Field House Drive and featured a decades-old standard-issue desk, two metal chairs of even older vintage, and a phone. For weeks, I would work long hours from this space as I struggled to keep my head above the deluge of press calls

A few days after Kathleen Blanco defeated Bobby Jindal in the 2003 governor's race, I was at her LSU transition headquarters checking out the new digs. This former dorm room in Hatcher Hall would be her office for the next two months. (Photo courtesy of *The Advocate/*Bill Feig)

and messages from friends and acquaintances, and entreaties from rank strangers who wanted to get their resumes before the governor-elect. It never stopped. My phone rang all day and part of the night. One person even pushed her resume into my hands at church one Sunday morning.

I should have been back in Breaux's office. I had not told him I planned to leave his staff and work for Blanco because I soon had second thoughts about accepting her job offer. At first, she suggested making me policy director, a position for which I did not feel qualified. I knew a little about policy, but it wasn't in my wheelhouse, and the idea of leading a policy shop, especially for a governor, gave me heartburn. I also considered the financial implications of walking away from my Senate retirement just three years shy of the twenty-year mark in Senate service. If I could get two decades, I could start collecting retirement when I turned fifty. Falling short of that milestone meant I wouldn't be eligible for benefits until I turned sixty-two. It was a big decision that could cost me hundreds of thousands of dollars. There was also the fact that I enjoyed working for Breaux. I'd been with him in one role or another for seventeen years. He was not only the most gifted politician in Louisiana; he was also a great boss and a friend. He was easy to work for and cared about his staffers. I always thought Breaux was like how Paul Begala once described Bill Clinton to me: "Clinton made us all look like geniuses." Breaux's natural political gifts made me look a lot smarter than I was. For all those reasons and more, I went to see Blanco to tell her I had changed my mind. I needed to go back to Breaux's staff. She and Coach said they understood and wished me well, while asking me to at least stay through the transition. With Breaux's blessing, I agreed.

And then I got wind from a few people in the DC office that Breaux was thinking of retiring from the Senate at the end of his third term, in January 2005. Fred Hatfield, our chief of staff, told me he was unsure what Breaux would do, but he would decide before year's end. He asked me to draft a statement in which Breaux announced his reelection. I'd helped write two of these speeches for Breaux over the years, so a third would be easy. Somehow, amid all my crushing workload in the transition office that late November-early December, I found time to draft a reelection statement. But as the days went on, my instincts suggested he wouldn't need it.

Breaux came to Baton Rouge on Wednesday, December 17, and told staff members he would announce his decision to the public the following day. After more than thirty years in Congress, eighteen of them in the Senate, he wouldn't run again. I was prepared for it. He had toyed with not running the previous election, and he had even once tried to persuade President Bill Clinton to appoint him ambassador to France. Breaux was a social animal who thrived on hunting down legislative deals. He was as dedicated to the principle of bipartisan progress as anyone I've ever known. By 2003, many of the moderate Republicans and Democrats

My parents, Robert and Charlene Mann, with Senator John Breaux.

who were allies during his first two Senate terms were gone, replaced by more partisan politicians. To some of these committed liberals and conservatives, "compromise" was a dirty word. Breaux detested the partisanship that infected Congress, and he knew that a fourth term would be even more frustrating than his third.

There was also the fact that after three terms, he was still not the chair of a major legislative committee. For several years, he had made the most of chairing the Senate's Select Committee on Aging, but that panel could not pass legislation. When elected in 1986, Breaux had the misfortune of joining the Finance and Commerce committees behind several Democrats who were about his age and not going anywhere. He might not get a chairmanship until a fifth Senate term. As Russell Long once told me, "You've not fully experienced being a US senator until you've chaired a committee."

On the morning of December 18—my eleventh wedding anniversary—I watched Breaux walk to the lectern in a room at the downtown Sheraton Hotel and make his announcement. He struggled through his brief statement, almost breaking down at several points. We all struggled to maintain our composure as he spoke. "There comes a time in every career when it is time to step aside," Breaux said. "And for my family and me that time has arrived." Breaux was only fifty-nine, three years younger than me as I write this. Even now, as he remains energetic in his mid-seventies, it's hard for me to believe he no longer represents Louisiana in Congress. His successor, David Vitter, was an embarrassment to the state and unpopular with his Senate colleagues, even Republicans (this was also true when Vitter served in the state House). Louisiana fell in firepower, influence, and intellectual heft in Washington. In his retirement announcement, Breaux noted: "Throughout my years in Congress, I have been guided by a simple philosophy to make government work for everyone. My sincere hope is that future Congresses will be able to pursue the center-out coalitions that I advocated. It is my hope that cooperation and legitimate compromise between our political parties will not be seen as political failure but as a means of building a stronger democracy that serves our nation." Today, it's clear Breaux's "sincere hope" was only a dream. Our parties are farther apart and less cooperative than ever. Few leaders like Breaux are left.

January 2005 would not only be the end of an era in Louisiana politics; it would be the end of my Senate employment. I reconsidered the wisdom of turning down that job offer from Blanco. I still had my Senate job for another year, but I knew I'd spend much of 2004 looking for work. Better to jump to a job I hoped was still on the table than wait around for something else to develop. I went back to Blanco and told her I'd changed my mind again. The policy director job was no longer available, but I hoped there might be a role for me in her administration. Within a few days, she asked me to serve as her communications director.

A few days later, Blanco announced my appointment and several others to her senior staff. Andy Kopplin, who had been Governor Mike Foster's chief of staff, would serve in the same role for her. It was an unorthodox decision. I had been friends with Andy since his first days in Baton Rouge and knew him to be a liberal-leaning policy wonk. He cared so much about making good policy that he had gone to work for the Republican Foster, as policy director and, later, as his chief of staff. Blanco knew Andy well enough to know he'd be loyal to her while continuing to work on the issues he cared about. Andy's good friend Terry Ryder, formerly Foster's deputy chief of staff and special counsel, also joined Blanco's staff. Blanco gave me some latitude to help her hire a press secretary. It took me two minutes to identify whom we needed: Denise Bottcher. A former television reporter from Houston, she was communications director for Attorney General Richard Ieyoub when I met her. We had been good friends for years and members of the same Sunday school class at our church. Nobody was better for this challenging job.

The period between election day and Blanco's January 12 inauguration was a blur, but it was nothing like the whirlwind of working in a governor's office in the first few months of a new administration. Many of us were learning our way around the building, assembling our offices and staffs, finding office space, securing parking spots, and unveiling and defending a new state budget, all while dealing with an expected $684 million budget shortfall and preparing for Blanco's first legislative session that spring.

Unlike Foster, who was known for his dislike of travel, even on behalf of economic development, Blanco was well versed in traversing the state and supporting Louisiana tourism. Promoting Louisiana's businesses and working hard to lure new industry to the state came naturally to her. Even before she was sworn in as governor, she was moving around Louisiana, meeting with political and business leaders and signaling she would be the activist governor Foster never was. In her first six weeks as governor, we traveled to places like Shreveport and Monroe more than Foster had in his eight years running the state. I saw how easy it was to impress people by just showing up. Civic leaders in cities large and small felt neglected by a governor who, while managing government competently, had little interest in getting out and meeting new people. Instead of traveling the state, Foster found time to enroll in evening law classes at Southern University during his second term. A homebody, he rarely spent the night in the Governor's Mansion, flying by State

Police helicopter to his antebellum mansion in Franklin most evenings. When Blanco showed up in places like Mansfield, Sulphur, Hammond, or Bastrop, it was often the first time anyone there had seen a governor in years. And people there were charmed by her attention to them. It mattered not so much what she did and said. Her presence was enough.

"Hats off to our new governor for the interest she is showing in the business of North Louisiana," a reader wrote in a letter published in the *Shreveport Times* in late January, just ten days after Blanco took office. "Although I did not cast my vote for Kathleen Blanco, I am impressed with her so far. Her genuine concern in the area of the state that has been ignored is refreshing." A few days later, John Hill, who covered politics for the state's Gannett papers, noted that "two days after taking her oath of office, [Blanco] was on the road, going to Minden." Blanco's wide travels around the state were "the sort of thing every governor—well, almost every governor—would do," Hill observed. "The reason it seems so remarkable is that it just hasn't been done for so long that we in Louisiana have forgotten what it's like to have a governor traveling to assist local economic development projects."

Blanco was so approachable and self-effacing that it was sometimes easy to forget she was the governor of Louisiana. On our first trip to Shreveport in 2004, at a reception at a private club with local leaders, she pulled me aside and whispered that a senior aide to the mayor kept calling her "Kathleen" in front of others. "Can you tell her address me as 'Governor'"? she asked. I swallowed hard and pulled the woman aside. "Look, I know she's always been 'Kathleen' to you," I said. "She was to me, too. But she's the governor now and deserves the respect of the title." I'm agnostic on the practice of calling elected officials by their first names, especially in informal settings. Because of our age difference and his exalted status, I never addressed Russell Long as anything other than "Senator Long" or, sometimes, "Boss." In private, I had usually addressed Breaux as "John" and, later, "JB." He never seemed to mind and never insisted on us using his title. But a governor was in a different orbit of public official. Even though I had called her "Kathleen" for years, it now seemed improper to address as her anything but "Governor."

In almost every way, Blanco was a delight to work for. She was rarely demanding and never overbearing. She was eager to listen to the views of others. In meetings with legislators or business executives, she often did the least talking of anyone in the room. She knew the names of the spouses and children of her staff members. When someone got sick, lost a loved one, or suffered tragedy, she was at her best. She was always a person of deep faith and impressive empathy, but the sudden and horrific loss of her son Ben had shown her a side of grief and loss that she now channeled into counseling and holding—literally—others in their time of trial. Over the years, I lost count of the number of people who told me about Kathleen and Coach showing up to a funeral or calling hospital rooms to pay respects or show their concern.

Both Blancos knew that faith was an important part of my life. Coach often jokingly called me "The Methodist," while Blanco and I often talked about our respective faiths in deeper ways. After a while, at staff luncheons and other events at the Mansion where a meal was being served, she would often call on me to say grace before the eating commenced. I thought that I was serious about my faith, but Kathleen Blanco was as devout a Catholic as I'll ever meet. She was proud of the prayer stand that an inmate built for her in the Mansion's basement woodworking shop. I think she used it often. Some of our conversations about faith concerned Cindy's and my involvement in the Kairos Prison Ministry and Cindy's role as executive director of the Louisiana Prison Chapel Foundation. When Cindy asked, Blanco eagerly agreed to serve as honorary chair of the foundation's board and hosted a fundraiser for the foundation on the Mansion's front lawn.

Because she believed I understood her faith, Blanco summoned me to her office one afternoon in the spring of 2004 to talk about the first Governor's Prayer Breakfast of her term. It was an annual event, held in a local hotel ballroom before the beginning of each legislative session. Hundreds of pastors, laypeople, legislators, and other elected officials showed up to hear a guest speaker and pray for the state's leaders. Blanco, however, was taken aback by the overwhelming White Evangelical flavor of the event. There was not a single Catholic priest on the dais. She instructed me to go see Senate President Pro Tempore Sharon Weston Broome (later mayor-president of East Baton Rouge Parish), relay her complaints, and work out a better program for the following year. Broome, a devout Evangelical, was among the planners of the annual event.

"You go tell Sharon if they want me to show up next year," she said, "they need to make some changes." Among her requests, she wanted a priest and a rabbi on the program. She wanted to transform the Evangelical event into an interfaith function. And she wanted more racial diversity. My meeting with Broome was not easy. Sharon was skeptical of several of the governor's ideas about transforming the event. "This is what she wants," I told Broome. "She was pretty clear that she won't come back next year if the committee doesn't make some changes." Within a few weeks, I got word that the planning committee appreciated the governor's input. The next year's program, to her delight, had a decidedly more interfaith flavor.

WHILE MY RELATIONSHIP with Blanco became a bit more formal, nothing much changed with Coach. For years, we had encountered each other at political events around the state. While Breaux and Blanco worked the room, Coach would often sidle up and regale me with stories about his impoverished childhood in Birmingham, Alabama, or talk about his days coaching high school and college football. Mostly, he shared his thoughts about Louisiana politics. In the history of Louisiana, I'm certain there has never been a political spouse more active in politics than Raymond Blanco. From sunup to midnight, he devoured politics and political intrigue like a starving man. His appetite for political news and gossip was insatiable. A bear of man, he was boisterous, never shy with his opinions, and encyclopedic in his knowledge of Louisiana and American political history.

Coach often seemed to assume I knew exactly what he was talking about. A conversation with him, especially by phone, was sometimes a breathtaking, confounding experience. It often seemed as if he had started the conversation with me five minutes before he dialed my number. I sometimes had to tell him to stop, back up, and start from the beginning or simply explain what the heck he was talking about. He also had an amazing capacity to absorb and process personal criticism or disagreement. If I thought he was wrong—and I often did—he made it clear I was perfectly within my rights to tell him so. He was self-assured enough that criticism and strong disagreement never bothered him. More than anything, he was delightful company. He loved to laugh, cry, shout, and sing—sometimes all in the span of ten minutes. He was and remains one of the most interesting and compelling people I ever knew in politics. While he sometimes drove me crazy with his phone calls and hectoring, I loved his company. And I loved him.

GOVERNOR BLANCO WAS not only traveling widely in Louisiana. In early February, she and Coach summoned me to the Mansion one afternoon to inform me that President George W. Bush had invited her to travel to Iraq to visit Louisiana troops. She would fly, in secret, with five other governors on a military plane. We could tell no one about the trip, for safety reasons. The Pentagon would announce the delegation's visit after they landed in Baghdad. There was only one problem. When the Defense Department told Blanco she could invite one home-state journalist to join her, she chose Gannett's John Hill. John and I were longtime friends. He was a well-respected veteran of press row and one of Blanco's favorites. He was not only a great reporter; he was also excellent company. But we soon found that his selection angered most reporters on press row. He was a friendly competitor but a competitor nonetheless.

As much as they liked John—and he agreed to share his notes with other reporters—Blanco was giving an advantage to one group of newspapers, including the *Shreveport Times*, the *Monroe News-Star*, and the *Lafayette Daily Advertiser*. The safer choice would have been to take an Associated Press reporter, like Melinda Deslatte or Adam Nossiter. All the major papers in the state were AP members and would get equal access to the wire service's coverage of the trip. All we could do was listen to the complaints from the *Advocate, Times-Picayune,* and Associated Press and tell them we were sorry. It was a valuable reminder about the dangers of giving one reporter a scoop unavailable to others.

Back home after a few days, Blanco dived right back into her new job, with an emphasis on energizing Louisiana's economy. Within days, she called a special legislative session to push through bills eliminating two corporate taxes (a seven-year phase-out of the state tax on corporate debt and the sales tax on machinery and equipment), which fulfilled a major campaign promise. The taxes weren't major business killers, but they weren't helping create jobs, either. And her decision to address them during a special session (the state's constitution allows fiscal bills in odd-numbered years only) proved that she was serious about promoting business development and job creation.

With the governor behind them, both houses passed her bills, even though the business community wanted an immediate repeal of the corporate debt tax. Blanco, however, held out for a gradual phase-out that wouldn't knock a bigger hole in the state's budget. She proposed eight years and settled for seven. She also took the same fiscally sound approach to another item in the special session, the renewal of a sales tax on business utilities that some businesses—particularly the chemical industry—hated. With a budget crunch, the state could not give up the $160 million a year the taxes generated. All three of the business and tax bills passed. Even state Senator Robert Barham, an Oak Ridge Republican and not a Blanco supporter, was impressed. "I have to praise her for doing what I could only dream about," Barham told a reporter. As chair of the Senate's Revenue and Fiscal Affairs Committee under Mike Foster, Barham had moved the same bills out of the Senate, only to have Foster—a Republican—block them in the House.

Blanco also focused on the plight of those without health insurance. In early March, she invited John Breaux to co-chair a two-day statewide summit in New Orleans to draw attention to Louisiana's high percentage of people without health insurance, and to brainstorm solutions. This was five years before President Barack Obama would push his healthcare plan through Congress giving states the funds to expand Medicaid. And it was twelve long years before Bobby Jindal's two terms would expire and a new governor, John Bel Edwards, would take advantage of the law to extend lifesaving health coverage to more than 400,000 individuals. Over seven hundred people attended the summit, but broad agreement on solutions was impossible without the federal involvement Obamacare eventually provided.

While Blanco also focused on reforming the state's juvenile justice system—it was often violent and dysfunctional, and did more harm than good to young offenders—and expanding early childhood education, nothing consumed her time more than creating and attracting new jobs. In March 2005, she led a controversial-but-productive trade mission to Cuba. In Havana, she signed a deal to sell $15 million in Louisiana agriculture goods to Cuba over the following eighteen months. After a private lunch with Fidel Castro, she left with a fistful of cigars the Cuban dictator fished from his desk humidor and handed to her. I'm not sure if bringing them back to the United States broke any law, but when Blanco returned, she gave the cigars to several staff members. I got one and have always regretted I didn't keep and frame mine. Instead, I handed it over to a friend who was an avid cigar smoker. The Cuba trip won Blanco praise. "Kathleen Blanco has made economic development and bolstering the economy main elements during her first term as governor," the *Monroe News-Star* said in an editorial. "She has shown an eager willingness to travel to promote Louisiana and what it has to offer."

While traveling to Cuba and eliminating some taxes would bring us good press and win some friends and new admirers, nothing bolstered Blanco's bona fides as a "jobs governor" more than the blockbuster announcement she made in June 2004. For months, she and her Economic Development team, including Louisiana Economic Development Secretary Mike Olivier, worked to persuade Chicago-based Union Tank Car Co., which manufactured railroad tank cars, to open its new plant in Alexandria. The proposed $100 million facility would employ 850 workers who would earn good salaries. Blanco was dogged and tireless in her pursuit of the company. She not only offered $65 million in state financial incentives—we called the state's campaign "Project U"—to induce company officials to locate in Louisiana; she got involved in the project in ways that previous governors, especially Foster, would not have imagined.

When the company announced in early March 2004 that it would deal exclusively with Texas for the new plant location, it appeared we had lost. But Blanco refused to take no for an answer. She wrote, then phoned, the company's president and forced Louisiana back into the negotiations. Within a few months, the state won the contract. "The only reason the company is coming to Louisiana," Gannett's John Hill wrote in June, "is

Blanco's aggressive pursuit of the company." Said the *Alexandria Town-Talk* in an editorial: "Blanco's success in winning over [the company] may be the object lesson that other Louisiana governors failed to learn: that dealing honestly and aggressively with business leaders pays off."

On the day we got the news about the deal, I was looking out the window of my corner office on the fifth floor of the Capitol building, almost directly above Blanco's spacious fourth-floor office. From my perch, looking south and west, I could see the Mississippi River and the railroad tracks than ran along the levee between the river and River Road. There, a long freight train had stopped. On a hunch, Denise and I sent a staffer to see if any of the cars had the Union Tank Car logo on them. To our delight, they did. The train would be a perfect backdrop for the press conference announcing the state's deal with the company. After a phone call to the railroad to ensure it would not move the train for a few hours, we hustled to set up a podium in front of one of the cars and alerted the press to the impromptu site. "Project U has made a U-turn," Blanco told reporters.

Even when she failed to attract a business prospect, Blanco came off looking strong and compassionate. For example, only a month into her term, State Farm Insurance announced it would close its large facility in Monroe. It was a blow to Blanco and her LED team, who fought hard to persuade the company to stay in northeast Louisiana. Most governors might have issued a statement of regret and moved on. Blanco's instinct was different. She flew immediately to Monroe, where she met with local leaders and assured them she would do everything she could to help the community recover. We weren't entirely sure how local officials would receive her. The loss of State Farm would be a massive hit to the area's economy. To my delight, when she walked into the room for the meeting, everyone stood and applauded her. It was a fitting tribute to the governor that this crowd knew she was with them and would not abandon them. Even we she "failed," Blanco found a way turn it into a win.

We were off to a good start.

16

I'M GOING TO KILL BOB MANN!

The summer of 2004 also featured the heated presidential election between incumbent George W. Bush and Democratic nominee John Kerry, then a US senator from Massachusetts. US troops were embroiled in Bush's ill-fated war in Iraq, which became less popular every day as US casualties increased and Americans learned Iraq never had the weapons of mass destruction that Bush and his aides claimed.

While Kerry attacked Bush over the war, Bush's allies smeared Kerry over his service in the Vietnam War, saying he did not deserve his Bronze Star for heroic actions in battle, nor his Purple Hearts for injuries sustained while he captained an American Swift Boat in South Vietnam. Bush didn't escape scrutiny over his own record during Vietnam. While he avoided combat in Vietnam by enlisting in the Texas Air National Guard in 1968, it appeared that he failed to attend flight drills, as required, in 1972. The race was ugly, as both candidates traded insults. Bush called Kerry a "Massachusetts liberal" and a "flip-flopper," while Kerry labeled Bush a "bully" who went to war in Iraq without building a bona fide international coalition.

Blanco had not endorsed a candidate during the crowded Democratic primaries, but by early March 2004 it was clear Kerry would win the Democratic nomination. When Kerry visited Baton Rouge before the state's March 11 party primary, his campaign asked Blanco if she would host a rally for the presumptive nominee. She agreed. She and Kerry had not met before, but they enjoyed an easy rapport as they talked inside the Mansion before the rally. Outside, on a stage erected in the Mansion's parking lot, Blanco introduced the Democratic candidate as "the next president."

Four months later, in July, she and Coach attended the Democratic National Convention in Boston, where delegates would nominate Kerry. Having attended the 1988, 1992, and 2000 Democratic conventions with Breaux, I was eager to add one more to my resume. I volunteered to staff

Blanco on the trip. We flew up on Bell South's corporate jet with the company's top Louisiana executive, Bill Oliver, who hosted us the first night at the most lavish dinner I ever attended. Bill rented out a room at an exclusive club near the Boston Common. Each of seven or eight courses featured a different wine. It must have set the company back a small fortune. It took me three days to recover from the meal.

The only real drama that week involved the governor's husband. One day, with the governor off shopping or meeting with someone, I had a little free time. I wandered down from Tremont Hotel, where Blanco and the Louisiana delegation stayed, to a small diner for lunch. Before I could order, my phone rang. It was Coach. "Where are you?" he asked. I told him I was at lunch and had just sat down. "I'm on my way," he said. Within five minutes, he was sliding into my booth. We ate and talked for more than an hour. Towards the end of the meal, the head of Coach's State Police detail called me. "Do you know where Coach is?" he asked. I could hear a hint of panic in his voice. "Sure," I replied, "he's right here with me, having lunch." Relieved, he exhaled and said, "Stay there. I'm coming." A few minutes later, when the breathless trooper burst into the restaurant, I learned that Coach had escaped his hotel room without alerting the trooper. For more than an hour, this distraught fellow—whose job was to keep his eyes on the governor's husband at all times—could not find him. Later, with Coach back in his room, the trooper pulled me aside. "Next time he shows up somewhere without a trooper," he pleaded, "can you *please* let one of us know?" Understanding that he could have lost his job for losing sight of his protectee, I assured him I would.

The highlight of the convention came in retrospect. I didn't know it, but as I sat in the upper deck on the convention's first night watching the keynote address by an unfamiliar Illinois state senator, I was seeing a future president of the United States. I also had no idea that Barack Obama's masterful speech, which won widespread praise and propelled him to immediate national prominence, would be so memorable that I would one day show it to my students at LSU.

That November, Kerry came close but fell just short of victory. Bush crushed Kerry in Louisiana, 57 percent to 42 percent. Worse, Republican US Representative David Vitter captured Breaux's Senate seat. The next morning, Blanco held an impromptu press conference after attending an education forum in the fourth-floor Governor's Press Room. When we left the room and headed back to her office, we ran into a scrum of reporters who had questions for her about the presidential election. Tyler Bridges, a former *Times-Picayune* reporter, was in town researching a feature story on Blanco for *Gambit Weekly* of New Orleans. She and Coach were so fond of Tyler that they had invited him to stay with them at the Mansion during his visit. When Tyler asked Blanco for whom she voted, she demurred. "I'd rather not say," she said. Despite having hosted a Kerry rally at the Mansion and joining him on the stage in Boston at the convention's end, she refused to disclose her vote. Tyler repeated his question. She refused to answer. "Come on, Governor," Tyler sputtered. "That's a copout."

Finally, after allowing that she thought Kerry was too liberal for Louisiana—especially his position on abortion—Blanco fled to the sanctuary of her office. I followed her, expecting she would order me to expel Tyler from the Mansion. Instead, she was her usual cheerful self and seemed to forget the embarrassing confrontation that just occurred. As I would find out in the years to come, Kathleen Blanco might get mad at you, but she did not hold grudges. She might yell or fuss, but she would get over it quickly.

That morning, she turned to what seemed to her a more important matter—taking care of my five-year-old son, Robert. With Cindy out of town, I had him and his sister, Avery, to myself. The night before, however, Robert developed a slight fever, and I couldn't let him go to kindergarten with his sister. He would have to come to work with me. And that was a problem. I was accustomed to having a boss who didn't mind it when I showed up with kids, but this would be different, I worried.

On the State Police helicopter with Governor Kathleen Blanco and journalist Tyler Bridges in November 2004.

I couldn't leave Robert in my office by himself. He was too intimidated by the strange environment. He wanted to stay close to me. And now I had an hourlong meeting with the governor and other staff members. I would have no choice but to take him into her office. I worried she and others might see a sick kid and grumble about the intrusion. "I'm sorry, Governor," I said, holding Robert's hand. "Robert is sick and I had to bring him to work with me today. I hope it's okay—." Before I could say another word, she shut me down and scurried from the office. She soon returned with a fistful of crayons and a coloring book. Next, she sat Robert in her chair at the head of the large conference table in her office. She made sure he was comfortable and happy before she started the meeting.

WHILE SHE FOCUSED on luring corporations to Louisiana, and helping existing businesses expand, Blanco also wanted to bring together state officials, business and nonprofits, and activists to talk about the overriding problem that created so many of the state's woes—poverty. In December 2004, she convened a poverty summit at the civic center in Monroe. We chose Monroe because it was the largest city in northeast

Governor Kathleen Blanco shares a laugh with two state legislators after speaking to the Louisiana Association of Business and Industry in Baton Rouge in January 2004. Left to right: state Representative Monica Walker of Marksville, state Representative Gary Beard of Baton Rouge, me, and Blanco. (Photo courtesy of *The Advocate*/Arthur D. Lauck)

Louisiana, the poorest region of the state. The poverty summit drew attention to the necessity of new solutions to the state's chronic problem, but before it began, we faced a small crisis—or, at least, a crisis in Coach's eyes. For months, Andy Kopplin, our chief of staff, and I met with representatives of the state's LGBTQ community. During the campaign, Blanco spoke with several key LGBTQ leaders and promised, if elected, she would reinstate the executive order that included "sexual orientation" in a ban on harassment or discrimination in state hiring and promotion. The language would also apply to any company that had a contract with the state. Governor Edwin Edwards had signed such an order in 1992, but executive orders only last for the term of the governor who signed them. Mike Foster let this one expire when he took office.

In this area, Blanco's caution got the best of her. While gay rights organizations kept asking us when she would sign the promised order, Blanco delayed. Coach was surely one reason. I suspect he never wanted her to agree to it in the first place. I thought it was good politics *and* the right thing to do. Discrimination was wrong and, just as important, she promised to ban it. I sat in her office one afternoon in the summer of 2004 with Joe Traigle, a former Baton Rouge bank president who had served as Revenue secretary under Buddy Roemer. Joe had been president of the Baton Rouge Chamber. He was also gay and in a long-term relationship with his now-husband, Carey Long. For some time, Joe worried about Louisiana's stagnant population growth. There were many reasons for it, but Joe argued that the bigotry of state and local governments towards gays and lesbians was a factor. Young people, he knew, wanted to live in a tolerant place that welcomed and accepted all kinds of people. I agreed and arranged for him to make his case to Blanco. He did and made an eloquent and passionate presentation. But I knew that Coach was more influential than Joe. And when he played to his wife's caution, as he was doing now, she became even more careful.

Meanwhile, Andy and I were getting pressure from the LGBT community to expand the order to include transgender persons. I supported that and so did Andy, but Blanco was not ready to go that far. We coaxed her to a place where she would issue the order in early December. But the deal she and Coach insisted upon was that the gay-rights organizations would not release a statement about it. In other words, they did not want gays and lesbians to celebrate an executive order banning discrimination against gays and lesbians. I hated telling the group about the deal, but I was quick to add that while the governor didn't want them to celebrate it too much, I knew there was no way we could insist upon their silence. I hoped they heard what I was trying to tell them—which was, "Do whatever you have to do."

Blanco signed the order on the morning of Monday, December 6, and then we flew by State Police helicopter to Monroe for the poverty summit. During our flight, the gay rights group released a statement applauding the governor for signing the order. When we landed, we went to our hotel, the Holiday Inn's Holidome, south of town. My room was next to the governor and Coach. Around four o'clock, as I was getting ready for that night's events, I heard shouting through the wall next door. I couldn't make out every word, but I knew it was Coach. In a flash, his words penetrated the wall and became clear: "I'm going to kill Bob Mann!" A couple of minutes later, I heard a knock at my door. It was one of the governor's state troopers. "The governor would like to see you," he said. When I walked into her room, I stepped into a buzz saw of anger, mostly from Coach. "They told us there'd be no press release or statement about Kathleen's order," Coach said. "How could you let this happen?"

"Look," I said, "you cannot expect this group to stay quiet about an order they've wanted for eight years. This is huge to them and they're just supposed to ignore it? Neither you or I can control what they do or say about an executive order. Besides, this is not going to hurt the governor." I tried to persuade Coach that his concerns were overblown. The governor, as she often did when Coach was on a tear, remained quiet. "What's done is done," I told them both. "Even if this is as bad as you fear, it's a one-day story. No one will be talking about this day after tomorrow." And I was right. Any outrage over a decent and humane executive order faded in days. Blanco's executive order remained on the books until her successor, Bobby Jindal, let it expire in January 2008.

WORKING IN A governor's office might not have been as demanding as working in the White House, but it was far more demanding on my personal time. I spent the last eleven years of my time on Breaux's staff working from Baton Rouge, where the rhythms of the job were far different from the rat race on the Hill. In Washington, it was nothing to work until eight or nine. Even when I resolved to leave the office around six, I went to the Library of Congress to research my Russell Long biography. I was always working. In Baton Rouge, I had a family and a flexible job that allowed me plenty of time at home. Except for the weeks and weekends that Breaux was in Louisiana, I was home for dinner by five or six. Weekends were mine to spend at home with the kids. When I went to work for Blanco, things changed. My life went into overdrive.

I was overseeing several areas of the governor's office, besides staffing her on many of her trips around the state and elsewhere. During nights and weekends, it was not unusual to receive a flurry of emails and texts from staffers about something that needed our immediate attention. While

I tried my best to make every basketball, baseball, and soccer game that Avery and Robert played during their elementary school days, I was often watching my BlackBerry instead of the game. One day, a few years after I'd left the governor's staff, I was chatting with Bridger Eglin, the grandfather of one of my son's friends and teammates. "My memory of you at most of those games," Bridger said with a tinge of pity, "was you on the phone or with your head buried in that BlackBerry." I had not realized that everyone, including my children, noticed how much I was not present.

Every weekday morning, the governor's senior staffers convened for a thirty-minute call to plan the upcoming day and talk about other issues on her radar. Most mornings, I would drive the kids to school, and during that five-minute journey to the LSU Lab School, I was almost always on the conference call when I dropped them off. I mouthed, "I love you," as they clambered out of my car. Some nights, I would get home so late from work that Cindy had already put them to bed. On those days, I would see my children for less than an hour. It was no way to live. Some people are great at making that work. I was not. It was demanding on Cindy, who also had a full-time job. Her flexible schedule and the ability to work from home made it easier on her, but too much of the child-raising responsibilities fell on her.

Then, there was the fact that Blanco and Coach were night owls. It was not unusual to receive a call from her at ten o'clock. And these were not quick affairs. Some conversations went on for an hour. I signed up for this life, I knew, but it was tiring, especially during the legislative sessions, when work life went into high gear. Having legislators always in the building complicated life. One morning, in the ground-floor lobby of the Capitol, I ran into Jim Cofer, then-president of my alma mater, the University of Louisiana at Monroe. He asked how I liked my new job. "This is the first time in my life," I confessed, "that I work in a building where it seems half the people here want me and my colleagues to fail."

NOTHING SEEMED TO occupy our thoughts in the first year of Blanco's term more than keeping the New Orleans Saints in Louisiana. For years, team owner Tom Benson had complained about the condition of the Superdome, where the Saints played their home games. Completed in 1975, the Dome underwent some sprucing up over the years, but by the late 1990s it needed serious renovations. More than anything, the Saints wanted a fancier Dome so they could generate more revenue for the team. Team officials and Governor Mike Foster negotiated a $187 million deal in 2002 that kept Benson's organization happy and in town for the short term, but the owner now insisted on a new stadium—something we concluded would cost the state as much as $700 million.

While Blanco did more for economic development than Foster, unlike Foster she was not in thrall to business leaders like Benson. Benson seemed to have Foster's number. And at the beginning of their negotiations, Benson acted as if Blanco would be an even bigger pushover than Foster. People misjudged her like this often because she was a soft-spoken, older woman. Men frequently treated her as though she was not the serious, resolute person her staff and friends knew her to be. In this case, however, she was eager to gain the upper hand on Benson from the start, knowing she must show him she was not as meek as he suspected.

Malcolm Ehrhardt, who ran a New Orleans public relations firm and was a trusted advisor, offered some useful insight into Benson's personality and business traits. "One of his tactics to gain the upper hand in negotiations, when he's not getting his way," Malcolm told Blanco a few days before her first official meeting with Benson, "is to clap shut his folder, stand up, and pretend he's ending the negotiations." Benson had apparently stunned competitors into compliance with this trick many times through the years. So, Malcolm suggested Blanco might beat Benson at his own game. Upon hearing this, Blanco's eyes lit up and she cackled at the thought of shocking Benson with such a stunt. Not long into their first meeting at team headquarters in Metairie, Benson tossed out a few unreasonable requests. Blanco responded that his demands were impossible. Benson pressed harder. So, she stood up and slammed shut her folder. "Well, then," she said, "I guess that means we're done here." Benson was stunned. He knew, instantly, he had a worthy opponent in Kathleen Blanco. He could do nothing but plead with her to stay and continue talking.

Negotiating with Benson and his team was often maddening. A famously cranky man, he had little interest in small talk or observing the usual niceties of casual conversation. Still vivid in my mind is a meeting in the family dining room of the Governor's Mansion early in our negotiations in 2004. The conversation veered into the types of amusements and attractions a renovated Superdome might include to draw bigger crowds to Saints games. Benson thought this was a preposterous idea. It was all I could do to suppress a guffaw when he shut down that line of talk, saying, "I don't know why we're talking about all this stuff. It's not like I'm in the entertainment business!" Given his team's mediocre 8-8 record the previous season, he was probably right.

To her credit, Blanco refused to give Benson the new stadium he craved. "I'm willing to do reasonable things," she said in November 2004, as it became clear to Benson and others he would not get the deal the Saints wanted. It would take Hurricane Katrina, and the severe damage it inflicted on the building, to spur a major renovation of the stadium.

While Blanco would seize the opportunity of the crisis to use federal dollars for repairing the Dome, Benson saw the crisis in another light. He would try to use the storm as an excuse to take his team elsewhere. Only the intervention of NFL Commissioner Paul Tagliabue would force him to drop that plan and keep the Saints in New Orleans.

More than once over the years that I worked for Blanco, I saw how men—especially powerful and rich men—treated women politicians differently. I was guilty of it myself. On an economic development trip to San Antonio in November 2004, I wandered down the hall to the governor's hotel room and rapped on the door. "You ready to go, Governor?" I asked, aware that the famously late Blanco was especially tardy for this evening's event.

She opened the door and invited me in. She was still fussing with her hair. "You're not ready?" I asked, with a slightly disapproving air.

"You worked for John Breaux too long," she shot back. "It's easy for men to get dressed. You just had to put that suit on and comb your hair. Do you realize how much longer it takes for someone like me to get ready for this event?"

I was embarrassed. I had not considered how much more harshly people judged women politicians, especially for their dress and appearance, and the pressure and self-doubt some female politicians experienced because of this double standard. No one would have cared if John Breaux or Russell Long wore the same suit and tie four days running. If their hair had not looked perfect, it would have mattered to no one. However, if Blanco wore the same outfit two days in a row, people would notice and some would judge her severely for it. If her hair was less than perfect, people would tut-tut and whisper about it.

Blanco also knew that male politicians often disregarded and spoke with condescension to female politicians. I saw that clearly at the meeting of the National Governors Association in Washington, DC, in January 2005, at the JW Marriott hotel. At the end of one day's session, Blanco convened a private meeting of five Gulf-state governors to discuss coastal erosion and protection issues. Mississippi Governor Haley Barbour, a former lobbyist and national chair of the Republican Party, could not have acted more resentful of having been summoned to this meeting by a woman. His annoyance at everything Blanco said was evident from the beginning. "I'm not really sure why we are here," the plump Mississippi governor drawled, shortly after Blanco made her opening pitch for collective action on the issue by the governors in the room. After about twenty minutes of Barbour's sexist tantrum, an infuriated Blanco gave up and ended the meeting. I followed her as she stormed towards the hallway. I almost ran into her as she opened the large door, only to stop suddenly and turn towards Barbour. As she shot him daggers with her eyes, she muttered loud enough for only me to hear, "Asshole." I had to agree.

AS THE SUMMER of 2005 approached, Coach was already in reelection mode, running polls and calling me and other staff members several times a day to talk about strategy and urge us to push even harder to keep the governor's poll numbers high. That pressure to continue pushing and expanding Blanco's political standing brought out the demons I thought I'd buried at the end of the 2003 campaign. My competitive spirit led me to not only propose an unethical plan; it caused me to deceive a reporter and betray one of my closest friends. All these years later, it's the episode in my political life about which I am most ashamed.

I first met John Copes when I went to work for the *Shreveport Journal* in 1983. A tall, brilliant, and laconic man, John grew up in Baton Rouge but had studied journalism at Louisiana Tech in Ruston. That's where he met Diane Hollenshead, a smart, shy student who was also in the journalism program. After graduation, they both found jobs at the *Journal*—about the time I arrived. John, who covered Shreveport City Hall, sat across from me. Diane, who was the paper's education reporter, occupied the desk to my right. After a few months, John and Diane got engaged and, later, married. Like most people who knew John, I was immediately drawn to him.

"Copes was a model of understated elegance, personally and professionally," Wiley Hilburn, head of Louisiana Tech's journalism program, wrote of his former student in 2006. "Copes had Eagle Scout patrician good looks, was tall, and wore expensive jackets over ancient blue jeans and brown brogans. His brown hair was fashionably long. He always had dark circles under his eyes. He was, in a word, cool." John "could quote James Joyce or Ezra Pound, if it was appropriate," Wiley also recalled. "A born Yellow-Dog Democrat, he was making fun of the Moral Majority in his *Tech Talk* column long before we elected a faith-based president. He was always ahead of his time."

It was not just that John was cool, brilliant, one of the most incisive writers I knew, and a great reporter; he had a devastating, quick wit and, sometimes, a quicker temper, especially with those who did not tell him the truth. I will never forget the day his interview with a Shreveport council member went south. Sitting across from me, on the phone with the politician, John tried to elicit the information he needed. He shot from his chair. It appeared the councilman was dodging his questions about some alleged misconduct. John had enough of the misinformation. He roared into the phone, "That's bullshit! That's bullshit." He slammed the receiver down and, with perfect calm, lit a cigarette and went back to work on the story.

John and Diane became my good friends. And when I left the *Journal* for Washington, John took over my role as political writer. Within a few years, he and Diane moved to Washington so Diane could study law at Georgetown University. The *Journal* named John its Washington correspondent. In those years, John and I grew even closer, playing golf many weekends and early mornings. We would tee off at Rock Creek Park Golf Course before dawn, play a quick nine holes, and I would be at my desk in the Hart Senate Office Building by nine o'clock. Jim Oakes and I would meet John and Diane for dinner somewhere almost every week. In 1994, they moved back to Louisiana. Diane got a job as an assistant US attorney for the Eastern District of Louisiana, working out of the Hale Boggs Federal Building in New Orleans. John worked from their Mandeville home and began writing a novel.

In 1999, however, John started a political blog. We were all new to the Internet, and creating a blog was much more difficult than it is today. In those days, there were no ready-made templates offered by tech companies. As a one-person operation, John didn't have the bandwidth to cover the news like the *Baton Rouge Advocate* or the *New Orleans Times-Picayune*, but he could share their stories and critique them. He called his new site "The Deduct Box," taking the name from Huey Long's famous treasury where he kept campaign contributions that his cronies coerced from state workers. It was one of the first versions of what would become common in journalism: a daily online news summary. After a few months of writing these summaries, John developed a growing and loyal following as he compared and commented on the coverage of various events by Louisiana news organizations. He was the best media critic Louisiana has had, and he became a prominent commentator on the news.

Just as his website took off, John got dreadful news. He had colon cancer and it spread to his liver. One doctor told him it was terminal and he had less than a year to live. John refused to accept that diagnosis and began researching therapies. He found doctors at Memorial Sloan-Kettering in New York City who had developed a new treatment for his disease. He and Diane went to New York for a surgery, and they stayed for several weeks as he recovered. Gannett Capitol reporter John Hill and I flew up one weekend to see them. We were then hopeful John could beat the disease. All his friends were excited he was not only fighting the cancer but seemed to be winning. That was even more important to the Copeses because they now had a young son, Jack, born about the same time as my children.

To focus on restoring his health, John suspended "The Deduct Box" in 2000, about three years before I went to work for Blanco. But because he was one of the smartest people I knew and had a sharp mind for politics, I kept calling him, almost daily, to talk over the challenges of communicating on behalf of a governor. I was still stung by the 2005 battle over Blanco's proposal to fund a teacher pay raise with a cigarette tax hike. In that legislative session, Blanco got most of what she asked for—she didn't ask for much—but we lost the fight to fund a pay raise for teachers and college faculty. After that defeat, I worried the governor did not have enough people coming to her defense and almost no external allies willing to help amplify our messages about important issues. Maybe we hadn't asked the Legislature for more, I worried, because we had so few supporters willing to fight for us.

I was also talking with John about all this because I wanted to get him back in the game, offer him a renewed purpose, and take advantage of his remarkable writing skills. In July 2005, we developed the idea—mostly mine—of a website promoting Blanco and attacking her opponents. Because Diane was a federal worker, we wanted to keep John's involvement quiet. There was nothing illegal or unethical about the husband of a prosecutor working in politics, but we both thought it wise to keep John's name out of it. We also agreed the Louisiana Democratic Party would be the best organization to support the enterprise. To get things moving, I asked John to write a memo proposing the broad outlines of the website and how it might work. A few days later, he emailed it to me and I forwarded it to the executive director of the party.

And then all hell broke loose.

One afternoon in mid-August, when I was in Shreveport with Blanco, John called me. He was distressed. "There's a New Orleans radio talk show host talking about our plan," he told me. He wanted to know with whom I'd shared the memo. I told him only the executive director of the party. "Don't worry," I said. "The whole thing will blow over." The next day, a reporter with the Associated Press called and asked me about the extent of my involvement in the plan to create an anonymous website designed to attack the governor's political opponents. I still could not believe that this memo fell into the hands of reporters and was flying around the Internet. Speaking with this reporter, however, I panicked. And in answering her question, I destroyed one of the best friendships I ever had and hurt a man fighting cancer, with little more than a year to live.

"I get lots of ideas from people," I responded, confirming to the reporter that Copes wrote the memo. I thought I was protecting the governor, who knew nothing about the proposed website. Later that day, a story moved on the AP wire describing the memo and our scheme. It featured this from John's memo: "Currently, Democrats have no comparable structure from which to return fire, or even to begin correcting the calumnies hurled against us daily." The story didn't quote me, but it ended with this sentence: "Mann, who confirmed that Copes wrote the memo, refused to comment on it, beyond saying that he often receives suggestions and advice from people. Copes also declined to talk about the four-page document."

With that, I had betrayed a good friend. In the moment, I had to choose between owning my mistake or throwing a friend under the bus. So, I threw John under the bus. The ensuing controversy was not pleasant, but after twenty years in politics, I knew it would fade and be forgotten when some other storm erupted. That literal storm, ten days later, would be Hurricane Katrina. Even though I did something dumb and unethical, I was prepared for the heat I would get. John, who was fighting cancer, was not. His wife was embarrassed by the controversy. More than anything, John was hurt I had responded to the reporter's question by treating him like a crackpot who had slipped me an unsolicited suggestion.

Regretting my initial comment, I confessed my role to other journalists who asked me about the memo, and I tried to explain to John that I would take my lumps for my part in this. He wouldn't return my calls, so I put it all in a lengthy email. He didn't reply. The damage was done. I called and emailed him several more times in the weeks after the incident, apologizing for my inexcusable behavior. I wanted him to know I owned my actions. But John didn't want to talk and so I finally dropped the matter. Within a couple of weeks, Katrina hit and everyone's life changed. No reporter asked me about the memo again. But during the last year of my dear friend's life, we were estranged. He did not want to see me or hear from me. Through mutual friends, I kept up with his condition and tried to convey my concern and affection—and my continuing regret and humiliation over my behavior.

We finally spoke by phone a few weeks before his death on October 19, 2006, at age forty-nine. His voice was weak, but he told me he forgave me. It was a generous act of grace he did not have to offer but for which I will be forever grateful. In 2017, in a column for the *New Orleans Times-Picayune*, I wrote about how I destroyed our friendship. It was a bit of public penance I thought I owed to John. I closed the column:

> Politics ain't beanbag, someone once observed. That is true. But there are basic standards of decorum and human decency that one should uphold: Don't steal. Don't cheat. Don't lie. Keep your promises. Don't betray your friends. Winning isn't everything. If it feels wrong, it probably is.
>
> As I think about my act of betrayal and how it hurt my friend and destroyed our relationship, the words of Jesus echo in my ears: "For what shall it profit a man, if he gain the whole world, and suffer the loss of his soul?"

With journalist John Copes in 1992. John and I worked together at the Shreveport Journal *in the early 1980s. John, to whom this book is dedicated, died in 2006. He was only forty-nine.*

There is no political victory worth more than your soul or a friend. Nothing in life is worth the cost of gaining it by dishonorable means.

Hardly a day goes by I don't think of John. I regret losing our friendship and mourn his death at such a young age. There is so much I would like to say to him and share with him. Through the dismal Jindal years and Donald Trump's presidency, Louisiana needed John's criticism and insight. He was a bright, shooting star who blazed through the lives of so many people who admired his singular voice and personality.

It had been thirty years or more since I assured my mother—and myself—that I could work in politics without sacrificing my principles. Now, I realized, it was a promise I failed to keep. I thought about her justified fretting about how the political life might tempt me to compromise my principles; I also thought about a conversation I had in 1989 with former Louisiana Lieutenant Governor Bill Dodd, whom I had interviewed for my biography of Russell Long.

"You're living in DC?" he asked me.

"Yes, sir."

"Well," he said, "if you spend too much time up there among all those people cutting deals and compromising their principles, before long you'll be just like them. It won't happen all at once. It's a gradual thing. And you don't know you've changed into a person willing to cheat and cut corners until it's too late. Don't let that happen to you." Now, I wondered, had Dodd's prophecy and my mother's apprehension about my future borne bitter fruit? And if it had, was it too late, as Dodd had suggested, to change my ways? I wasn't sure. Within a couple of weeks of the website controversy, however, Hurricane Katrina would slam into Louisiana and change everything—including my personal and professional lives. I didn't know it, but my political career was about to end.

17

We Need Everything You've Got

The first inkling of the levee collapses and the approaching catastrophe in New Orleans reached the Emergency Operations Center (EOC) in Baton Rouge late Monday morning, August 29, 2005, a few hours after Hurricane Katrina made landfall in Buras, Louisiana. By the time it slammed into the coast, the storm had dissipated, if only slightly. It was no longer the 175-mile-per-hour category-four storm of a few days earlier, but it was still a strong category-three hurricane. The storm's brutal winds drove a wall of water into the low-lying coastal region south of New Orleans. The city wasn't as vulnerable to storm surge as the coast, but it would still suffer much of the storm's fury. Much of New Orleans rested below sea level on a narrow strip of land between the Mississippi River and Lake Pontchartrain. If the levees that protected the city failed or were topped, disaster was certain.

Around nine that morning, a FEMA official in New Orleans began hearing about the spreading levee collapses that would inundate most of the city, kill almost two thousand people, and destroy tens of thousands of homes. He relayed the news to colleagues at the EOC, where I rode out the storm with Blanco and her staff. Before that, the early news was that Katrina might blow through the city without great consequence. And that's what happened, in a way. The winds from Katrina did not inflict catastrophic damage. Some windows on hotels were blown out. Part of the Superdome's roof sustained significant damage. But most structures in the city survived the storm's worst winds.

Miles to the east, meanwhile, storm surge destroyed large portions of several coastal Mississippi towns, including Waveland, Biloxi, and Pascagoula. Raging water also flooded unprotected Louisiana towns southeast of New Orleans and on the north shore of Lake Pontchartrain. But if the federally built levees and drainage-canal walls had been better constructed and maintained properly, most people in New Orleans proper would have wandered outside, cleaned up the debris, assessed their roof damage, and begun moving on with their lives. Instead, the levee collapses turned a severe inconvenience into a cataclysm.

The gravity of the situation became clear by late Monday morning. "Water is inundating everywhere," Joey DiFatta, chair of the St. Bernard Parish Council, told the *Times-Picayune*. "We have buildings and roofs collapsing. We're preparing rescue efforts and as soon as the wind subsides we'll start trying to get people out of St. Bernard." In nearby Gretna, Mayor Ronnie Harris reported that the storm had torn away a piece of his City Hall's roof. Not long thereafter came word that portions of the Lower Ninth Ward, a poverty-stricken area of southeastern New Orleans, were taking on six to eight feet of water. Meanwhile, we learned that, not far away, Jackson Barracks—home to the Louisiana National Guard—was nearly underwater. By eleven o'clock that morning, news arrived that in St. Bernard Parish surging water had forced many residents into their attics and onto rooftops. By early afternoon, we began hearing that hundreds of people were on their roofs and clinging to trees in the Lower Ninth Ward. At that point, a group of reporters from the *Times-Picayune* ventured out from the paper's offices on Howard Avenue, not far from downtown. Their report, filed midafternoon, was sobering. "Within four blocks of the office, the storm scenes were still raw and astonishing," they wrote. They reported widespread devastation—cars with smashed windows, downed light poles along I-10, billboards "shredded and flailing in the wind," and trees uprooted everywhere.

Around eight o'clock, the paper reported: "Even as reports of damage continued coming in Monday night, the full extent of the destruction in Katrina's wake was hard to gauge. But one thing was clear: Gentilly, Treme, Bywater and the 9th Ward had been swallowed." In another story, a *Picayune* reporter wrote: "Treme and the city's 8th and 9th Wards were severely flooded. Eastern New Orleans was inaccessible by car due to the high water on Interstate 10 East. The farther one drove east on Interstates 10 and 610, the deeper the water and the danger. . . . For miles in the 9th Ward, there were only rooftops, with floodwaters lapping at the eaves, visible from I-10. Rows of homes were swallowed by water. Standing outside on the concrete interstate, in the whipping winds, signs could be spotted that so many of the city's residents did not evacuate."

The catastrophe that was Katrina—and there's no better word to describe it—was manmade. The levees failed, and a city flooded. That's the story of Monday, August 29, 2005, in southeast Louisiana. What happened before and after that day compounded the suffering of so many people. Looking back on the days leading up to the storm's landfall, I realized I should have recognized the warning signs. First, there was

Mayor Ray Nagin's reluctance to order a mandatory evacuation of New Orleans on Friday and Saturday, when it appeared the storm would be much larger and deadlier than it turned out to be. Because of Blanco's desire to have a good relationship with the New Orleans mayor on the cusp of a possible disaster, she did not overrule him and order an evacuation. Legally, she might have had the authority to do so.[1] She could have held a press conference and urged everyone to leave. But that would not have worked without all the area parish presidents and Nagin working in concert to facilitate a staged evacuation that allowed those south of the city to leave first and those in northern Jefferson Parish, especially Metairie and Kenner, to leave last. By four o'clock on Saturday, however, Blanco ordered contraflow out of New Orleans to speed up the city's evacuation.

Things hadn't gone so well the year before, in September 2004, when people in the region hit the road all at once when Hurricane Ivan, a category-three storm, appeared headed for New Orleans. The storm turned north towards Florida before landfall and spared the city. But the botched evacuation—some families spent twelve torturous hours in cars inching their way to Baton Rouge—was a blessing in disguise. It persuaded state and New Orleans-area officials we must be smarter about getting people out of the city if the "big one" ever approached.

I didn't want to admit we had failed to evacuate the city properly for Ivan, but it was true. On the afternoon of September 16, 2004, the day after Interstate 10 between New Orleans and Baton Rouge turned into a parking lot, an angry Senator Mary Landrieu called to tell me—in the plainspoken, urgent language that was her hallmark—that we must do a better job next time. I argued with her for about ten minutes, but when I hung up I had to admit she was right. Everyone knew she was right. Our administration spent the next year working on contraflow out of New Orleans. While Department of Transportation traffic engineers worked on the details, I worked with the State Police to design a map that we could distribute to every household in south Louisiana. Once we had the map, I wanted to ensure people could read it and quickly decide where to drive. I persuaded the State Police to hire Malcolm Ehrhardt and his public relations firm to conduct a series of focus groups during which average citizens were shown the map and invited to critique it. By the time hurricane season 2005 arrived, we were comfortable we could evacuate the city, given enough time.

And Blanco needed more time on Saturday, August 27, 2005, two days before the storm would hit. Worried that Nagin still did not appreciate the urgency of the situation, on Friday she had persuaded Max Mayfield, who ran the National Hurricane Center, to call the mayor and impress upon him Katrina's severity and danger. By Saturday morning, Nagin and officials in surrounding parishes ordered an evacuation.

On Saturday morning, I flew by helicopter to Jefferson Parish with Blanco and Coach, where we met with parish President Aaron Broussard, who had ordered a premature evacuation the year earlier that caused many to fear he might do so again and unleash mayhem on the interstate. Blanco secured Broussard's assurance he would follow the plan and wait his parish's turn. After a press conference with him and other officials in Kenner, we flew on to the Superdome's heliport and then took a short drive to New Orleans City Hall for a similar press conference with Nagin. The message was simple. Take the storm seriously. Prepare. Leave town. "We can always restore property," Blanco said. "We cannot restore life." Thanks to Mayfield's call, Nagin also got the message. "Ladies and gentlemen, this is not a test," he said. "This is the real deal."

On Sunday, less than twenty-four hours before the storm would hit, Blanco returned to New Orleans. This time, her message was even more urgent. She and others had persuaded Nagin to order an evacuation the previous day, but we still needed to make sure people left town, as we could not force them to leave. On Saturday, a few Blanco staff members worked the phones, lobbying local pastors and priests to urge congregants and parishioners to leave town on Sunday after church.

Over about forty-eight hours, most people with the means and desire to leave New Orleans would depart the city without incident. But thousands of residents would be stranded because they did not have time to arrange transportation. Maybe their car was broken, or they didn't have a car. Their neighbors or family members might have evacuated the day before. For whatever reason, they couldn't leave. Many who wouldn't evacuate stayed because they couldn't afford a hotel room for two or three days. Some had pets, and they knew that the shelters would turn them away and most hotels wouldn't rent them a room with a dog or cat in tow. Many just didn't know where they might go, having never ventured far from New Orleans. Others—and I think this made up most of the people who stayed behind—just didn't believe the storm would be that bad.

On Sunday morning—with Katrina's sustained winds at 175 mph and even higher gusts—the National Weather Service in New Orleans issued a stunning advisory that left no doubt the region needed to be evacuated quickly. Yet, even that advisory never mentioned the possibility of widespread flooding:

HURRICANE KATRINA . . . A MOST POWERFUL HURRICANE WITH UNPRECEDENTED STRENGTH . . . RIVALING THE INTENSITY OF HURRICANE CAMILLE OF 1969. MOST OF THE

AREA WILL BE UNINHABITABLE FOR WEEKS . . . PERHAPS LONGER. AT LEAST ONE HALF OF WELL CONSTRUCTED HOMES WILL HAVE ROOF AND WALL FAILURE. ALL GABLED ROOFS WILL FAIL . . . LEAVING THOSE HOMES SEVERELY DAMAGED OR DESTROYED. THE MAJORITY OF INDUSTRIAL BUILDINGS WILL BECOME NON FUNCTIONAL. PARTIAL TO COMPLETE WALL AND ROOF FAILURE IS EXPECTED. ALL WOOD FRAMED LOW RISING APARTMENT BUILDINGS WILL BE DESTROYED. CONCRETE BLOCK LOW RISE APARTMENTS WILL SUSTAIN MAJOR DAMAGE . . . INCLUDING SOME WALL AND ROOF FAILURE. HIGH RISE OFFICE AND APARTMENT BUILDINGS WILL SWAY DANGEROUSLY . . . A FEW TO THE POINT OF TOTAL COLLAPSE. ALL WINDOWS WILL BLOW OUT. AIRBORNE DEBRIS WILL BE WIDESPREAD . . . AND MAY INCLUDE HEAVY ITEMS SUCH AS HOUSEHOLD APPLIANCES AND EVEN LIGHT VEHICLES. SPORT UTILITY VEHICLES AND LIGHT TRUCKS WILL BE MOVED. THE BLOWN DEBRIS WILL CREATE ADDITIONAL DESTRUCTION. PERSONS . . . PETS . . . AND LIVESTOCK EXPOSED TO THE WINDS WILL FACE CERTAIN DEATH IF STRUCK. POWER OUTAGES WILL LAST FOR WEEKS . . . AS MOST POWER POLES WILL BE DOWN AND TRANSFORMERS DESTROYED. WATER SHORTAGES WILL MAKE HUMAN SUFFERING INCREDIBLE BY MODERN STANDARDS. THE VAST MAJORITY OF NATIVE TREES WILL BE SNAPPED OR UPROOTED. ONLY THE HEARTIEST WILL REMAIN STANDING . . . BUT BE TOTALLY DEFOLIATED. FEW CROPS WILL REMAIN. LIVESTOCK LEFT EXPOSED TO THE WINDS WILL BE KILLED.

Nagin's initial relaxed approach to the storm was the first indication we were headed for big trouble. It was not, however, the last. Back in Baton Rouge on Sunday night, Michael Brown—the former head of the International Arabian Horse Association and now the director of FEMA—arrived at the EOC to meet with Blanco. At the time, I was only vaguely aware of Brown. I had no idea what job he held before President Bush named him to FEMA. I had some hazy notion he was a former governor. That may have been because of the way he spoke to Blanco. It was off-putting. Brown was supremely self-assured. He evinced not a worry or concern in the world. In their conversation, he gave Blanco what I guess he thought was wise advice: "Be sure to get eight hours of sleep." The idea that a night owl like Kathleen Blanco might sleep for eight hours was preposterous. More than anything, I remember watching Brown talk to Blanco and thinking to myself, "This guy is a b.s. artist." Brown was the president's emissary and the person Bush and Homeland

Security Secretary Michael Chertoff would ask for advice about how to deal with the storm's aftermath. He would tell the president what Louisiana needed in the coming days. And it dawned on me that we were in the hands of a blowhard.

I didn't perceive just how awful and incompetent Brown was until later, but I had the feeling he was not someone worth trusting. I don't regard myself as perceptive about people like this. The only other time I would have this sixth sense about someone was in Ames, Iowa, in January 2008, at a rally for North Carolina Senator John Edwards. I had taken a couple dozen of my students to Iowa for the presidential caucuses and, as I watched Edwards speak that morning, I thought how much he reminded me of Mike Brown. In other words, a phony. I was right about both men.

ON MONDAY MORNING, the atmosphere at the EOC was controlled mayhem, as everyone waited for news about how New Orleans had fared. Already, all communication—cell and landline—between Baton Rouge and New Orleans was down. We had only spotty reports about what was happening just eighty miles down the road. Katrina would hit Baton Rouge, too. The day before, Cindy took our children to Lafayette, where she stayed for several days with her parents. I came home that evening to a neighborhood in total darkness. The only sound through the pitch black was the occasional rumble of a home generator providing power and blessed air conditioning to a house's fortunate inhabitants. A large water oak rested across the front of our dead-end street, a casualty of the high winds. So, I parked as close as I could and groped my way down the dark street until I arrived at what I thought was our house. It was hard to know. Until I fumbled my way inside, I couldn't tell the extent of the damage. I found a flashlight and explored. The house was unscathed. I would sleep there the first night and then, in pursuit of air conditioning, I sought refuge at the Governor's Mansion for the second night. When Cindy and the kids returned on Wednesday, we moved in with friends for a few days until our power was restored.

THE EOC WAS a large, sprawling, one-story building built next to the State Police headquarters, six miles east of downtown Baton Rouge. It had an enormous, high-ceilinged room with large television screens on the wall where the dozens of agency representatives could watch the weather and news coverage while monitoring their piece of state government. Off this room was a spacious, utilitarian conference room where Blanco could meet with her cabinet and other officials to discuss the state's response to the storm. And to one side of that room was a smaller space she could use as an office. It had no desk, only telephones, a television, a sofa, wingback chairs, and a small restroom. (Elsewhere in the EOC was a large, proper office reserved for her, which she would use rarely. Within a few weeks, she would move to a large RV, parked behind the building, which we used as a field office.) On the other side of the conference room was a small room that, beginning in the days leading up to the storm, we used for press briefings.

This press room was less than ideal. A few months earlier, Denise Bottcher and I had scouted out a large auditorium at a city facility nearby where we might hold press conferences if a catastrophic hurricane, or some other disaster, struck Louisiana and the national press descended on us. The idea was the governor and her staff would continue to operate from the EOC but we would stage the press a few blocks away at the ad hoc media center. This plan would have worked if we had held the first briefings at the auditorium. But because we held them in the small EOC room in the days before and after August 29, it became impossible to move once the national press descended on Baton Rouge. Although we would have made their lives more pleasant, reporters would have surely interpreted the move unfavorably. They would conclude we were kicking them out of the building and hiding the governor. It would create animosity and suspicion. So, we would have to live with the press looking over our shoulders for weeks.

For several days, Blanco arrived each morning in her black State Police sedan, which pulled up to the front door of the EOC. For the next twenty minutes, she ran a gauntlet of television and newspaper reporters who were camped on the lawn and in the building's lobby. It was only on day three or four that it occurred to me that the building had a back entrance the press could not reach. We started entering by that door. We weren't trying to avoid the press—the governor had three or four briefings every day for several weeks. I just wanted to move her into the building and to her work without answering the same question twenty times.

IT WASN'T LONG before the national press turned on Blanco, Bush, and Nagin. That's because the situation on the ground in New Orleans and throughout the region, even into Mississippi, was complete confusion compounded by an almost-total absence of federal assistance. For the first few days, the US Coast Guard helped Louisiana Wildlife and Fisheries agents, National Guardsmen, and average citizens in fishing boats rescue tens of thousands who were stranded on rooftops. But once the rescues were over, the Superdome and the New Orleans Convention Center were full of thousands of suffering souls. Other thousands weren't stuck on their roofs, but they were still living in their homes without fresh water or food and with no way to evacuate to safety. Some city streets were like the Wild West. Looters roamed the areas most impacted by the storm, but national news reports of widespread chaos and looting were exaggerated. Yet, the New Orleans Police Department was shattered. And all the federal help Blanco and other state officials requested of Bush, Brown, Chertoff, and others was nowhere to be found.

"We need everything you've got," Blanco told Bush when she spoke to him by phone on August 29, the day the storm hit Louisiana. That day, federal officials told Blanco 500 buses were "standing by" to help evacuate citizens stranded in New Orleans. The next day, when our chief of staff, Andy Kopplin, asked for the buses to begin moving people out of the city, he was informed they would not arrive in New Orleans for several days. We were astonished. Those federal buses never came in time to do much good. The state only got people out of the Dome and the Convention Center after Blanco signed an executive order commandeering school buses around the state to drive to New Orleans and fetch them. It was a deplorable failure by the federal government to live up to its commitment under the National Response Plan negotiated and issued by the Bush administration the previous year. Had Blanco known that Brown was giving her false hope about the buses, she could have made other arrangements much earlier. It would have relieved great human suffering.

At almost every turn, whenever Blanco requested something from the federal government, the complaint from FEMA or other federal agencies was that she hadn't gone through the proper channels, hadn't been specific enough, or hadn't put it in writing. It was like we were playing an elaborate game in which it was more important to ask the question using just the right language than to answer it correctly—a disaster version of "Jeopardy."

Although FEMA embedded officials in the EOC so they could advise Blanco on what federal resources she could and should request, much of what we needed arrived late. As press secretary Denise Bottcher told the *New York Times*, "We wanted soldiers, helicopters, food and water. They wanted to negotiate an organizational chart."

We weren't the only ones complaining. Adam Sharp, Senator Mary Landrieu's communications director, spoke for his boss and agreed with Blanco. The problem was not the lines of authority in Louisiana, he noted, but that FEMA was holding up aid to people in Louisiana. "FEMA has just been very slow to make these decisions," Sharp said in early September. Even Nagin, with whom Blanco would soon clash, pointed the finger at the federal government's inability to deliver what it guaranteed us. "They kept promising and saying things would happen," he told the *New York Times*. "I was getting excited and telling people that. They kept making promises and promises." US Representative Charlie Melançon, frustrated by what he saw as the White House's excessive attention to public relations rather than helping people, emailed several Blanco staffers on the afternoon of Friday, September 2, as the governor prepared to meet with the president. He was furious and complained that Bush's "entire effort on behalf of the federal government has been reflected in his and his people's nonchalant attitude to the people of [Louisiana]." He added, "You may give him this to read."

That day, September 2—five days into the crisis—we were still waiting for the FEMA aid that federal officials promised us but hadn't materialized. Days earlier, Blanco requested 40,000 more troops, ice, water, food, buses, base camps, staging areas, amphibious vehicles, mobile morgues, rescue teams, housing, airlift, and communications systems. She was frustrated, distrustful of what Brown and Chertoff were telling her, and doubtful the White House or our Republican representatives would help her navigate the federal bureaucracy. She knew she needed sound advice about what to ask for and what to expect from FEMA. So, she hired James Lee Witt, who served as FEMA director under President Bill Clinton. That decision helped, but it also bred distrust between us and the White House. That was no doubt exacerbated by fierce partisans like presidential advisor Karl Rove, US Senator David Vitter, US Representative Bobby Jindal, and former US Representative Bob Livingston, who all saw the chance to take advantage of Blanco's vulnerability while also serving the White House's efforts to deflect the blame from Bush's failures.

I WILL NOT try to tell the complete story of Katrina's aftermath. I leave that to the historians. My perspective was too narrow to afford me the knowledge and understanding of events that I would need to provide a definitive account of these events. For many days in those early weeks, in fact, I sometimes thought I was the least-informed person in the world about Katrina. (Blanco's executive counsel, Terry Ryder, later told me he had the same feeling.) I had little time to watch the wall-to-wall coverage on television. I tried to keep up with the newspaper accounts of events, but even that was hard. Particularly frustrating was knowing that the national press, especially the cable networks, were often getting things wrong, repeating rumors, and peddling falsehoods given them by well-meaning but uninformed sources or by our political enemies. The problem was I would usually not learn about a false report until the next day. A few friends would call or email me when they saw something egregious, but I knew we needed a better system.

That's when Mark Looker entered the scene. An agricultural public relations executive from California, Mark once worked for Democratic US

Representative Tony Coelho of California. One of his colleagues in that House office had been Fred Hatfield, who was now Senator John Breaux's chief of staff. Fred called me one afternoon and said Mark had contacted him. Mark was watching the news reports about the devastation and, like the good Methodist he was, wanted to help. I called Mark and asked him how soon he could be in Baton Rouge. He arrived within a couple of days. For two weeks, Mark slept in our son's upstairs bedroom. During the day, he would sit before a bank of televisions, each tuned to a different news channel. When he saw something that seemed wrong or just needed our attention, he would let Denise or me know. By then, Chris Frink, Blanco's speechwriter, had arrived to help. So had Malcolm Ehrhardt, the New Orleans public relations executive whom Blanco and I often consulted.

Often when Mark would see something wrong, it was coming from a television reporter repeating inaccurate information on our front lawn. I could walk outside, find the journalist, and try to correct the record. What I learned in those encounters was that, to many television reporters, truth was just a work in progress. Almost no one went to the trouble of correcting the record, even when I proved to their satisfaction they were wrong. The best I could hope for was they would get it right the next time they were on the air. That would have to be enough.

Mark wasn't the only person who bunked at our house in the weeks after the storm. For a while, Matt Furman, a public relations advisor to James Lee Witt, was our guest. A few weeks later, the Louisiana National Guard's public affairs director, Col. Peter Schneider, now a brigadier general in the Louisiana Guard, stayed with us. Other angels descended on Baton Rouge to help, including officials from National Guards in other states and William Leighty, the chief of staff to Virginia Governor Mark Warner, who brought a colleague with him and slept on the floor in the EOC for days. And then there was Aprill Springfield, a former aide to Senator Hillary Clinton, who came to assist with various tasks, including speechwriting and press relations. A few years later, she would marry Blanco's son Ray.

WHAT I DID not realize until much later was that, in the days and weeks following Hurricane Katrina, the distorted picture the world saw was of a drowned city, gripped by chaos, bordering on anarchy. *Newsweek*'s description was typical: "Only despair. The news could not have been more dispiriting: The reports of gunfire at medical-relief helicopters. The stories of pirates capturing rescue boats. The reports of police standing and watching looters—or joining them. The TV images of hundreds and thousands of people, Black and poor, trapped in the shadow of the Superdome. And most horrific: the photographs of dead people floating facedown in the sewage or sitting in wheelchairs where they died, some from lack of water." *U.S. News & World Report* also painted a dystopian portrait of the city: "It didn't look like America, the exodus of stunned refugees wading through turbid, waist-high water, carrying only what mattered most: sick relatives, bundled babies, storm-soaked family Bibles. It looked like another country, the kind of place where armed bandits outnumber police and desperate families search garbage dumpsters for food. A place where the poorest of the poor die in the heat, their corpses ignored on the side of the road."

No doubt conditions were primitive, and sometimes dangerous. Information was sketchy, especially in the hours and days after the storm hit. It seemed as challenging as reporting from a war zone, only without constant gunfire. Out of this chaos rose false rumors. And many in the media took these rumors and shared them as fact. This included stories of rape and murder in the Superdome, tall tales about stranded citizens firing guns at their rescuers, and inaccurate information about the toxicity of the water (some called it "a toxic soup"). Most of the stories—especially those about rescuers as the targets of violence—hindered rescue efforts by discouraging some first responders, relief workers, bus drivers, and others from helping.

National media organizations printed inaccurate statements by Bush administration officials who were attempting to absolve themselves of blame. For example, the *New York Times*, in a September 2 story headlined "Government Saw Flood Risk But Not Levee Failure," quoted Bush's claim, "I don't think anyone anticipated the breach of the levees." The *Times* accepted the statement, although there was published evidence before the storm suggesting the levees might not hold. In fact, the previous year, Blanco warned federal officials about the threat a catastrophic hurricane posed to New Orleans. In an op-ed in the *Washington Post* on December 8, 2004, she wrote: "My state dodged a massive natural disaster in September when Hurricane Ivan, which seemed on course to hit New Orleans, veered away at the last minute. . . . Even with the massive evacuation, thousands could have died in the storm surge, trapped in a city that is largely below sea level."

Fox News, on September 7, and ABC News, on September 11, repeated the false report that "there were 2,000 buses under water" in New Orleans that had not been used for the evacuation. Reports later determined that the city owned only 324 school buses. If the city's public transit buses were added to that number, the total would have been about 700. The inaccurate figure appears to have come from a *New York Times* story on September 4 that quoted Louisiana emergency planners who believed it would have required up to 2,000 buses to evacuate 100,000 elderly and disabled citizens from New Orleans in the event of an approaching catastrophic hurricane. But as the *Times* reported, this was "far more than New Orleans possessed."

Fox News and the Knight Ridder news service reported that Blanco blocked the American Red Cross from sending relief supplies to the Louisiana Superdome. The Louisiana National Guard had not prevented the Red Cross from entering New Orleans but had merely advised Red Cross officials that it could not guarantee the safety of the organization's workers and volunteers should they enter the city.

I bear responsibility for some of this misreporting, because the state did not permit most reporters to enter New Orleans and denied them access to National Guard helicopters and Louisiana Wildlife and Fisheries boats. In the days after the storm, most reporters with automobiles were stopped at checkpoints and could not proceed. The news media were generally not allowed into New Orleans from Monday, August 29, through the afternoon of Thursday, September 1. While some media organizations circumvented the checkpoints, many of those who reported from New Orleans for the first three days after the storm were individuals who entered the city prior to Katrina and weathered the storm. One day early that week, sitting at my desk in the EOC, I looked up to see Bob Woodruff, then the anchor of ABC's "World News Tonight," standing before me. He pleaded for help in getting permission to drive into New Orleans with his crew. I hurried to the other side of the building and found Col. Henry Whitehorn, head of the State Police. I asked him to give Woodruff the permission and necessary paperwork to pass through the checkpoints. He agreed. I wish I had been more aggressive in helping reporters like Woodruff get into the city to see things for themselves.

Although Blanco sent hundreds of Wildlife and Fisheries boats into the storm zone on the afternoon of Monday, August 29—just after the hurricane had passed over the region—no reporters, photographers, and videographers were allowed on these boats. The state also banned media from National Guard helicopters that began rescue missions that afternoon. It was wrong to not make an accommodation for media on boats and choppers. Saving lives was the priority, but public confidence in government is also crucial. During times of crisis and danger, citizens deserve to know that public servants are working on their behalf—and *showing* them is far more effective than *telling* them.

It wasn't just that our public relations were lacking. We also had our public affairs resources in the wrong place. With few exceptions, all of Louisiana's public information officers were in Baton Rouge, which was the site of a large part of the story. But a much more important story was unfolding eighty miles to the south, and we had almost no one managing communications for the governor, the National Guard, the State Police, and the Department of Wildlife and Fisheries. Even if I had sent public affairs officers into the storm zone, they would have been isolated and out of touch much of the time because of the total breakdown in communication between New Orleans and Baton Rouge. We *prevented* access to New Orleans when we should have *controlled* access to the city. That meant the story of the state's role in the rescue was not reported widely, or at least not recorded by still and video photographers.

This shutdown of movement into the city meant that, in the days after the storm, the principal images from New Orleans were those of flooded homes with desperate residents stranded on rooftops, apparent widespread looting, dead bodies floating in floodwaters, uncontrolled fires, flooded school buses, the Superdome and Convention Center crowded with suffering evacuees, and confused and overwhelmed public officials unable to deal with the crisis.

While these images were accurate, they did not represent the whole story. For example, what was not often reported was that more than 90 percent of the residents of the New Orleans region safely evacuated before the storm. There's no doubt the city, state, and federal governments did not do enough to evacuate the remaining residents. Officials documented and acknowledged this at every level. And yet, despite these failures, the safe evacuation of more than one million citizens in less than forty-eight hours was a remarkable feat. State and local officials had accomplished the largest exodus of an urban center in the nation's history and the first wholesale evacuation of a major American city since the Civil War. As the disastrous evacuation of Houston prior to Hurricane Rita a few weeks later showed, evacuating such a large population is difficult and can be deadly.

Just as significant, the national media gave viewers around the country the impression that state officials were paralyzed by fear and indecision and that no one was being evacuated or rescued, except by the US Coast Guard. In fact, thousands of citizens were being rescued each day—probably more than fifty thousand people during the week after the storm—by the Louisiana National Guard, by the Louisiana Department of Wildlife and Fisheries, and by average citizens in their boats. That story did not receive the attention it deserved because the media were not allowed to accompany the rescuers. At one point, a day or two into the recovery, I went to a top National Guard official and begged him to let us send a few reporters, photographers, and videographers into the hurricane zone to record the rescue. He shook his head. "Every extra person I put on a boat or helicopter is one less person we can save from a rooftop," he said in denying my request. I should have pushed harder.

Maybe I could have persuaded Blanco to overrule him. I'm sure these reporters would have let someone sit on their laps for a few miles. The reasoning for these decisions was sound. However, because the television audiences saw so few images of these rescues, viewers got the impression that almost nothing was being done to save lives when, in fact, heroic public servants laboring in obscurity were saving thousands.

When Blanco visited the Superdome that first week—on Tuesday evening after the storm—she barred media coverage of the visit. For understandable reasons, she wanted to speak with these suffering people outside the glare of the television lights. She respected their dignity and cared about their hardship too much to be seen exploiting them. Looking back on this moment, I find it's one reason I'll always love Kathleen Blanco. She approached situations like this as a human being first. The political considerations were often secondary in her reasoning. So, we excluded reporters from the trip and missed an opportunity to demonstrate the state's concern for those stranded at the Superdome. I know my attention to these public perceptions of our work might seem callous or superficial, but I've always believed otherwise. That's because we sometimes left the impression that government officials either did not care or were incapable of dealing with the enormous challenges presented by the disaster.

ALL THESE YEARS later, it is still hard to believe that the governor of Louisiana and the mayor of New Orleans could not communicate in the week after the storm. For days, if Blanco wanted to get word about something to Nagin, she had to write a letter or note and have it hand-delivered to him. In the early days, I sometimes phoned an employee in Nagin's press office who had evacuated to Houston. She could communicate with Nagin. I called her several times with messages to pass along to the mayor. The most reliable way to reach Nagin in those early days was for Blanco to board one of the National Guard's Blackhawk helicopters and fly to the city. One late afternoon, I went with her into New Orleans. We swooped over the drowned city and landed at the helipad next to the Superdome. From there, the National Guard picked us up and drove us in a large high-water vehicle to City Hall, across the street from the Dome. Nagin was nowhere to be found. So, we met with US Army Lt. Gen. Russel Honoré, commander of Joint Task Force Katrina, and the chief of police. We never saw the mayor on that visit.

That the state, the federal government, and the city of New Orleans could not cooperate—nor communicate—in the days after the storm compounded the negative image of the state. For that, Nagin was largely responsible. Many of us on Blanco's staff suspected he was working with the White House in its effort to smear the state. As Senator Mary

Landrieu would tell a reporter for *Salon* in 2008, "[The White House] looked around and they found a Democratic governor and an African American Democratic mayor who had never held office before in his life before he was mayor of New Orleans—someone they knew they could manipulate." I had heard that Nagin was bragging about being in touch with "The Man," i.e., President Bush. From the early days of the crisis, we heard that Nagin was in constant communication with the White House, speaking with Bush and his close aide, Karl Rove, and also with another Bush ally, Senator David Vitter. As Mary Landrieu later said, "I knew Ray Nagin could be easily manipulated," adding, "I could see where Rove was going: Blame Blanco. Blame the levee board. Blame the corruption in New Orleans."

To her credit, Blanco never uttered an unkind public word about Nagin in the weeks after Katrina. When he was having what many believed was an emotional breakdown—his meltdown on WWL-AM that week was disturbing—she resisted the urge to feud with him, because she knew it would only further undermine public confidence in the response and recovery. The fact is, however, that the inability of Blanco and Nagin to communicate reinforced an image of failure and overwhelming incompetence. Because federal officials—particularly those working for FEMA and the Department of Homeland Security—were engaged in the White House's efforts to undermine Blanco, the relationship between the governor's office and federal officials was strained and added to the dysfunction of the coordinated response.

As badly as the press treated Blanco in the first two weeks of the catastrophe, it would be nothing compared to the Republican smear campaign that would soon engulf her and all of us.

18

WE ARE NOT GOING TO PICK A FIGHT WITH THIS WHITE HOUSE

In the storm's aftermath, many national reporters had a myopic view of the unfolding story in New Orleans because of the severe constraints we imposed upon them, including limiting their access to the city and not allowing them to accompany state employees on rescue missions. But this was not the only reason people had such a negative view of how Blanco and other state officials handled the crisis. In the days following the storm, the White House conducted a campaign to shift the blame for its blunders onto state and local officials. Blanco, Nagin, and others in Louisiana deserved criticism for their mistakes. But when White House and other federal files are eventually opened to the public, I'm confident we'll find that, during the worst natural disaster in American history, White House aides devoted themselves not to helping local and state officials save lives but to saving the president's political life.

Just two days after the storm, it was clear to everyone on Blanco's staff that the operation to shift blame was in full swing. Denise Bottcher and I spent most of our time answering inaccurate press reports coming out of Washington about the state response. Sometimes, the reporters would identify the source of this misinformation as "senior White House officials." In one of the most egregious examples of this, the *Washington Post* on September 4 quoted an anonymous "senior Bush official" who alleged Blanco had not yet declared a state of emergency. "Louisiana Gov. Kathleen Babineaux Blanco seemed uncertain and sluggish," *Newsweek* reported, "hesitant to declare martial law or a state of emergency, which would have opened the door to more Pentagon help." The clear implication, accepted as fact by the *Post* and by *Newsweek* and never confirmed by any source in Louisiana, was that Blanco was so inept she could not declare a state of emergency. However, as the *Post* reported on September 5 in a correction, Blanco had declared a state of emergency on August 26, three days before the storm. *Newsweek* issued a correction, too.

Some of the strategy behind the White House campaign of blame shifting was revealed in the *New York Times* on September 5. "Under the command of President Bush's two senior political advisors, the White House rolled out a plan this weekend to contain the political damage from the administration's response to Hurricane Katrina," reporters Adam Nagourney and Anne E. Kornblut wrote. These advisors, the journalists reported, "directed administration officials not to respond to attacks from Democrats on the relief efforts, and sought to move the blame for the slow response to Louisiana state officials, according to Republicans familiar with the White House plan." The reporters noted that "the administration is also working to shift the blame away from the White House and toward officials of New Orleans and Louisiana who, as it happens, are Democrats."

In one example of administration officials who were adhering to Karl Rove's communications philosophy, the *Times* reporters quoted Secretary Michael Chertoff of the US Department of Homeland Security: "The way that emergency operations act under the law is the responsibility and the power, the authority, to order an evacuation rests with state and local officials. . . . The federal government comes in and supports those officials." The reporters observed that this "line of argument was echoed throughout the day, in harsher language, by Republicans reflecting the White House line." As Terry Ryder, then Blanco's executive counsel, pointed out to me later, "While it is generally accurate that primary response is with the locals," the federal National Response Plan "called for almost-automatic actions at all levels—like activation of the 82nd Airborne to respond—whereas, in this case, Secretary of Defense Donald Rumsfeld refused to send General Honoré for days." Terry also noted that "Louisiana did not then, nor now, have 'martial law' powers."

After twenty years in politics, I thought I was sophisticated about how these games worked, but one brief encounter still haunts me as a reminder of my naiveté. About two weeks into the crisis—as the White House's effort to trash the state remained in full swing—then-House Republican Minority Leader Tom DeLay of Texas visited the EOC in Baton Rouge. I was desperate to impress upon someone in Washington that the political attacks on Blanco prevented state and local officials from doing their jobs. And they damaged the state's credibility as we prepared to ask Washington for billions in assistance to rebuild Louisiana's shattered infrastructure and economy. Our tormentors included Bob Livingston and David Vitter, who put naked partisanship ahead of helping their state. I pulled DeLay aside in the EOC's big conference room. "Look, we are doing our best to deal with a disaster of epic proportions, but our job is being made so much harder by all the political backstabbing," I said. "Can you do anything to help stop it?" DeLay looked me in the eyes, smiled earnestly, nodded, and assured me he would try to help. I now understand he was probably thinking: "Who is this idiot, and why does he think we won't destroy his boss if we have the chance?"

Much of the nation saw a state in which officials were unable to deal with the catastrophe. Some of this was based on valid criticism of the city and state's inability to evacuate those without transportation and who were later stranded in the Dome and Convention Center. But a substantial part of it resulted from an effective blame game played by the White House.

In a speech to graduate students at the Metropolitan College of New York in January 2007, former FEMA Director Mike Brown admitted that politics were a major factor in Bush's desire to federalize Louisiana's National Guard during the first week of September 2005 (as I have described in chapter one). "Unbeknownst to me," Brown said, "certain people in the White House were thinking, 'We had to federalize Louisiana because she's a White, female Democratic governor and we have a chance to rub her nose in it.'" When the complete story is told, I believe it will be apparent the White House did to Blanco what Bush's operatives did to Senator John McCain in the South Carolina primary in 2000—they said whatever was necessary to smear and destroy those who presented threats to Bush's political standing, and they used every useful tool at their disposal.

I've always thought we should have challenged aggressively the White House's blame shifting. The landscape is littered with the dead careers of politicians who did not respond effectively when under attack. Michael Dukakis (see Willie Horton and prison furloughs) and John Kerry (see Swift Boat Veterans for Truth) come immediately to mind. Because Blanco feared offending Bush when the state desperately needed federal help, we were forced to disarm. I and others on the staff argued against that. "We've got to set the record straight," I told her in a meeting at the EOC late that first week. Denise Bottcher and Andy Kopplin agreed. But Blanco was adamant that we not engage in what she considered partisan sniping. "We are not going to pick a fight with this White House," she declared. "We're on our knees. We need President Bush's help to rebuild this state."

We did everything possible to set the record straight without going to war with the Bush administration. But it was impossible to persuade her and Coach to allow us to challenge aggressively a tsunami of blame moving in the state's direction, instigated by the White House, its allies, and spokespeople. I thought she was making a terrible decision. I believed we had to fight back and defend the work she and other state officials were doing in the face of the White House's efforts to slander her.

Blanco was also determined not to do anything that looked like she was concerned about the politics of Katrina. If others wished to politicize the disaster, she thought, they would have that on their conscience, but hers would be clear. For that reason, when I told her a group of Democratic operatives wanted to conduct a statewide poll in late September to assess the political damage the storm inflicted on her and other Louisiana Democrats, she rejected the idea. "I don't want anything to do with that poll," she said. "Tell them I don't want any poll like that run in Louisiana." I shared her sentiments with my contact, but it was a free country, and he and I knew that Blanco couldn't prevent him from ordering a survey. A few weeks later, the individual sent me the poll numbers. Blanco was furious when she learned the survey had gone forward against her orders. I was with her in Houston that day. She was about to board our state plane for the return trip to Baton Rouge, and I was aboard a separate aircraft with several journalists who accompanied us for the day. When she heard about the poll, she summoned me off my plane. For about ten minutes, she chewed me out for my failure to shut down the enterprise. I tried to protest that I had been powerless to do so, but she was in no mood to hear my explanation. It was as thorough a chewing-out as I've ever received. That night around ten o'clock she called to berate me all over again. I heard the message loud and clear: no politics.

Blanco was wise to operate above the political maelstrom. It is not clear our small communications staff could have competed against the vast resources of the White House and federal government. The governor's communications operation had no more than five people. Our unilateral disarmament in the face of a blatant, well-orchestrated effort to blame her for the Bush administration's failures meant that history, at least for the next decade, would blame Blanco as much as Bush for breakdowns in the Katrina response. Historians are already kinder to her and have reassessed the role she played in leading the recovery and rebuilding of southeast Louisiana.

Again, I'm not arguing that the state was blameless. State and local officials made many mistakes in the planning and response to Katrina. Those have been well documented. In fact, because Blanco was the only public official to release voluntarily every document requested by the US House and Senate investigating committees, we know more about Louisiana's failures than those of any other government entity.

Unfortunately, Blanco's public image during this time was not one of strength and resolve but fatigue. I wish I had insisted we restrict her to one—maybe two—daily press briefings in the early days of the crisis. She was a good politician, but public speaking was not her strongest suit. In too many briefings, she did not speak with authority. Within a few days, exhaustion and enormous pressure created a communications nightmare for us. The many press briefings during the week after the storm exposed her to questions she was often not prepared to answer. They highlighted the strain in her voice and the pain in her demeanor.

Even when we tried to keep her press briefings to a minimum, we sometimes failed. One day, someone brought me word the Reverend Jesse Jackson was on his way from New Orleans to the EOC and wanted a meeting with Blanco. I greeted Jackson when he arrived, and he promptly told me he wanted Blanco to appear with him in a joint press conference to discuss the developments of the day. I was noncommittal but thought this might be a mistake, because we had no idea what Jackson might say. Before I ushered him into the governor's small office, I pulled Blanco aside.

"Just a warning," I told her. "Jackson will ask you to join him at the podium. That's not a great idea. Let me decline for you when he asks." She agreed. At the end of their visit, Jackson said, "Governor, I'm going to hold a little press briefing. Would you join me?" I quickly jumped in. "Reverend," I said, "I'm not sure that's a good idea. We haven't had time to brief the governor on all the latest developments and I don't think it's wise to send her out there to answer questions without a good briefing. Why don't you go ahead without her?" That seemed to mollify Jackson, who said he understood. Blanco, however, had another idea. "I'll do it with you," she responded. And five minutes later, she was holding a joint press briefing for which she had not prepared.

THE BLANCO ADMINISTRATION had two periods. There was pre-Katrina, during which Blanco devoted herself, among other things, to creating jobs and reforming education and juvenile justice. Post-Katrina, there was nothing but recovering from Katrina and Rita. After the search-and-recovery phase, the work of restoring south Louisiana began. To secure the billions in recovery aid Louisiana needed from the federal government meant Blanco would be forced to testify before congressional committees investigating the errors and missteps by officials at every level of government. She also would have to make a dozen or so trips to Washington to lobby congressional leaders and Bush administration officials for the money, especially after the initial appropriations bill awarded much more per capita to Mississippi than Louisiana. That had something to do with the fact that Mississippi's senior US senator, Thad Cochran, chaired the Senate Appropriations Committee. He and other Senate leaders initially shortchanged Louisiana. Blanco and the congressional delegation, led by Senator Mary Landrieu, fought for months to get Louisiana residents the assistance they deserved.

For Blanco, the job was grueling and often humbling. On virtually every trip, she went to the White House to plead for funding from officials who attacked her or who doubted that Louisiana government was honest or efficient enough to spend properly the rebuilding dollars we requested. In these visits, she showed her steel, once threatening to blast Bush in a press conference on the White House driveway if his aides did not give Louisiana what it needed. They quickly relented when they realized she wasn't bluffing. Then, she would trudge over to Capitol Hill for meetings with Democratic and Republican leaders.

I got a little taste of what Blanco sometimes endured in December 2005 when Cindy and I spent a long weekend outside Nashville with our friends Harvill and Lois Eaton. Harvill, a former LSU vice chancellor, was then president of Cumberland University in Lebanon, Tennessee. US Representative Jim Cooper, a conservative Democrat, represented the Nashville area and was a strong Cumberland supporter. Harvill arranged for me to meet with Cooper in his district office one morning. From the first minute until the last, Cooper attacked me for what he considered the botched Katrina response. He never inquired about my family's wellbeing or evinced the slightest concern for Louisiana residents. And he never asked about my boss and her health. He was angry, and I was his target. I came away understanding some of the indignities Blanco suffered in her meetings in Washington.

The stress on Blanco was clear. The suffering she witnessed weighed on her constantly. She had to know that Katrina would be her legacy, for good or bad. And bad it was, at least in the early months. During this time, I think she looked for and treasured moments when she could forget about Katrina and Rita for a few hours. And she understood when others needed to do the same. She allowed me a week off in mid-October 2005 to take my family on a long-scheduled, prepaid vacation to Disney World. It was surreal, living a "normal" life in Orlando that week. I came back refreshed and revitalized, but also aware that, since I was a staffer, the press wouldn't care much if I took off a week so my kids could see Mickey Mouse. As governor, Blanco could not enjoy a break like this for months.

Days or evenings during which she could truly relax were rare, but I witnessed one of them on a trip with her to Washington in December 2005. Blanco spent all day testifying before congressional committees and meeting with members of the House and Senate appropriations committees. Like all these days in DC, it was long and exhausting. That evening, she and the staff went to dinner and then retired to a large condo in northwest Washington owned by a friend of Aprill Springfield (Blanco's future daughter-in-law who had recently joined the staff). After a review of the day, Aprill and the other staffers drifted away for bed. Finally, it was just Blanco and me. She was as relaxed as I had seen her in months. We talked for a while. Even though I was sleepy and looking for an excuse to retire, I couldn't leave her until she was ready to turn in. Eventually, we discovered that the owner of the place had a media room with an impressive collection of movies on DVD. "You want to watch a movie?" I asked. I knew she was a night owl, so her answer was not in doubt. We combed through the DVDs and settled on *Pirates of the Caribbean: The Curse of the Black Pearl*, a hilarious film starring Johnny Depp. For over two hours, we laughed like children.

It was a reminder that, at her essence, Blanco was a normal person who hadn't expected that her legacy would be helping an entire state get up off its knees. But as a person of deep faith, she believed that God called her to serve in that way. I don't mean that Blanco thought God made her governor. She didn't have a grandiose view of public service. But like many believers, she saw herself as one of God's instruments. If her lot in life was to be the governor who responded to Katrina, she would do it with resolve and let her faith guide her.

More typical of Blanco's schedule was her whirlwind trip to the Netherlands in January 2006—along with Senators Mary Landrieu and David Vitter, several New Orleans-area parish leaders, and other local officials—to learn how the Dutch deal with the constant, centuries-old threat of water. This small, low-lying country on the North Sea is vulnerable to flooding like much of south Louisiana. With its many miles of intersecting canals, Amsterdam is a beautiful example of a city that coexists with water, unlike New Orleans, which depended only on floodwalls and levees, hoping the barriers held. A state trooper and I accompanied Blanco on this trip. The delegation left New Orleans on a Monday, arrived in Amsterdam on Tuesday morning, toured the country over Tuesday, Wednesday, and Thursday, and flew back on Friday. Blanco returned a day early, on Thursday morning, leaving me to represent her on the final day. She never recovered from the jet lag caused by flying east over the Atlantic before she endured the jet lag of flying in the opposite direction. She must have been exhausted when she returned to work on Friday. I don't know how she did it.

EVEN IF OUR communications in the weeks and months after the storm had been perfect, they would not have overcome the nightmare that was Louisiana's rebuilding effort, which the administration at first called "Governor Kathleen Blanco's Road Home Program." When Blanco and the Louisiana congressional delegation finally secured the $10 billion to help homeowners rebuild, the money often got caught up in maddening red tape. No state had ever had to administer a program like this. No company—Virginia-based ICF International won the contract—had ever distributed that much to more than 100,000 homeowners. There were bound to be problems, bad stories, and thousands of frustrated and angry citizens. And there were all of those. As the delays and problems mounted, so did Blanco's political woes. Had the rebuilding effort gone perfectly, she might have survived and overcome Katrina's aftermath. It didn't, so she couldn't, even though the Road Home eventually did what it was created to do. As *Times-Picayune* reporter David Hammer would write almost ten years later, in August 2015: "For all but a small minority of the 130,000 Louisiana homeowners who reached out to it, the state's $10 billion Road Home rebuilding program left them with what it was supposed to: a reconstructed house or money to buy a new one, even if there were potholes and detours on the road to recovery."

By the time Blanco would die fourteen years later, the assessment of her leadership had softened. Historians and others who examined what happened during and after Katrina began to recognize that Blanco's leadership—while not perfect—was far better than Bush's, who left the White House in disgrace, and Ray Nagin's, who went to federal prison a few years later. Those who looked at Blanco more dispassionately applauded her for leading the state with dedication and integrity during its most difficult days. They recognized she fought for Louisiana when some in Washington—including the Republican speaker of the House—wanted to give up on New Orleans and the rest of the state. Blanco never gave up. Until the last day of her term, she worked with relentless passion to restore her beloved state.

Thirteen years after Katrina, on December 20, 2018, as Blanco was dying of the cancer that would take her life in August 2019, I wrote her a letter:

> I was listening this morning to the [New Orleans] public radio podcast about you, the media, and Katrina. And it reminded me of how proud I was to work for you at that time. And it made me regret all the ways I might have failed you, too. Those were hard times for so many people and your wise, compassionate decision not to declare war on Bush was the right one—although it seemed wrong to me at the time.
>
> What I really want to tell you is that Louisiana was blessed to have you as governor at that time in history. Your legacy will be one that your children and grandchildren will be proud of. If I have anything to do with the writing about the history of that time (and I plan to), I will do my best to make it abundantly clear what a wise and tireless leader you were for our state.
>
> Thank you for trusting me with the job you gave me in your administration. I'm proud to have served you and, more than anything, proud to know you—the real you. A person of true kindness, compassion,

and profound faith in God. You are in my prayers and I want you to know that I love you and will always treasure our friendship.

I'm happy Blanco lived long enough to see the assessment of her leadership evolve. Because everyone knew she only had a year or two to live when her cancer returned in late 2017, she read and heard some of this reassessment, including from then-*Times-Picayune* columnist Jarvis DeBerry, who said he regretted writing a column critical of Blanco. "Blanco is a fundamentally honest person who happened to be governor at one of the most difficult times in Louisiana history," DeBerry wrote in December 2017. "If we'd had the kind of federal response the crisis required, then there wouldn't have been so much anger directed at her. We shouldn't lose sight of how humongous the job was and how much criticism—justified and otherwise—was directed at her." Historian Douglas Brinkley, who taught at Tulane University at the time of Katrina, said in April 2019, "I think Kathleen Blanco was a true hero of Katrina." Republican state Senator Danny Martiny of Metairie was also kind in describing her leadership. "In the end," he said in 2016, "I think you'll find that this lady was a leader who was dealt a bad hand, and did the best she could."

As I wrote in the New Orleans paper *Gambit* the day she died, "[She] wasn't the boldest or most charismatic politician Louisiana ever produced, but Kathleen Blanco may have been the most empathetic, compassionate person to serve as Louisiana governor. That's no insignificant distinction. Knowing her as I did, I suspect she would be fine with that legacy. Even in her role as governor during and after hurricanes Katrina and Rita in 2005—which will, for good or bad, define her term as governor—Blanco's compassion and her humanity were always clear." I told a few personal stories about her humanity, some that I have related in this book.

I ended thus: "The last few times I saw Kathleen Blanco, I was overwhelmed with her sense of peace. She was fighting cancer, to be sure, but I sensed a feeling of ease with her fate. She knew her time was short and, as a person of profound faith in God, she wanted to show everyone around her how to die. In other words, to her very end, she acted with concern for others. Kathleen Babineaux Blanco gave us this great and wonderful gift in the way she lived her final days with grace, dignity and, always, compassion."

19

You're Losing This Class

By early 2006, my effectiveness as Blanco's communications director was over. She and Coach blamed me for her poor public image in the wake of Katrina. It usually showed in their faces and interactions with me. They increasingly excluded me from meetings and decisions about communications and policy. Many days in early 2006, I showed up at work with almost nothing to do because Blanco and other senior staffers shut me out of meetings.

Whatever they blamed me for, I blamed myself, too. I still do. I could have done more. I could have managed better the communications assets we had. It didn't compare to what the White House could throw at us, but it wasn't nothing. I wasn't creative enough to present Blanco as a decisive leader. I should have found more ways to show the press and the public she was in command. Instead, people often saw her stumble through press briefings. In smaller settings, she was always more effective and forceful. I wish I had practiced more often what I'd preached: get her out from behind the lectern and put her in smaller settings.

At times, Blanco also suspected I was disloyal to her. In a staff conference call in early 2006, I had disagreed vehemently with a proposal to spend state money on a pet project of a legislative ally from Morehouse Parish that had nothing to do with Katrina relief. I thought it would be a disaster if she were seen spending state money on pork-barrel projects in north Louisiana while the southeastern part of the state was still on its knees. "If we do this, all of us might as well start polishing our resumes, because she won't get reelected," I said. The comment was hyperbole, but I wanted to make my point with force. Someone on the call went to Coach or the governor and told one or both what I said. Later that day, she summoned me to her office in the Governor's Mansion, with several staffers present. She had chewed me out before but never in front of others. "What are you doing telling people you don't think I can get reelected?!" she raged. I tried to explain, but she wasn't listening. She was shouting so loudly I was sure people in the foyer could hear her. Worse, she was berating me in front of several staffers.

I left the meeting shaken. I knew that anything I said on a conference call might be distorted by someone who wanted to undermine me. And I now knew Blanco was willing to believe the worst about me. More than anything, I knew I had lost her confidence. I had to leave.

Among the friends I consulted about job opportunities was John Maxwell "Jack" Hamilton, dean of the Manship School of Mass Communication at LSU. He told me his school would soon hire someone for a two-year appointment (it later became permanent) to the school's Manship Chair in Journalism. He encouraged me to apply. The position would allow me to teach, research, and write books as part of my job, not a part-time endeavor. I had dreamed about a job like this for years. For my last two years on Breaux's staff, I had taught at the Manship School as an adjunct and loved it. I knew I would enjoy faculty life. In February 2006, Jack called to schedule my interview with the school's faculty.

I had not told Blanco I was looking for another job, but I suspected it would not surprise her. Still, I wanted her to hear it directly from me. The *Baton Rouge Advocate* almost ruined that. The day before my LSU interview, the school circulated my schedule among faculty and staff. Copied on the email was at least one *Advocate* writer who taught as an adjunct. Within minutes, a reporter called about my interview. I knew that what I had assumed would be a confidential job talk was now a news story. I rushed to see Blanco. She was gracious and wished me luck. The next morning, as I prepared to spend the day at the school, the *Advocate* announced in a story on page 15-A, "Blanco advisor seeks LSU endowed chair." I had to laugh. Most people don't have their job interviews announced in the local paper. Within a few weeks, Jack called to say the faculty voted to offer me the position.

On my last day working for her, Blanco hosted a going-away dinner for me at a local Italian restaurant. As a parting gift, she presented me with a lovely leather-bound book. She wrote inside it, in part: "It has been a long two and a half years and our journey has been an incredible one. I'm glad you were part of this story. . . . I hope that your years at the Manship School will be at least as interesting as those years spent with me in the Governor's Office—but perhaps not as stressful."

TEACHING AT LSU was everything I hoped it would be, and more. I loved the freedom to spend my nonteaching hours at the school's library doing research on my next book project, a history of American wartime dissent. I loved teaching political communication. And I loved my students, who were eager and smart.

With Governor Kathleen Blanco and her husband, Raymond "Coach" Blanco, at my going-away dinner in the spring of 2006.

I realize now one of the reasons I love teaching is that I never really enjoyed political press relations as much as I pretended. And that was for one simple reason: I wasn't very good at it. To excel in public relations, you must be comfortable with selling. I don't mean to say that all PR people are salespeople, but the best probably are. In press relations, you're always spinning, sometimes putting the best face on a bad situation, or trying to sell skeptical reporters on a story idea. In the best of cases, you're selling something, or someone, you believe in. In the worst cases, you've got to sell something you know is wrong or imperfect. That's the part of the job I hated and never performed well. Maybe it's because I had been a reporter, but I could always imagine the journalist on the other end of the line thinking, "Yeah, this is bunk."

I hated the idea of calling anyone and pitching them on something they might not want. As competent as I consider myself with words, I often stumble when I try to peddle something. And I really fall apart when I know that person is skeptical of me or what I'm hawking. Maybe it's a little bit of low self-esteem (or imposter syndrome), but I've never had much confidence in my ability to persuade people, at least in one-on-one situations. I've masked that with some coping mechanisms and a dash of razzle-dazzle. I don't mind putting my arguments on paper, but even writing my opinions in a newspaper column or blog post wasn't easy at first.

Teaching, however, came naturally to me. I was comfortable in the classroom, where I wasn't selling ideas or policy proposals but talking about the elements of good writing. While I'm not as comfortable selling a single person on an idea, I've never had trouble speaking to audiences, large or small.

Not that I was perfect at it. One day, about midway through my first semester at LSU, a student dropped by for a visit.

"Can I be honest with you?" he asked.

"Sure," I said, with trepidation.

"You're losing this class," he told me. "You need to make some changes in the way you teach."

As the student and I talked, I realized I was teaching the course all wrong. I was not focusing enough on giving them useful, professional skills that would help them get a job upon graduation. Based on this student's sound advice, I retooled the syllabus and pulled myself back from the abyss. Ever since, I've told students about this episode and implored them to tell me if they think my teaching isn't serving them.

At LSU, my life shrank in welcome ways. We lived five minutes from University Lab School, which our children, Avery and Robert, attended. Most mornings, I dropped them off and then drove to my office just a short distance across the LSU campus. The entire journey took less than ten minutes. Because the school was so close to my office—a ten-minute walk—I could stroll down the street and join them for lunch once or twice a month. It was a joy to go from being an absentee dad to having the luxury of sharing lunch with my children whenever I wanted. They loved having Dad show up at their classroom and walk with them to the cafeteria—and I loved it, too. Suddenly, much of our lives were confined to a one-mile radius around LSU.

My office was a small, sparsely furnished room on the first floor of the LSU's Journalism Building, one of the oldest structures on campus but newly renovated. For the first time in several years, my workday proceeded at a leisurely pace—sometimes too leisurely. But I also no longer had an assistant to field my phone calls or a BlackBerry to remind me about scheduled meetings. I was on my own, which meant I was sometimes late for appointments or missed them completely. But I enjoyed spending time with students between classes, as well as with new faculty colleagues. Most of all, I loved that I was responsible for nothing at LSU beyond teaching my classes and grading papers. Unless the Journalism Building burned to the ground on a Friday night, no one at the school would ever think to call me over the weekend, which was a welcome relief from my once-frantic work life. Weekends were mine to do with as I wished.

AS I SETTLED into the job, however, another potential campaign called. In early 2007, Blanco faced the reality that Hurricane Katrina and its aftermath—particularly what many people considered her botched Road Home Program—had undermined any chance she had of reelection. In March 2007, she announced she would not run again. "While so many still suffer," she said, "I am choosing to do what I believe is best for my state. I will focus my time and energy for the next nine months on the people's work, not politics." Within a few weeks, Democrats began casting about for someone who might hold on to the governor's office. Some of them settled on John Breaux, who had expected Blanco would not run and was exploring the possibility of a campaign. He was then about a year into his Senate retirement, working for a government relations firm with his old friend and former Republican Senate colleague from Mississippi, Trent Lott. Like several Louisiana senators over the years, Breaux had long nursed a desire to become governor. The lure of the office is easy to understand. It has far more power and influence than any other statewide office, including US senator. A governor skilled in the art of persuasion— and Breaux knew how to do that as well as anyone—could achieve much.

From the beginning, the idea appealed to me, too. Breaux had the stature to clear the Democratic field. He could raise money—and lots of it. If elected, he would have the public's support. Most voters knew Breaux as a bipartisan leader who always looked for practical solutions to problems. While Republican lawmakers would work hard to elect Bobby Jindal or some other Republican, Breaux had forged good relationships with many of them over the years. After decades of working both sides of the aisle in DC, Breaux knew—in his bones—how to work with lawmakers from the opposite party.

Breaux quickly warmed to the idea. Some prominent supporters and former staff members were doing what we could to test the waters. We convened meetings and conference calls, sometimes several a week, to discuss how to get Breaux into the race. But there was one problem we could not overcome. After he left the Senate, Breaux thought he was done with electoral politics. And the job he had taken required him to be in Washington most of the time. So he did not own a house in Louisiana, unless one considered his part-ownership of his childhood home in Crowley. Breaux's elderly father, Ezra, still lived in that simple wood-framed house. Sure enough, his residency quickly became an issue. Voters might understand why a member of Congress might not maintain a large home in Louisiana (even that expectation was changing), but they would want their governor to be a full-time resident of the state.

The legal advice Breaux got on this question was favorable. He could probably win a court challenge to his residency. But that was just the problem: there would be an ugly and protracted legal challenge. No doubt the Louisiana Republican Party, or some Republican activist, would sue. Breaux, and probably his father, would be forced to testify about how much time he spent in the state, where he paid property taxes, and where he voted. Breaux decided not to run. I wanted him to, but I also hoped he would be in the best position to win the race. It was clear he would spend much of fall 2007 arguing in court that he was a resident of Louisiana. It was not the ideal way to launch a statewide campaign.

Looking back on the eight years of Governor Bobby Jindal's misrule, I mourn the absence of a competent, honest leader like Breaux. He would have worked hard for sound policy accomplishments, not cheap political points. Unlike Jindal, he would not have injected partisan Washington politics into Baton Rouge. He would not have slashed income taxes and blown a hole in the state budget. He would have never decimated state funding for higher education. He would not have attacked public school teachers. After Obamacare passed, he would have moved quickly to expand Medicaid for hundreds of thousands of people who needed healthcare. He would not have geared his governorship to setting himself up for a presidential race. He would have stayed in Louisiana and minded the store. He would have devoted himself to building on the substantial progress Blanco began and fashioned a bipartisan governing coalition to deliver sound results. Knowing Breaux as well as I do, I know Louisiana lost eight crucial years when it elected, and reelected, Jindal.

IN THE FALL of 2013, I learned of my election to the Louisiana Political Hall of Fame. Created by the legislature in 1987 and located in Winnfield— hometown of Huey and Earl Long—the Hall of Fame honors the best-known politicians and political journalists in the state. My friend Dan Borné was generous enough to nominate me. Ted Jones, who had worked for Governors Earl Long and Jimmie Davis, and Russell Long Mosely, grandson of Russell Long, served on the Hall's board. They shepherded my nomination. Over the years, I had attended several induction ceremonies in Winnfield. I attended the first ceremony in 1993 on Long's behalf, accepting his award during a dinner that also featured former Governors Edwin Edwards and John McKeithen. I attended again in 2003, when Breaux was inducted. Knowing I would join them and a pantheon of other Louisiana political giants was humbling and satisfying beyond measure. I knew I didn't deserve the recognition, but I never considered declining it.

In February 2014, with my family and several lifelong friends in the audience—including Jim Oakes and a dear friend from college, former Sulphur Mayor Ron LeLeux—Cindy and I sat on the stage where I would accept my plaque and deliver brief remarks. That night, future Governor John Bel Edwards was there to accept for his family, which was installed in the "Political Family" category. When my time came to speak, I made it clear I was not worthy. "I feel tonight a little like Barack Obama when they called from Oslo with news that he'd won the Nobel Peace Prize," I said. "I'm pretty sure I don't deserve it, but there's no way I'm not going to come and pick up my award."

After thanking my family and friends, I arrived at the essence of my remarks. I tried to capture what had been most meaningful to me during

When I was installed in the Louisiana Political Hall of Fame in 2014, old friends Jim Oakes (left) and former Sulphur Mayor Ron LeLeux (right) joined me and my family for the ceremony in Winnfield.

my three decades in and around politics. I also hoped I had proved that my mother was wrong when she warned me more than forty years before that politics would eventually corrupt everyone. As I wrote my acceptance speech, I knew I had not always behaved admirably. I'd cut corners. I hurt people. Several times, I had let my temper or my desire to win get the best of me. On balance, however, I believed that I had served honorably. I had learned from my mistakes. I had apologized to those whom I had unfairly attacked or maligned. And I now did my best to teach my students not to make the mistakes I made. To the audience and other honorees that night, I said:

> Twenty-three years ago, I took a leave of absence from my job as press secretary to Senator John Breaux to come back to Baton Rouge and work as press secretary on the reelection campaign of Senator J. Bennett Johnston. Nothing I've done in politics before or since has given me more satisfaction than helping defeat David Duke.
>
> Those of you in politics can testify to this: there aren't many days in your career when you see clearly—with absolute certainty—that one road is the right way and the other road is the wrong way. Life isn't usually like that. Our choices aren't usually so clear-cut. So, when you're presented with such an easy decision—progress versus the past; tolerance versus hatred; justice versus injustice—you really want to make sure you don't miss that opportunity. You want to seize it. And that's what I did. I've never regretted working in that campaign. And I've clung to the belief that I played a small part in helping save our state.
>
> Sometimes doing the right thing has benefits beyond saving your state. Were it not for coming home to work in that campaign, I wouldn't be married to my wife. It was during those six months in the spring and summer of 1990 that we really got to know each other. When I returned to DC in November of that year, I left my heart in New Orleans, where Cindy was living at the time. So, my heart for Louisiana brought me down here and my heart for the woman I love wouldn't let me stay long in DC. Within a year and a half, I packed up a U-Haul truck and moved my possessions to Baton Rouge to get married and, God bless him, continue working for John Breaux.
>
> Paul Begala, who helped Bill Clinton get elected president, told me once that President Clinton made them all look better than they deserved to look. And I've decided that I feel the same way about John Breaux and Russell Long. I was never half as clever or effective as those two political masters made me appear. They not only made me look better and smarter than I deserved; they taught a young kid some very important lessons about politics and life and I'm so blessed to have had them as mentors.
>
> I learned don't take your politics too seriously. And don't take yourself too seriously. I learned that today's adversary might be tomorrow's ally.

That politics and government *is* serious business, but don't forget to have fun. And I learned to remember that we're just temporary occupants of our offices. We don't own the place; it owns us. John Breaux and Russell Long taught me all that and more. And I'm grateful for the trust they had in me and the responsibility they gave me. Were it not for them, I wouldn't be standing here at this moment accepting this amazing honor.

And were it not for the experience these two leaders gave me, I wouldn't have had the opportunity to do what I do now and which gives me more pleasure and satisfaction than any job I've had. And that is the honor to spend my days among our state's future political leaders as a faculty member at LSU's Manship School. Every day, I'm among the young men and women who will one day lead this state and this nation. I know this sounds trite, but it's true: this next generation may be the one that saves this state.

As storied as our politics are, they haven't always served our people well. We may have the best and funniest politicians, but let's be honest—our poverty and our education systems are sad testimonies to the failures of our political system in recent generations. While we may have the most colorful politics, that hasn't always meant that we've had the noblest leaders. I pray that our next generation of leaders will continue to aspire to a career in politics. It is a noble profession. We just need more noble people in it. I'm hopeful that that next generation—the young people I work with every day—will ennoble our politics and lead our state into a new era of prosperity and equality and justice. That's my hope and I know it's yours, too.

So thank you so much for this honor. As I said, I don't feel like I deserve it. But don't anyone try taking this plaque out of my hands.

These days, the plaque—a beautiful and impressive memento—hangs on the wall in my LSU office in Hodges Hall. Students and visitors sometimes admire it. I love it when the occasional student, visiting my office for the first time, notices the plaque and then looks at me, quizzically, as if to ask, "*You* were once in politics?!" I chuckle inside a bit because those days seem like a lifetime ago. When my children were very young, they bounced on John Breaux's knee and hung out with Kathleen Blanco in her office. But like many of my students, Robert and Avery think of me as a college professor. That's really all they've ever known that I do. And while I'm proud of my former life and what I accomplished, teaching LSU students has been, by far, the most rewarding work I've ever done.

It may surprise some to learn that I rarely talk about my former life in class. I hardly ever tell political war stories to my students. Most current or former students of mine will have learned of these stories only by reading this book. I never wanted to be a teacher whose relevance was his or her past life. That said, my life, my stories, and the lessons I've

My family at Washington Mardi Gras in January 2019. Left to right: Robert, Cindy, Avery, and me.

learned along the way are worth sharing with my students and others, which is why I wanted to write this book. I hope that anyone who reads this understands that I regard politics as a noble and essential profession. It has too many rogues and self-dealers, to be sure, but most people I worked with were attracted to public service by a sincere desire to serve others.

I spend most of my days around young people who still have faith in our government and other institutions. They want to serve in government jobs or help elect good people to office by working in campaigns. Others want to defend the poor and the powerless by becoming lawyers or working for nonprofit organizations. A few still want to become crusading journalists. I hope those students who read this will come away a little wiser about the pitfalls of politics and better aware of the consequences of cutting corners and forgetting one's principles. For those who aspire to a life in public service, I hope they will work not just for anyone but for leaders who are honest, caring, and compassionate. I hope my former students who run for public office will listen to their consciences and surround themselves with ethical advisors and staff members unafraid to tell them the truth.

As much as anything, I hope the generation I'm teaching now will reach higher and crave more than I ever imagined possible. I regret having too often accepted the status quo. I did not, until late in my career, begin to question and challenge Louisiana's shameful acceptance of poverty and racism. In the words of the United Methodist prayer of confession, for too long I "did not hear the cry of the needy." I listened to the "important" people—business leaders, lobbyists, politicians—and far less to those on the margins of life. I gave little thought to the dangers of climate change. All this and more shame me.

More than anything, I hope my students will stop treating their elders with so much reverence. As I tell them at the beginning of each semester, "You're all good Southern young men and women. You've all been raised to treat your elders with deference and respect. From the earliest age, your parents drilled it into you to say 'yes, sir' and 'no, ma'am' to people older than you. But just because someone has gray hair or an office with nice leather furniture doesn't mean they're competent or know what they are talking about. Just look around this campus, this community, or this state. Tell me, where did you get the idea that the people in charge know what they are doing? In too many cases, they don't. They need to be challenged. You need to ask them why they are failing you. You need to demand they start listening to you. And you probably need to communicate it with more anger and less deference than your parents drilled into you."

In so many ways, the people running Louisiana and this country have not earned the respect of my students and my children. The leaders of my generation have failed them. I failed them. That's why I hope to spend the rest of my teaching days instilling in them a healthy disrespect for those in power and a greater understanding that the *real power* to change things in Louisiana and nationally resides in the vision and ability of the people to make their voices heard to those in power. If I learned anything from my several decades working in politics and government, it's that the "leaders" will lead if the people will tell them where to go.

ACKNOWLEDGMENTS

I owe much to many people who have helped make my happy life, and this book, possible—none more so than my wife, Cindy, who loves me more than I deserve. Her love is my daily reminder of God's grace. I'm also grateful for the love and example of my parents, Robert and Charlene Mann; my in-laws, Alfred and Gerry Horaist; my sister, Sarah Luker; my brother, Paul Mann, and his wife, Marlo Meuli; my sister-in-law, Jan Skinner, and her husband, Michael Skinner; and my brother-in-law, David Horaist. My children, Robert and Avery, are a source of enormous pride and love in my life. I pray they have learned from me that it's okay to make mistakes if you acknowledge them and try to make amends.

I'm also grateful for the many mentors and friends (living and deceased) in my life who taught me valuable lessons that I have passed along to my children and students. Compiling a list like this is dangerous. I'm bound to omit someone who deserves to be named. They include: Hattie Mae Wellhausen, Annie Mann, Nell Mullin, Betty Cornelius, Bill Wellhausen, H. Lynn Russell, Richard Baxter, Dave Norris, Stan Tiner, Russell and Carolyn Long, John and Lois Breaux, Kathleen and Raymond Blanco, J. Bennett and Mary Johnston, Daryl Owen, Jim and Karen Brady, Wiley Hilburn, Ted Jones, Roger and Gayle Guissinger, Clyde Taylor, Jerry and Margaret Johnson, Delise Battenfield, Jim and Tammie Oakes, John Copes, Ron and Renee LeLeux, Jim Nickel, Kyle France, Jerry Ceppos, Martin Johnson, Ross Atkins, Hal Kilshaw, Kris Kirkpatrick, Dan Borné, Richard Stiltner, A. J. Meek, Denise Bottcher, Lanny Keller, Kevin McGill, Ed Anderson, Jim Amoss, Rafael Bermudez, Chris Peacock, Michael Jefferson, Martin Walke, Chris Andrews, Terry Ryder, Jack Hamilton, David Kurpius, F. King Alexander, James Carville, Louis Day, Bob and Marguerite Ritter, Aly Neel, and David and Becky Poor.

Several individuals read all or part of this book and offered helpful criticisms, corrections, and suggestions. They are: Cindy Mann, Terry Ryder, Jim Oakes, Alisa Plant, Sarah Procopio, Denise Bottcher, Dave

Norris, Jerry Ceppos, and David Ferris. Any remaining mistakes, misjudgments, errors of grammar and style, and faulty memories are mine alone.

At Pelican Publishing, I am grateful to publisher Scott Campbell and editor in chief Nina Kooij for their enthusiasm for this book—and also to Nina for her fine job of editing the manuscript.

I dedicate this book to my late friend John Copes, who left us much too early. I hope his son, Jack, appreciates the extraordinary person his father was, as well as the profound and lasting influence he had on everyone who knew and loved him.

Notes

Chapter 2

1. More than forty years later, I would bring those items to St. Paul, Minnesota, when I spoke to a group of Humphrey's family and former staff—including former Vice President Walter Mondale and Humphrey's son Robert—at the premiere of a documentary about Humphrey's life. After I finished, I took my seat next to a former Humphrey aide, who leaned over, pointed to the booklet, and whispered, "I wrote that."

2. I later realized that most of the correspondence I received from politicians were form letters, signed by autopen or an aide. In my adulthood, I would become proficient in signing Senator John Breaux's name to correspondence sent to constituents from our Baton Rouge office.

Chapter 3

1. Like me, Dale would go into politics. After graduating Tulane Law School, he worked as an assistant district attorney in Vernon Parish, served as district manager for Republican US Representative Jim McCrery of Shreveport, and was a senior aide to two Shreveport mayors.

2. During his years hosting the popular country music radio show in Shreveport, Logan had introduced Elvis Presley, Johnny Cash, and Hank Williams to national audiences. He was also the first to utter, "Elvis has left the building."

Chapter 6

1. Twenty-one years later, I would take a phone call one morning from Fox as I stood outside the governor's office on the fourth floor. Now Louisiana's secretary of state, Fox thought I had persuaded Governor Kathleen Blanco to oppose a pay raise for all statewide elected officials. I was innocent, but McKeithen wanted the pay increase and decided I was the problem. "You're just a clerk," he spat into the phone as he chewed me

out for about five minutes. For the first three minutes, at least, I had no idea what he was talking about.

2. Kathy and I would work together a few years later, when she left *CQ* to move to Capitol Hill as press secretary to Republican Senator William Cohen of Maine.

Chapter 7

1. Also in that race was Kris Kirkpatrick's father, Claude, a former state representative from Jennings.

Chapter 8

1. In December 1985, Edwards' federal trial would end in a mistrial. Prosecutors would put him on trial again in the spring of 1986.

Chapter 9

1. I spoke with Kennedy about Crowley once at a reception at the home of the Australian ambassador. After telling him I worked for Breaux, I asked if he enjoyed spending time in Crowley when he and Vicki went home to see his father-in-law, retired city judge Edmund Reggie. "Well, there's not much to do there," he said with a shrug and a smile. "I play some tennis and that's about all there is."

Chapter 11

1. Later that year, Duke would approach my future wife, Cindy, at a tailgate outside LSU's Tiger Stadium before a football game. When he went to shake her hand, Cindy refused. Duke didn't frown or scowl. He spat no insult at her. He nodded his head and moved along.

Chapter 12

1. A year or two later, while I was working on my next book, I spoke with Clinton during a visit he made to Barksdale Air Force Base. He was interested to hear I discovered a memo in J. William Fulbright's papers from the mid-sixties that mentioned him among the clerks in the Arkansas senator's Washington office.

Chapter 13

1. These included Landrieu, Blanco, Margaret Lowenthal of Lake Charles, and Diana Bajoie, Jackie Clarkson, and Renee Gill Pratt of New Orleans.

Chapter 14

1. In 2007, when Jindal would run for governor again, the stories would make news. By then, however, his election was inevitable, and they

did him little harm. The only time his bizarre writings would hurt him would be in 2012, when he was on the short list to be GOP presidential nominee Mitt Romney's running mate. I've always thought the idea of a Mormon running with a Catholic who'd performed an exorcism hurt Jindal's chances.

Chapter 15

1. This decades-old practice ended when Democrat John Bel Edwards became governor in 2016.

Chapter 17

1. This does not address the implications and shortcomings of a proposed "mandatory" evacuation of the city, which Blanco has been criticized for not ordering. The only way to enforce such an order would be to send police and other law enforcement door to door throughout a large American city and force people out of their homes and onto nonexistent buses, planes, and trains. Even if there was time for a large-scale operation of that sort—and there wasn't—it is folly to think anyone could have implemented it.

INDEX